Prophecy, Fate and Memory in the Early and Medieval Celtic World

Sydney Series in Celtic Studies

Dr Pamela O'Neill and Professor Jonathan Wooding, Series Editors

The Sydney Series in Celtic Studies publishes monographs and edited collections of original research in the field of Celtic Studies including archaeology, art, history, law, languages and literature. The series encompasses early and medieval subjects, as well as the modern Celtic nations with their diasporas, and encourages innovative approaches to traditional questions in its major field.

1 *Early Irish Contract Law* by N. McLeod
2 *The Celts in Europe* by A. Cremin
3 *Origins and Revivals: Proceedings of the First Australian Conference of Celtic Studies* by G. Evans, B. Martin & J. M. Wooding (eds)
4 *Literature and Politics in the Celtic World: Papers from the Third Australian Conference of Celtic Studies* by P. O'Neill & J. M. Wooding (eds)
5 *Celtic-Australian Identities: Irish- and Welsh-Australian Studies from the 'Australian Identities' Conference, University College Dublin, July 1996* by J. M. Wooding & D. Day (eds)
6 *Nation and Federation in the Celtic World: Papers from the Fourth Australian Conference of Celtic Studies* by P. O'Neill (ed.)
7 *Between Intrusions: Britain and Ireland between the Romans and the Normans* by P. O'Neill (ed.)
8 *Exile and Homecoming: Papers from the Fifth Australian Conference of Celtic Studies* by P. O'Neill (ed.)
9 *Celts in Legend and Reality: Papers from the Sixth Australian Conference of Celtic Studies* by P. O'Neill (ed.)
10 *Language and Power in the Celtic World: Papers from the Seventh Australian Conference of Celtic Studies* by A. Ahlqvist & P. O'Neill (eds)
11 *Celts and their Cultures at Home and Abroad: A Festschrift for Malcolm Broun* by A. Ahlqvist & P. O'Neill (eds)
12 *The Land beneath the Sea: Essays in Honour of Anders Ahlqvist's Contribution to Celtic Studies in Australia* P. O'Neill (ed.)
13 *Late Medieval Irish Law Manuscripts: A Reappraisal of Methodology and Content* by R. Finnane
14 *Medieval Irish Law: Text and Context* by A. Ahlqvist & P. O'Neill (eds)
15 *Grammatical Tables for Old Irish* compiled by A. Ahlqvist
16 *Germano-Celtica: A Festschrift for Brian Taylor* by A. Ahlqvist & P. O'Neill (eds)
17 *Fir Fesso: A Festschrift for Neil McLeod* by A. Ahlqvist & P. O'Neill (eds)

Prophecy, Fate and Memory in the Early and Medieval Celtic World

Edited by

Jonathan M. Wooding and
Lynette Olson

Sydney Series in Celtic Studies 18

SYDNEY UNIVERSITY PRESS

First published by Sydney University Press
© Individual contributors 2020
© Sydney University Press 2020

Reproduction and Communication for other purposes
Except as permitted under the Act, no part of this edition may be reproduced, stored in a retrieval system, or communicated in any form or by any means without prior written permission. All requests for reproduction or communication should be made to Sydney University Press at the address below:

Sydney University Press
Fisher Library F03
University of Sydney NSW 2006
AUSTRALIA
sup.info@sydney.edu.au
sydneyuniversitypress.com.au

 A catalogue record for this book is available from the National Library of Australia.

ISBN 9781743326732 (paperback)
ISBN 9781743326794 (epub)
ISBN 9781743326879 (mobi)

Cover image: Stairway to the monastery on the island of Skellig Michael, Co. Kerry, Ireland. Photo by J. M. Wooding (2002).
Cover design by Miguel Yamin.

Contents

Figures		vii
Introduction: Crafted Memories and Binding Futures *Jonathan M. Wooding*		1
1	Poeninus and the Romanisation of the Celtic Alps *Bernard Mees*	15
2	Landscapes, Myth-Making and Memory: Ecclesiastical Landholding in Early Medieval Ireland *Tomás Ó Carragáin*	35
3	Remembering and Forgetting Holy Men and their Places: An Inscription from Llanllŷr, Wales *Jonathan M. Wooding*	53
4	Early Irish *Peregrinatio* as Salvation History *Meredith D. Cutrer*	77
5	Insular Influences on Carolingian and Ottonian Literature and Art *Penelope Nash*	93

6 The *De xii abusivis saeculi* and Prophetic Tradition in 125
   Seventh-Century Ireland
   Constant J. Mews

7 Memories of Gildas: Gildas and the *Collectio canonum* 149
   Hibernensis
   Stephen Joyce

8 *Armes Prydein* as a Legacy of Gildas 171
   Lynette Olson

9 A Woman's Fate: Deirdre and Gráinne throughout 189
   Literature
   Roxanne T. Bodsworth

10 'No Remission without Satisfaction': Canonical Influences 209
   on Secular Lawmaking in High Medieval Scotland
   Cynthia J. Neville

11 Esoteric Tourism in Scotland: Rosslyn Chapel, *The Da Vinci* 247
   Code, and the Appeal of the 'New Age'
   Carole M. Cusack

About the Authors 271

Index 275

Figures

Figure 1.1 The Liddes inscription. 18

Figure 1.2 A votive from the temple at the Great St Bernard Pass. 20

Figure 1.3 Dedications to Poininos from the Val Brembana. 23

Figure 1.4 The Berne zinc tablet inscription. 30

Figure 1.5 The Manching Boios inscription. 31

Figure 2.1 The core estate of Inch Labhrainne showing early medieval settlements and route-side monuments. 43

Figure 2.2 Crosses inscribed into standing stones at Emlagh, Brackloon, Ballintermon and Ballynacourty. 45

Figure 2.3 Standing stone in Brackloon with nearby rock outcrop decorated with prehistoric rock-art. 46

Figure 2.4 Standing stone in Ballintermon. 49

Figure 2.5 Other cross sculpture on the lands of Inch Labhrainne in Gortacurraun, Ballinclare and Inch West. 51

Figure 3.1 The Llanllŷr inscription. 56

Figure 3.2 The flood-plain of Llanllŷr. 59

Figure 5.1 Map of Europe showing places mentioned in the text. 103

Figure 5.2 Carpet page, Book of Durrow. 104

Figure 5.3 The Lion, symbol of Saint Mark, Echternach Gospels of St Willibrord. 108

Figure 5.4 Gospel Book, initial page with figured frame. Franco-Saxon School. 109

Figure 5.5 Initial Ini(tium), St Mark, Book of Durrow. 110

Figure 5.6 Crucifixion, St Gall Gospels. 115

Figure 5.7 Adelheid, Theophanu, Otto III and Lamb of God. Initial page, Matthew Evangelistary, Gospel of Saint-Gereon. 120

Figure 11.1 Rosslyn Chapel, south side. 249

Figure 11.2 Rosslyn Chapel, west end. 254

Figure 11.3 Rosslyn Chapel, north side. 258

Figure 11.4 Gargoyle, Rosslyn Chapel. 262

Figure 11.5 Roslin Hotel. 267

Introduction: Crafted Memories and Binding Futures

Jonathan M. Wooding

There are various challenges particular to the study of early and medieval Celtic cultures. One is simply a problem of evidence. Celtic-speaking populations came late into the mainstream of European history and often only in the process of their colonisation by neighbouring peoples. Even for the later Middle Ages and Early Modern era the preservation of records is uneven. For the earlier periods we often have only fragmentary data. I suppose many of us quite like it that way, as there is a particular interest to the type of detective-work involved in studying non-narrative sources—not to mention sources in which historical data are engagingly mixed up with the mystical or the prophetic. Such sources are, however, difficult to contextualise. How much do they speak to past events and how much to the present? How much do they owe to traditional and how much to external influences? What connections can we draw between sources that are separated by considerable distances of time, space, and language? In our struggle to extract basic meaning from exiguous sources we may be prone to beg wider questions, including theoretical approaches. 'Celtic' historiography and source-criticism have indeed at times been notably conservative, often reluctant to seek meaning beyond philology—or at least those hermeneutics that are hard-wired to philology. The nationalism that frequently has been a backdrop to Celtic scholarship inspires a focus on secular politics and native tradition. There is a need to embrace new approaches, though not necessarily at the expense of our established methods. This may include a reach into neglected, sometimes non-narrative sources, or embracing methods from contemporary religious as well as literary hermeneutics.

The present volume marks a reboot of the venerable Sydney Series in Celtic Studies, now under the aegis of Sydney University Press. An essential element in its renewed mission is that it 'encourages innovative approaches to traditional questions in its major field'. The choice of themes and topics of the present collection speaks to our ambition to innovate without compromise to the scholarly values that are essential to our discipline. One of our chosen themes is memory—a theme that has proved highly productive in some areas of modern Celtic historiography.[1] Thinking about how people remember also can help us to question traditional ideas in earlier Celtic studies. Cynthia Neville in her chapter demonstrates through masterful, exhaustive analysis the subtle process by which the Scottish court, in seeking to affirm Malcolm III and his descendants as the legitimate rulers of Scotland, set out 'to recast, reshape and rewrite the collective memory'. Lynette Olson in her chapter asks provocative questions concerning how early-medieval people crafted identities through conscious memorialising of past loss. Older historiographical visions which saw Celtic nations as being largely in thrall to tradition, or having only an intermittent knowledge of a more sophisticated world, will not be found here.

Yet in seeking to liberate the medieval Celtic nations from assumptions of nativism and worthy unsophistication we must be wary of treating them as if they were simply modern nations. The worldview of medieval people was undoubtedly quite different to ours. When an early-medieval historian such as Bede described visions of heaven and hell in his *Ecclesiastical History* it was because these visions of the future were perceived as being 'history'. His audience believed that prophetic visions could reveal future history and that travellers who claimed to

---

1 See, for example, Frawley, O. editor 2010–2014 *Memory Ireland*, 4 vols, Syracuse NY: Syracuse University Press; Beiner, Guy 2018 *Forgetful Remembrance: Social Forgetting and Vernacular Historiography of a Rebellion in Ulster*, Oxford and New York: Oxford University Press.

have visited the heavens—for example the Irishman St Fursey—brought back real memories of future events. Some believed that powerful utterances, such as the *geisi* referenced by Roxanne Bodsworth in this volume, might even bind future events. Though the context of Bodsworth's analysis is a literary one, study of charms and curses recorded from wider society tell us that words and statements of power had a reality in social life.[2] Penance, one of the themes of Constant Mews' chapter, is shown to be the basis of influential social teaching that crossed over into the secular sphere and in which Gildas' 'prophetic criticism of secular and clerical behaviour was being transmuted into a body of thought structured around respect for law'. We have, accordingly, added fate and prophecy to the theme of memory here, so as to capture distinct qualities of the worldview of the early Celtic-speaking nations. It is notable that all the contributions find productive outcomes from one or more of these concepts.

Landscapes, Monuments and Memory

Inscribed monuments are one of the categories of non-narrative written data that increasingly feature in the rewriting of the ancient and medieval history of north-west Europe. Our collection opens with three studies with inscribed monuments at their centre. In the past *and* in the present, monuments have always been central to how things were remembered and which things were chosen to be remembered. Here they are the subject of approaches that consider them in their wider relational contexts—their placement in the landscape and the performances associated with them. Bernard Mees offers us a detailed reflection on the philology of some inscriptions from Northern Italy, which he places in the context of a process of Romanisation. These inscriptions fall within the broad group known as 'Lepontic', which contains Celtic texts dating back to the sixth century BC, but these are from a much later period, nearer to the end of the Roman Republic. Mees sees these texts as being 'not merely of linguistic interest, but

---

2   See Tuomi, I. *et al.* editors 2019 *Charms, Charmers and Charming in Ireland: From the Medieval to the Modern*, Cardiff: University of Wales Press.

also of broader socio-cultural importance, particularly those that are religious in nature'. The study of religious ideas in provincial Roman inscriptions is indeed one of the more dynamic fields in recent Celtic studies, where the work of the F.E.R.C.AN. project,[3] along with the re-theorising of what Ralph Häussler has termed *interpretatio indigena*, has affirmed the local quality of the processes of Romanisation to which these texts are witnesses—a provincial Romanisation that was by no means just 'top-down'.[4] Considering a group of texts from the region of St Bernard's Pass concerning the local deity Jupiter-Poeninus, Mees makes a contrast between the Latin *votum* ('vow') texts and the Liddes inscription, which, in omitting the Roman name and using a Celtic dedicatory verb, is different from other inscriptions from the locale. In his view it 'appears closer in style to a typical Gaulish dedication'. Comparing the Liddes *Poeninus* inscription with one to *Boios* at Manching he finds evidence of alphabet-switching (mixing graphemes from different alphabets), 'an expected feature of Romanisation', but the dedication of the Liddes inscription is itself native in character rather than Roman.

In a case study of western Ireland in the second half of the first millennium AD, Tomás Ó Carragáin considers some evidence for ecclesiastical land-holding. His wide-ranging introduction observes the disjunction of landscape data with some historical models that would synchronise churchyard burial with religious change or which equate density of churches with the regional character of pastoral care. In a particular case study of the estate of the Kerry saint Mochaellóc Mac Uibhleáin—a once obscure saint who carries a surprising weight of recent scholarship[5]—Ó Carragáin seeks to reconstruct the social and ritual processes in which monuments participated. He envisages a landscape not inertly demarcated by monuments, but monuments as

---

3   Fontes Epigraphici Religionum Celticarum Antiquarum.
4   Häussler, Ralph 2012 *Interpretatio indigena*: Reinventing Local Cults in a Global World, *Mediterraneo Antico* 15, 143–174.
5   See Ó Corráin, D. 2004 To Chellóc mac Oíbléni: Saint and Places, *Cin Chille Cuile: Texts, Saints and Places*, edited by J. Carey, K. Murray, M. Herbert, Aberystwyth: Celtic Studies Publications 258–67; Ó Caoimh, T. 2000 Mochaellóc Mac Uibhleáin of the Corco Dhuibhne, *Tuosist 6000*, Lauragh: Tuosist History and Newsletter Committee 79–84.

part of social processes, often on linear routes through territories rather than, as has often been assumed, around their perimeters. Inscription and re-inscription of monuments is interpreted in terms of periodic change and promotion of new owners and cults. For the defaced ogham on the Ballintermon stone, for example, he suggests

> the overwriting of one claim of ownership by another. Assuming it was erected in the prehistoric period, the first early medieval claimants probably saw this impressive pre-extant monument as a source of kudos. They may have sought to control, and even solicit, rather than to neutralise, its lingering power. The same may have been true of their ecclesiastical successors, notwithstanding the social and religious changes in the intervening period. After all, it was the previous claim represented by the ogham inscription that they defaced, not the monument itself.

The emphasis here on the 'mundane'—as Ó Carragáin describes it—event of land transaction might be seen as a further move away from mapping artefacts in terms of culture-historical discontinuities such as invasion or corporate conversion. One is also reminded of the modern historian Jay Winter's theorising of war memorials, in which he suggests 'shifting the scale of vision from the national and grandiose to the particular and mundane', to locate monuments in the sphere of local 'memory activists', whose causes are often more diverse and personal than 'stabilization' of society after major disruptions.[6]

In a study of a first-millennium site in Wales, the present writer (Jonathan Wooding), like Mees, finds glimpses of expected processes of change on an inscribed stone, but a less expected diversity of terms as well as names. At Llanllŷr there is possible evidence of commemorations of more than one religious figure. We have fairly recently left behind an historiography in which the names of holy people on a site would be blithely tracked back to their naming/ dedication in an 'age of the saints' c. AD 500–600. The detail of names

---

6   Winter, Jay 2006 *Remembering War: The Great War Between Memory and History in the Twentieth Century,* New Haven CT: Yale University Press 135.

at Llanllŷr, in a genuine first-millennium text, may provide a glimpse of the more complex and diverse models of cult-formation we now envisage in its place.[7] The use in the inscription of a rare term *tesquitus* also prompts us to think about how the Celtic-speaking churches drew upon a Latin tradition that they could have accessed through learning from abroad but also through an inheritance of Romano-British Latin.

Insular Visions

As we have observed above, there are few areas in which the study of Celtic texts has been so transformed across the last quarter century than the study of religious ideas. For many years the assumption of native origins for seemingly unusual Christian ideas was unhelpfully shored up by un-diverse perceptions of a 'Celtic Christianity' formed in isolation.[8] Here the groundbreaking revisionist studies by, among others, Thomas O'Loughlin, Richard Sharpe and Martin McNamara, have transformed our approaches.[9] Meredith Cutrer, one of a new generation working in this field, expands authoritatively on the Scriptural and Patristic bases of *peregrinatio*, which was a central motif of Insular religious culture. One might suspect that *peregrinatio* would be a well-worked topic, but Cutrer's research shows how much further

---

7   Sharpe, Richard 2002 Martyrs and Local Saints in Late Antique Britain, *Local Saints and Local Churches in the Early Medieval West*, edited by Alan Thacker and Richard Sharpe, Oxford: Oxford University Press 75–154; Thacker, Alan, *Loca sanctorum*: The Significance of Place in the Study of the Saints, *Local Saints and Local Churches* 1–43.
8   Meek, D. 2000 *The Quest for Celtic Christianity*, Edinburgh: Handsel Press 318–9; Morgan-Guy, V. 2019 Bypassing the Church: Some Reflections on Celtic Christianity and Orthodox Ecclesiology, *From the East to the Isles: Approaches to the Eastern Connections of the Early Churches of Britain and Ireland*, edited by J. Wooding and A. Louth, London: Fellowship of St Alban and St Sergius 149–64.
9   For example: O'Loughlin, Thomas 2000 *Celtic Theology*, London: Continuum; Sharpe, Richard 1984 Some Problems Concerning the Organization of the Church in Early Medieval Ireland, *Peritia* 3, 230–70; McNamara, Martin 2015 *The Bible and the Apocrypha in the Early Irish Church, AD 600–1200*, Turnhout: Brepols.

the critique of the theological conception of *peregrinatio* can be pursued when informed by a skilful reach into Scripture and Patristics. This approach from the theological side complements the recent historical work of scholars such as Alexander O'Hara and Elva Johnston on the historical careers of *peregrini*.[10] Considering the themes of memory and prophecy, Cutrer examines how the *peregrini* saw their historic journeying in the context of a teleological narrative of salvation history. Foretastes of the end of this narrative could be the fruits of a journey into the 'desert' space of an ocean in which the end of the world was physically, as well as temporally, imminent.[11]

Our perception of the ways in which the world of the *peregrini* connected Insular monastic culture to Continental has also changed markedly across the last half-century. The mythic vision that Johannes Duft once termed 'Iromania', the belief that the Irish handed down a sort of mystic genius into Continental culture, has given way to a more holistic approach to the encounter of two learned cultures.[12] When culture was perceived as spontaneous product of 'visionary Celts' or Classical geniuses, there was less cause to consider the nexus between philosophy and art.[13] Penny Nash shows that there were many

---

10   O'Hara, Alexander 2013 *Patria, Peregrinatio, and Paenitentia*: Identities of Alienation in the Seventh Century, *Post-Roman Transitions: Christian and Barbarian Identities in the Early Medieval West*, edited by Walter Pohl and Gerda Heydemann, Turnhout: Brepols 89–124; Johnston, Elva 2016 Exiles from the Edge? The Irish Contexts of *Peregrinatio*, *The Irish in Early Medieval Europe: Identity, Culture and Religion*, edited by Roy Flechner and Sven Meeder, Basingstoke: Palgrave Macmillan 38–52.

11   Stalmans, Nathalie and Charles-Edwards, T. M. 2007 Meath, Saints of (act. c.400–c.900), *New Oxford Dictionary of National Biography*, Oxford online, s. v. Cormac Ua Liatháin; O'Loughlin, *Celtic Theology* 36–7.

12   Duft, J. 1956 Iromanie—Irophobie: Fragen um die frühmittelalterliche Irenmission exemplifiziert an St Gallen und Alemannien, *Zeitschrift für schweizerische Kirchengeschichte* 50, 241–62; James, Edward 1982 Ireland and Western Gaul in the Merovingian Period, *Ireland in Early Medieval Europe: Studies in Memory of Kathleen Hughes*, edited by D. Whitelock *et al.* Cambridge: Cambridge University Press 362–86: 370–3.

13   The myth of the Classical genius of the Irish is humorously put into the mouth of a medieval monk in Eco, Umberto 1984 *The Name of the Rose*, London: Picador, 311–13. On the 'visionary Celt': Sims-Williams, P. 1986 The Visionary Celt, *Cambridge Medieval Celtic Studies* 11, 71–96. On some of the

relationships between Continental and Insular scholars, not all of which fit a single pattern. She addresses the less often considered 'why', rather than 'what', of Irish motifs that were remembered into Ottonian art. She also, like Cutrer, reflects on the narratives that inform development of iconography that was itself an aid to memory in reading books that were multimedia works, using text and image to convey their interpretations.

Gildas, Penance and Prophecy

Three chapters centre on the legacy of Gildas, our most prominent voice from sixth-century Britain—a figure who, in a similar way to Bede, veers between treatment as a historical and a theological voice, as well as someone whose concern was arguably monastic as well as secular. In many new studies of Gildas, including these ones, we see a welcome attempt to reconstruct Gildas as a holistic persona, finding explanation of his diverse concerns and expressions in his reception, rather than, as has sometimes been the case, in speculating on whether he wrote his works in the persona of a secular priest or a monk.[14]

Lynette Olson, in her study of the tenth-century Welsh prophetic poem *Armes Prydein Fawr* (Great Prophecy of Britain), considers the problem of constructed memory in claims of nationhood. Making a comparison with Vamik Volkan's psychological theorising of modern dispossession and genocide, she invites us to recall the real dispossession that led to the creation of a Britain shared between Celtic and English people. She observes that the author of *Armes Prydein* was predicating his call for rebellion on a 'chosen trauma', rooted in the loss

---

debates concerning Celtic and English claims to genius: Ó Cróinín, D. 1984 Rath Melsigi, Willibrord, and the Earliest Echternach Manuscripts, *Peritia*, 3, 17–49.

14 Chadwick, O. 1954 Gildas and the Monastic Order, *Journal of Theological Studies* n.s. 5, 78–80; cf. Herren, M. 1990 Gildas and early British monasticism, *Britain 400–600: Language and History,* edited by A. Bammesberger & A. Wollmann, Heidelberg: Universitätsverlag C. Winter 65–78.

of a sovereignty over the island, an idea she sees as one of a number of legacies of Gildas:[15]

> One was a prophetic cast to their history. Another was the concept of Britain as a unit, which had clearly been extended to Brittany and arguably to an even wider common culture in *Armes Prydein*. Another was concern for British unity rather than civil war. The greatest legacy was the 'Welsh historical myth', their 'chosen trauma' in Volkan's more dynamic concept, of the loss of much of Britain to the English, to which Gildas gave influential and enduring literary form.

The theme of Gildas as an authority moving between monastic and secular concerns is explored by Constant Mews. In his detailed study of the seventh-century Hiberno-Latin text *De xii abusivis saeculi* (On the Twelve Abuses of the Age), Mews finds in Gildas a silent partner in the process of laying down a path for kings. He traces an influence from Gildas upon the ideas of Cummian of Clonfert (Cumméne Fota) and of the latter upon the *De xii abusivis*:

> The Twelve Abuses offers a remarkable synthesis of ethical reflection in mid-seventh-century Ireland that extends the prophetic voice of Gildas in the *De excidio*, directed so much against bad kings and bishops (*sacerdotes*), into a concise, carefully structured reflection on moral responsibility for different groups in society. Ethical principles that had been formulated by Jerome and Cassian within a monastic milieu were now having to be made relevant to a much more ecclesiastically organized environment.

That the monastery and its ideas of penance could provide models for secular living is a contemporary theological theme.[16] Some recent

---

15 Also see O'Loughlin, T. 2001 One Island, One People, One Nation: Early Latin Evidence for this Motif in Ireland, *The ITB Journal* 2, 4–13.
16 See MacIntyre, Alasdair 2007 *After Virtue,* 3rd edition, London: Duckworth 257–63.

studies have argued that it was also one of the innovations that made Irish preaching popular in early medieval Europe—as Peter Brown has observed it makes a more plausible cause of the reputation of the Irish than as purveyors of visions of more mystical otherworlds.[17] As Mews observes, monastic virtues that had started as advice for monks in the work of John Cassian are made relevant by Cummian and the *De xii abusivis* to a range of non-monastic contexts. Mews also sees in the *De xii abusivis* a combination of the 'prophetic voice with respect for ecclesiastical authority' that again points to the memories of Gildas—a point taken up in Stephen Joyce's contribution.

The Irish collection of canon law, *Collectio canonum Hibernensis* (probably early 700s), was for a long time only accessed with difficulty through a rare, un-translated, edition.[18] A return to the detail of the *Hibernensis* was pivotal in creating the revisionist historiography for the early Celtic churches that emerged in the 1980s.[19] That Gildas is cited in this work with the authority of a Church Father was established in 1984 by Richard Sharpe.[20] Stephen Joyce further considers the identity of Gildas in the *Hibernensis*, where he finds Gildas cited only from his fragmentary correspondence (*Fragmenta*) with Finnian—which even then 'the *Hibernensis* did not slavishly copy'—and not from the better-known *De excidio*. This he sees as a response to a

> fundamental change in the nature of authority in Ireland, one that took the edification of secular and church leaders from monastic

---

17 Brown, Peter 1996 *The End of the Ancient Other World: Death and Afterlife between Late Antiquity and the Early Middle Ages,* New Haven CT: Yale University Press 34; Dunn, Marilyn 2000 Gregory the Great, the Vision of Fursey and the Origins of Purgatory, *Peritia* 14, 238–54.

18 Now see Flechner, Roy 2019 *The Hibernensis: Book 1: A Study and Edition,* Washington DC: Catholic University of America Press; for history of scholarship see O'Loughlin, T. 1996 The Latin Sources of Medieval Irish Culture: A Partial *Status Quaestionis, Progress in Medieval Irish Studies,* edited by K. McCone and K. Simms, Maynooth: Department of Old Irish 91–105.

19 Sharpe, Some Problems, *passim.* Etchingham, C. 1999 *Church Organisation in Ireland, AD 650 to 1000,* Naas: Laigin.

20 Sharpe, Richard 1984 Gildas as a Father of the Church, *Gildas: New Approaches,* edited by M. Lapidge and D. Dumville, Woodbridge: Boydell 193–205.

figures such as Columbanus and placed it in the hands of bishops, as exemplified by Patrick. The result, in an Irish context, was an emerging emphasis on Gildas as Gildas *Sapiens*, as the author of the *Fragmenta* and a contributor to canon law. Significantly, in a contemporary English context, a different image of Gildas was evolving, one that emphasised the *De excidio* and providential history: that of Gildas *Historicus*.

The Gildas whom we know from the *De excidio* as a harsh critic of kings and bishops is found in Joyce's and Mews' studies as a supporter of episcopal authority and the episcopate as the rightful critic of kings. They offer grounds to see this as a product of redaction, but also, as Joyce argues, possibly arising from a primary concern in all his works with the exercise of authority.

These three studies attempt to reconcile the diverse perceptions of Gildas through a reach into his reception and through a renewed focus on the less modern of his modes of expression: his prophetic voice as well as his theological ideas.

Fate, Salvation and Crafted Memories

In her contribution Roxanne Bodsworth considers the questions of fate and agency in a holistic critical study of the early Irish heroines Deirdre and Gráinne. These two heroines experience tragedy under broadly similar circumstances and both to a degree are found to be culpable in their own fates. They have, however, come to symbolise very different ideals of womanhood across time: Gráinne manipulative and selfish, but Deirdre immensely desirable in her fated victimhood. Bodsworth brings to this study a nuanced account of multiple versions past and present, seeing each as deliberatively conceived and received—in contrast to past critics who often saw the earlier tales as formed anonymously in 'tradition'. Her comparison reveals the perhaps sadly predictable conclusion that hostility to female protagonists did not, as she observes, change with the re-appropriation of these tales to late-nineteenth/early twentieth-century nationalism. The respective vilification and beatification of the two heroines, however, makes an intriguing analysis, enriched by taking this long perspective.

Cynthia Neville, in an immensely rich and detailed exploration of state building in thirteenth-century Scotland, reflects on the conventional models of state-formation followed by scholars such as David Carpenter, Alice Taylor and Dauvit Broun, which default to secular causes. She reconsiders these in the light of the 'complex and sophisticated network of nuncios, legates and judges-delegate' in the thirteenth century to argue that canon law, as much as secular, was at work in the building of a new Scottish kingship, with rulers appropriating

> to their own uses the clerical significance of ceremonies of personal subjection. They did so because the church's views gave added weight in the secular sphere to relations between ruler and ruled. The profound transformation that occurred in power relations between the crown and the Scottish aristocracy in this period—what Taylor has dubbed the 'shaping' of the Scottish state—was effected without benefit of the advantages associated with sacral kingship (unction) that were the norm almost everywhere else in Christendom. Public displays of lawmaking implicitly co-opted these attributes and served to emphasize the superior lordship of the king of Scots.

Neville argues that idea of compensation for injury, 'deeply ingrained' in customary law in Scotland, chimed with the ideas of redress and reparation inherent in Christian penance. The Scottish monarchy's investment in canon law schools facilitated the promotion of the Scottish kings as Christian rulers whose role was to ensure that sins were punished. Her study—which thus explores texts which have many parallels with the *De xii abusivis* (see above)—reflects on long historiographies that variously find the Scottish court both as a 'frontier area of Christendom', as well as one that actually 'kept abreast of the legal reforms of the Angevin rulers and their thirteenth-century successors'. Again we see a vision of a medieval Celtic world that developed a distinctive culture through connection with, rather than isolation from, a wider world.

In the final chapter, Carole Cusack, building on her long-standing work on esoteric religion as well as her interests in religious tourism, reflects on the way the fifteenth-century Rosslyn Chapel, near Edinburgh, has been represented in literature of esotericism. Its appeal to romantic writers at the beginning of the modern era was the precursor to complex legends of this site, linking it to anachronistic theories of the origins of the Freemasons and hidden, 'true' Christianities. Cusack intriguingly shows how these legends of complex memory gained traction in the mid-twentieth century, in a context in which the discoveries of the Dead Sea Scrolls and Nag Hammadi codices were progressively diversifying perceptions of early Christianity. While it might be wrong to say that in these matters all roads lead to Rennes-le-Chateau, it is perhaps no surprise, given its rich and sometimes ambiguous decoration, that the remarkable chapel was drawn into the orbit of the contentious book *Holy Blood and the Holy Grail,* and thence to Dan Brown's reinterpretation of these ideas in *The Da Vinci Code.* To historians of empirical method these types of associations of a monument can seem little more than frustrating diversions, but Cusack rightly acknowledges the force of the reception here and its implications for our understanding of how visitors apprehend the heritage of medieval buildings.

In reflecting on this whole collection, we might take Cynthia Neville's observations concerning the neglect of theological questions in royal historiography, as, *mutatis mutandis,* a leitmotif of much of our collection. Twentieth-century secularism and nativism are tempered here by a renewed appreciation of the importance of religious ideas in the worldview of early and medieval people. The late-twentieth century idea of 'Celtic' as primarily a vernacular-language identity is also tempered here by a renewed respect for the Latin sources for our subject—even if this requires us to wrestle with sources in pre-modern editions and typography. How people envisaged the future and remembered the past is productively reinterpreted in ways that reflect recent innovations in Celtic scholarship, but which also keep sight of the critical values which remain central to our field.

1
Poeninus and the Romanisation of the Celtic Alps

Bernard Mees

Since the time of the Celtic revival in the early nineteenth century, a key manner in which the memory of the Celtic past has been celebrated on the European continent is through the discovery, analysis and museological display of archaeological finds. And of these physical testaments of Celtic antiquity, finds that preserve epigraphic evidence are often the most treasured. Yet most of the inscriptions that are Celtic in language uncovered in recent years on the European continent have tended to be published in French, German or Italian, not in English-language accounts. And the evidence represented by recent finds of Continental Celtic inscriptions is often not merely of linguistic interest, but also of broader socio-cultural importance, particularly those that are religious in nature.

The 2008 publication, for instance, of epigraphic finds from the mountains above Liddes, Valais, and in the Val Brembana, Bergamo, has brought to light new evidence of dedications to Poeninus, the ancient god of the Great St Bernard Pass.[1] The inscriptions are written in epichoric letterforms and also preserve evidence for the process

---

1   Casini, Stephania, Fossati, Angelo and Motta, Filippo 2008 Incisioni protostoriche e inscrizioni leponzie su roccia alle sorgenti del Brembo (Val Camisana di Carona, Bergamo): note preliminary, *Notizie Archeologiche Bergomensi* 16, 75–101.

of Romanisation in the Celtic Alps. Although a Celto-Etruscan or Lepontic text, the Liddes inscription evidences Romanisation comparable to that attested in a Gallo-Greek votive plaque found in the 1980s in the northern suburbs of Berne. And the processes of Romanisation evidenced in the Liddes and Berne inscriptions can be analysed in light of recent approaches to linguistic and orthographic acculturation. Taken together, the Liddes, Berne and other local Alpine Celtic texts provide new evidence for orthographic Romanisation as a prelude to alphabetic and eventually also language shift.

The Dedications to Poeninus

The earliest writing system employed in the Alps was a derived form of the Etruscan alphabet and since the 1970s Celtic inscriptions from this Alpine Etruscan tradition have usually been described as Lepontic.[2] Most of the Lepontic texts are known from the area about and below the Lepontine Alps, but all manner of Celto-Etruscan texts are often loosely described as Lepontic. A recent epigraphic find from the mountains above Liddes, Valais, for example, was taken to be Lepontic by its first publishers even though it can scarcely have had much to do with the ancient Lepontic tribe who gave their name to the Val Leventina. The Liddes find is clearly a religious inscription, however, and is an orthographically as well as linguistically remarkable text.

Most Lepontic inscriptions can be described by a threefold typology: onomastic texts (featuring the name of the maker or owner of a find), funerary memorials and religious finds. This typology mirrors that found in archaic Greek epigraphy and seems typical of early forms of alphabetic use or craft literacy. When alphabetism is first adopted in ancient societies, its use tends to be restricted to certain specialist employments and craftsmen, and types of texts which represent public or civic expressions (such as law codes) are not found. Ancient societies tend to develop literacy along a common cline: non-literacy > craft literacy > semi-literacy > full literacy. The Liddes inscription is clearly

---

2 Lejeune, Michel 1971 *Lepontica*, Monographies linguistiques 1, Paris: Les Belles Lettres.

an expected type of Lepontic text, even if it seems peculiar in some other ways.[3]

First published in 2007 by a local Swiss historian, the Liddes inscription preserves several features that seem to reflect Romanisation.[4] The inscription is unambiguously Celtic linguistically, but looks to represent an epigraphic admixture of North Etruscan and Roman (and perhaps even Greek) writing. Its discovery led to the formation of an association called Recherches Archéologiques du Mur (dit) d'Hannibal (Ramha) in Liddes to undertake excavations of the wall and the site is still being excavated by local archaeologists.[5] The inscription was first thought by many Celticists to be a clever forgery, but the odd features of the inscription can all be explained by its late date and relative isolation.

The Liddes inscription was discovered in an Iron Age fortification known as Hannibal's Wall, a 270 m long defensive stonework 2650 m above sea level in the mountains above Liddes.[6] Found on a block of gneiss, it is housed in a small stone building that looks as if it may formerly have served as some kind of shrine. The Liddes text is difficult to date, but given the age of the fortification appears to stem from the late first century BC. Most Celto-Etruscan inscriptions stem more clearly from the middle of the La Tène era, with the earliest found in archaeological contexts from as early as the seventh century BC, but inscriptions from as late as the Julio-Claudian period are also known from Italian sites.[7] The wall seems to have been created by local Celts in reaction to Servius Galba's victory further to the north at Octodurus

---

3   Havelock, Eric A. 1963 *Preface to Plato*, History of the Greek Mind 1, Cambridge MA: Harvard University Press 38–41; Bodel, John P. 2001 Epigraphy and the Ancient Historian, *Epigraphic Evidence: Ancient History from Inscriptions*, edited by John P. Bodel, Approaching the Ancient World 10, London: Routledge 1–56: 10.
4   Quartier-La-Tente, Vincent 2007 L'énigme du Mur d'Annibal! Enfin une piste! *La vallée du Gd-St-Bernard: Liddes et Bourg-St-Pierre vous informent* ... 58, 12–13.
5   See the website www.ramha.ch.
6   Andenmatten, Romain and Paccolat, Olivier 2012 Le mur (dit) d'Hannibal: une site de haute montagne de la fin de l'âge de Fer, *Jahrbuch Archäologie Schweiz* 95, 77–95.

Figure 1.1 The Liddes inscription. Drawing by S. Casini-A.E. Fossati from Casini, Stephania, Fossati, Angelo and Motta, Filippo 2013 L'iscrizione in alfabeto di Lugano al Mur d'Hannibal (Liddes, Valais), *Notizie Archeologiche Bergomensi* 21, 157–65, fig. 7.

(Martigny) in 57 BC during Caesar's Gallic campaign. The Romans did not manage to subdue the *Vallis Poenina* (which gave its name to the modern-day Canton of Valais) until the reign of Augustus, however, and all manner of traces of last-century BC life have been found at the fortified site.

The local historian who first published the Liddes find (discovered by his wife in 2005) recognised that the inscription was orthogra-

---

7   Rubat Borel, Francesco 2005 Lingue e scritture delle Alpi occidentali prima della romanizzazione: stato della questione e nuove ricerche, *Bulletin d'études préhistoriques et archéologiques alpines* 16, 9–50.

phically Lepontic and the Italian team who first analysed its text formally transcribe its sinistroverse letterforms as:

poenino
ieuiseu[8]

The first term preserved in the Liddes inscription is clearly a dative form of the epithet of the god Iovus Poeninus recorded in Roman votive inscriptions from the environs of the Great St Bernard Pass. Known to the Romans as the *summus* or *mons Poeninus*, ancient accounts indicate that *Poeninus* was the name of a local god, long presumed to be Celtic in origin.[9] Another Lepontic text from further north in the same canton was discovered in 2003 at Argnou, near Sion, but its only partially preserved text seems to describe the find as the funerary stone of a man called *Ritilos*.[10] Rather than local epichoric inscriptions, the Liddes text seems best to be understood, in the first instance, in light of votive finds known from the area about the hospice founded in the eleventh century by St Bernard of Menthon, the patron saint of the Alps.[11]

Excavations in the area are first recorded from 1762–64 when Laurent-Joseph Murith, the prior of the Hospice of the Great St Bernard Pass, began investigating the local Roman remains of what had become known as the *mons Jovis* in late antiquity (Mt Joux in later French).[12] Numerous Latin dedications are known today, preserved on bronze

---

8 Casini, Stephania, Fossati, Angelo and Motta, Filippo 2013 L'iscrizione in alfabeto di Lugano al Mur d'Hannibal (Liddes, Valais), *Notizie Archeologiche Bergomensi* 21, 157–65.
9 Livy, *History of Rome* 21.38.9 translated by Foster, B. O. 1929 Loeb Classical Library, London: Heinemann V.112–13.
10 Rubat Borel, Franceso and Paccolat, Olivier 2008 Une inscription lépontique découverte à Argnou, commune d'Ayent VS, *Jahrbuch Archäologie Schweiz* 91, 127–33.
11 Donnet, André 1942 *Saint Bernard et les origines de l'Hospice du Mont-Joux (Grand-St-Bernard)*, St-Maurice: L'œuvre St-Augustin; Lucken, Christopher 2003 Exorciser la montagne: Saint Bernard de Menthon au sommet du Mont-Joux, *Actes des congrès de la Société des historiens médiévistes de l'enseignement supérieur public* 34, 99–120.
12 Walser, Gerold 1984 *Summus Poeninus: Beiträge zur Geschichte des Grossen St. Bernhard-Passes in römischer Zeit*, Historia-Einzelschriften 46, Wiesbaden:

Figure 1.2 A votive from the temple at the Great St Bernard Pass. After Castan, Auguste 1877 Vesontio colonie romaine, *Revue archéologique* n.s. 33, 373-80, figure on p. 377.

votive plaques, which seem to have come from a Roman temple to Jupiter Poeninus that was erected in antiquity just south of the pass, 2464 m above sea level. The small (11 x 7 m) temple was established in the Flavian period on the remains of a former sacred site, presumably an open-air *nemetos* of the Salassi.

The contents of the Great St Bernard Pass inscriptions are more diverse than is typically the case for texts found at other provincial Roman dedicatory sites, with one even explicitly mentioning that it has been dedicated *pro itu et reditu* 'for the journey and return' over the Alps.[13] But the Great St Bernard inscriptions generally take a typical

---

Steiner; Hunt, Patrick 1998 Summus Poeninus on the Grand St Bernard Pass, *Journal of Roman Archaeology* 11, 265–74.

13 *Corpus Inscriptionum Latinarum*, edited by Theodor Mommsen *et al.*, Academia litterarum regiae Borussica (and successor bodies), 17 vols, Berlin: Reimer/De Gruyter V no. 6875.

three-part Roman dedicatory form, i.e. that of a *votum* or 'vow' text; e.g.:

> Iovi Poenino
> Q(uintus) Silvius Peren
> -nis tabell(arius) colon(iae)
> Sequanor(um)
> v(otum) s(olvit) l(ibens) m(erito)
>
> To Jove Poeninus.
> Quintus Silvius Perennis,
> a courier from Colonia Sequanorum.
> In fulfilment of a vow, willingly and deservedly.[14]

In the Latin dedications, the name Poeninus is typically reduced to an epithet of Jupiter. Sometimes the votive plaques merely feature the name of the devotee or of the dedicator and a *votum* formula, mostly commonly *v(otum) s(olvit) l(ibens) m(erito)*.[15] The god venerated is often referred to just as *Poenino*, but also as *I(ovi) O(ptimo) M(aximo) Poenino*, i.e. 'to Jove Poeninus, the best and the greatest', *Optimo Maximo* being a common epithet of Jupiter.[16] Votive statuettes of Jupiter were also found in the sanctuary, among evidence of other cults, including bronze figurines of Minerva, Fortuna and Tutela, a horse, an eagle, a foot and a hand. It is a different matter in the epichoric inscription from above Liddes, however, where Poeninus' name appears without the corresponding Roman form and along with what seems most plainly to be understood as a Celtic dedicatory verb, not a reference to a vow. Inscriptions of the *votum* type are a peculiarly Latin development and are widely attested across the Roman provinces.[17] A different kind of religious expression from those found in the temple by

---

14 *Corpus Inscriptionum Latinarum* V no. 6887.
15 E.g. *Corpus Inscriptionum Latinarum* V nos 6863–64.
16 E.g. *Corpus Inscriptionum Latinarum* V nos 6865 and 77.
17 Derks, Ton 1998 *Gods, Temples and Religious Practices: The Transformation of Religious Ideas and Values in Roman Gaul*, Amsterdam Archaeological Studies 2, Amsterdam: Amsterdam University Press 215–39.

the Great St Bernard Pass, the epichoric Liddes text appears closer in style to a typical Gaulish dedication.

Gaulish dedications usually take a more typical (and simple) archaic style than do Roman *votum* texts.[18] The basic form of a Gaulish dedication includes the nominative name of the dedicator, the verb *ieuru* in second syntactic position, the name of the divinity in the dative and a description of the object being dedicated in the accusative. A dedication from Auxey, Côte d'Or found in the eighteenth century, for example, reads:

> Iccauos Op-
> pianicnos ieu
> -ru Brigindoni
> cantalon
>
> Iccauos son of
> Oppianos
> dedicated (this) *cantalon*
> to Brigindona[19]

The Liddes inscription seems best understood as a laconic form of a typical *ieuru* text, with the name of the dedicator and the object being dedicated not being expressed. The verb features in second position in line with the verb-second tendency widely observed in Gaulish.[20]

The name Poeninus, however, also seems to be attested in two inscriptions from the Val Brembana, Lombardy. The Val Brembana inscriptions hail from much further to the east, but feature two more apparent references to Poeninus (Celtic Poininos). First published in 2005 by members of the Centro Storico Culturale Valle Brembana, the Val Brembana inscriptions presumably date to the second or third

---

18 Lambert, Pierre-Yves 2003 *La langue gauloise: description linguistique, commentaire d'inscriptions choisies*, 2nd ed., Paris: Errance 93–109.
19 *Recueil des inscriptions gauloises*, XLVe supplément à «*Gallia*», edited by Paul-Marie Duval *et al.*, 4 vols, Paris: CNRS no. L-9.
20 See Koch, John T. 1985 Movement and Emphasis in the Gaulish Sentence, *Bulletin of the Board of Celtic Studies* 32, 1–37.

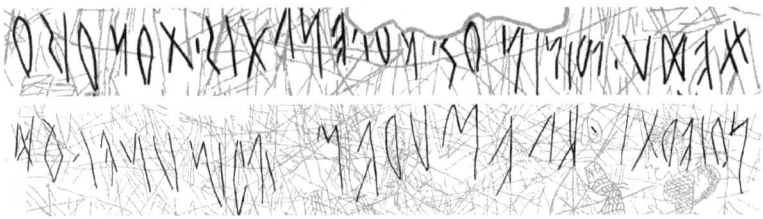

Figure 1.3 Dedications to Poininos from the Val Brembana. After Casini, Stephania and Fossati, Angelo 2013 Incisioni rupestri e iscrizioni preromane a Carona, Val Brembana (Bergamo), *Bulletin des études préhistorique et archéologique alpines* 24, 377–92: 380.

centuries BC and the references to Poeninus were both found on the same rock outcrop in the Val Camisana (above Carona) some 2248 m above sea level.[21] Comparable rupestrian inscriptions are a characteristic of the neighbouring Valcamonica and are generally thought to have had a religious function, but the Valcamonica texts are not obviously Celtic. One of the other rocks from the Val Camisana features Camunic inscriptions, however, and some of the characters used in the Lepontic texts from the Val Brembana look to have been influenced by Camunic letterforms.[22] The Val Camisana inscriptions are found along with images that date back as far as the fifth century BC and the carvings (which include those of medieval knights) were evidently still being added to the outcrops until quite recently.

The fifth of the Celto-Etruscan texts described in the Val Brembana find report appears to be written in the nominative and includes the form *poininos*:

---

21 Riceputi, Felice, and Dordoni, Francesco 2005 Incisioni rupestri sulle montagne di Carona, *Quaderni Brembani* 3, 8–17.
22 Motta, Filippo 2015 Incontri di genti e di culture: aggiornamento sui ritrovamenti epigrafici in Val Camisana (Carona), *Quaderni Brembani* 13, 35–43.

zaśu.poininos.kopenatis.tonoiso[23]

The second-last two forms in the Val Brembana *poininos* text clearly represent a binomen of the genitival kind: presumably Compenatis (son) of Donnos.[24] The form *zaśu* which precedes *poininos* looks to represent a derivative of **sta-* < Indo-European **steh₂-* 'stand', perhaps with a meaning comparable to Greek εὐ-σταθής 'well-built, steadfast, quiet'. An apparent oblique form of the second term *poininos*, however, appears in one of the longest lexically interpretable finds, the eleventh of the Val Brembana inscriptions:

noiarti.kpamuram.poinunei.oś[25]

This inscription seems to reflect a more regularly syntactic sentence, beginning with a verb *noiarti* followed by at least two nominal constituents. The oblique form *poinunei* follows an accusative *kpamuram* (of unclear meaning) and looks to be a morphological locative serving as a dative, a relatively common early Italian Celtic phenomenon.[26] Like the accusative form *kpamuram*, which is presumably best understood as *k(l)amuram* (and perhaps associated with Latin *clamō* 'call, cry out'), the locative seems more regularly to be understood as *poin(i)nei* with the *u* given in the find report representing an overly ambitious reading—although vocalic variation (apophony) might also explain the suffixal form. The expected dative at Liddes would be **poininū*, however—both the spelling of the diphthong and the dative inflection attested in the Liddes inscription are unexpected and look as if they may represent Latin influence.

---

23   Casini, Stephania and Fossati, Angelo 2013 Incisioni rupestri e iscrizioni preromane a Carona, Val Brembana (Bergamo), *Bulletin des études préhistorique et archéologique alpines* 24, 377–92: 380.
24   Casini, Fossati and Motta, Incisioni protostoriche 97.
25   Casini and Fossati 380.
26   Eska, Joseph F. and Wallace, Rex E. 2001 A Syncretism *in fieri* in Early Celtic, *Indogermanische Forschungen* 106, 229–40.

Yet the epichoric spellings *poin-* and *poen-* are difficult to reconcile with the nineteenth-century assumption that Poininos is somehow related to Welsh *pen*, Old Irish *cenn* < *$k^u enno$-* 'head'.[27] Instead, a relationship to Middle Irish *cin* 'guilt, crime, payment, respect, esteem', Lithuanian *káina* 'price', Greek ποινή 'compensation', Avestan *kaēnā-* 'vengeance, hatred' < *$k^u oin\bar{a}$* 'compensation' would seem more regular phonologically. Presumably, Poininos meant 'the respected one, the honoured one'; cf., similarly, Greek τιμή which means both 'honour, dignity' and 'compensation, penalty'.

The second line in the Liddes inscription more clearly features a form of the common Gaulish dedicatory verb *ieuru*, albeit with a Latinate *r* where the authors of the find report read *is*.[28] The inscription represents a dedication to Poeninus, written in a typically Gaulish manner, with the late spelling *-oe-* for Val Brembana *-oi-* comparable to the late spelling *-eo-* for earlier Lepontic *-io-*.[29] The verb *ieuru* is usually accepted to represent the functional equivalent of Latin *dedit* 'gave' where the *-u* is a perfective ending of unclear origin.[30] In a discussion with Tom Markey in 2011, Eric Hamp posited that the *-u* of *ieuru* was in origin merely (a facultative) part and parcel of the perfect also reflected in the perfect active Indo-European participle *-ue/os-/-u-/-u- which is typically (and most prominently) inserted after laryngeals; cf. Sanskrit *dadāu, paprāu* and the Magre form *dedeve*.[31]

Gaulish *ieuru* (also attested as *ieiuru, ieuri, iourus,* ειωρου and ειωραι) has long been connected with Old Irish *ro-ír* 'gave' and *-ern* 'grants, gives' < Indo-European *$perh_3$-* 'provide', and hence thought to continue *$pe-porh_3$-*.[32] The zero grade is preserved in the future tense

---

27 Zeuss, Johann Kaspar 1853 *Grammatica Celtica*, Berlin: Weidmann 77.
28 Cassini, Fossati and Motta, L'iscrizione in alfabeto di Lugano 158.
29 Lejeune 52.
30 Lambert 65–66.
31 Tom Markey, pers. comm., 26 January 2011; cf. Markey, Thomas L. 2006 Early Celticity in Slovenia and at Rhaetic Magrè (Schio), *Linguistica* 46, 145–71: 161.
32 Lambert, Pierre-Yves 1979 Gaulois IEVRV: irlandais *(ro)-ír* 'dicauit', *Zeitschrift für celtische Philologie* 37, 207–213; Rix, Helmut 2001 *Lexikon der indogermanischen Verben: Die Wurzeln und ihre Primärstammbildungen*, 2nd ed., Wiesbaden: Reichert 474–75.

Old Irish *ebra-* 'will give' < **pi-prā-* < **pi-prh₃-*, but Old Irish *nia*, genitive *niath* 'nephew' < **nepos, nepotes* suggests that *-ir* does not continue **pe-porh₃-*.³³ The Gaulish forms have also been held to feature a reflex of the preverb **epi-* with *īeur-* < **ei̯-eor-* < **epi-pe-porh₃-* and Gallo-Greek ειωρ- (i.e. *īōr-*) < *īeur-*.³⁴ A similar preverb is not clearly attested elsewhere in Celtic, however, and **ei* usually monophthongises to *ē*. A precise parallel for the presumed development of **epi-* > *ī-* has not as yet been discerned elsewhere in Celtic and connecting the Gallo-Latin dedicatory verb with the description *eurises* on the pillar of the boatmen does not explain the vocalism of *ieuru* either.³⁵

It is fairly clear, however, that the form *noiarti* in the second Val Brembana Poininos text is a compound form featuring a preverb *no-* and an infixed clitic or second preverb. The verbal root is self-evidently *ar-*, i.e. what seems best to be understood as a zero-grade variant of the form reflected in Old Irish *ro-ír* 'gave', *-ern* 'grants, gives' and *ebra-* 'will give'; cf. Latin *parō* 'prepare' < **prh₃-*. The *e*-vocalism in Old Irish *-ern* does not seem to be original and the expected nasal present is **-arn* < **pr̥néh₃-*.³⁶ The Val Brembana form *noiarti* looks much like it represents a *t*-preterite 'dedicated, gave' with a preverb *ī-* < **epi-* or infixed pronoun *-i-* < **id* following the element *no-*.³⁷

From an Insular Celtic perspective, the Val Brembana form *noiarti* seems most likely to feature an infixed pronoun, *no-* often being used in Old Irish as a 'dummy' preverb (i.e. as a semantically functionless host

---

33   Schumacher, Stefan 2004 *Die keltischen Primärverben: Ein vergleichendes, etymologisches und morphologisches Lexikon*, Innsbruck: Institut für Sprachen und Literaturen der Universität Innsbruck 509–10.
34   Schmidt, Karl Horst 1986 Zur Rekonstruktion des Keltischen: Festlandkeltisches und inselkeltisches Verbum, *Zeitschrift für celtische Philologie* 41, 159–79: 176.
35   *Recueil des inscriptions gauloises* no. L-2; Lambert, *Langue gauloise* 205 and cf. О'Шей, Наталья Андреевна 2005 Галльские и лепонтийские формы претерита—традиции, инновации и вопрос диалектного распределения, *Вопросы Языкознания* 6, 31–43: 36.
36   Cf. McCone, Kim 1991 *The Indo-European Origins of the Old Irish Nasal Presents, Subjunctives and Futures*, Innsbrucker Beiträge zur Sprachwissenschaft 66, Innsbruck: Institut für Sprachwissenschaft der Universität Innsbruck 27–29.
37   Cf. McCone 107.

for an object clitic). The final diphthong in the Liddes spelling *ieureu*, however, looks to be a phonologically more conservative form than that recorded in the Gallo-Greek orthographies ειωρου and ειωραι, and a connection of *eurises* with *ieuru* supports the impression that an infix or preverb is present in the usual form taken by the Gallo-Latin dedicatory verb. The Liddes spelling may indicate that the inherited perfective base was *i-or-* < **pe-porh₃-* with *ieur-* featuring an infixed object pronoun: i.e. *i-e-ur-* 'gave it' with **id* > *e* and **-e-o-* > *-e-u-*; cf. the Gaulish verb *readdas* which has been analysed as continuing **(p)ro-e(d)-ad-da-s-t*.[38] Pronouns infixed within reduplicated forms are otherwise unattested, however, suggesting that a better explanation of the middle element of *no-i-arti* is as a preverb, and that Old Irish *-ír*, Gallo-Greek ειωρ-, Gallo-Latin *ieuru* and the Liddes form *ieureu* all continue **īeor-* < **epi-pe-porh₃-*. The final term *oś* appears to be pronominal and to reflect the same element as appears in the Celtiberian pronouns *oscues, osias* etc.[39]

Epigraphic Romanisation

The epigraphic find from Liddes also sheds light on the process of Romanisation in the Celtic Alps, with the appearance of the Latinate *r* presumably reflecting a form of 'alphabet-switching'.[40] Gaulish inscriptions (particularly those which appear on coins) often feature graphemes taken from a mixture of epigraphic traditions and another dedicatory inscription which features influence from Latin was found in the 1980s on a tablet of zinc that was found by the user of a metal detector in the northern suburbs of the city of Berne.[41] Discovered in a park that lies on a pronounced loop in the Aare (the Enge peninsula),

---

38 Schrijver, Peter 1997 *Studies in the History of Celtic Pronouns and Particles*, Maynooth Studies in Celtic Linguistics 2, Maynooth: Department of Old Irish 178–79.

39 Meid, Wolfgang 1993 *Die erste Botorrita-Inschrift: Interpretation eines keltiberischen Sprachdenkmals*, Innsbrucker Beiträge zur Sprachwissenschaft 76, Innsbruck: Institut für Sprachwissenschaft der Universität Innsbruck 101–2.

40 Adams, James N. 2003 *Bilingualism and the Latin Language*, Cambridge University Press 70–76.

the zinc tablet preserves a predominately Gallo-Greek text, executed in a pointillist or *punctim* manner, but with its last line featuring Roman R's rather than regular Greek rhos. The whole Enge peninsular area (which has been the subject of numerous excavations since the nineteenth century) shows signs of Iron Age fortification and was presumably an *oppidum*—Roman and La Tène-era graves, a pre-Roman cult site (which featured a mass deposition of weapons), an arena, a thermal bath, some Roman religious buildings and even the remains of a Roman *vicus* have all been found in the environs.[42] The Berne inscription also consistently shows omicron or omega where a representation of /u/ would be expected, a matter treated somewhat inconclusively by previous examiners of the find:

ΔΟΒΝΟΡΗΔΟ
ΓΟΒΑΝΟ
ΒΡΕΝΟΔΩΡ
ΝΑΝΤΑΡΩΡ

Dobnorēdo Goban(n)o Bren(n)odor(o) Nantaror(o)[43]

In *Dobnorēdo*, for example, the *-o-* in the first syllable appears where Gaulish forms usually record *-u-* (cf. Old Irish *domun*, Welsh *dwfn* 'world') and final *-o* stands where Gaulish texts usually feature *-ū* < *-*ōi*. The inscription on the Berne tablet also fails to represent what other texts suggest were phonological geminates and the representation of /u/ in Greek inscriptions by a digraph of OY suggests that the spelling of expected /u/ with omicron and omega in the ancient Helvetic text

---

41 Fellmann, Rudolf 1991 Die Zinktafel von Bern-Thormebodenwald und ihre Inschrift, *Archäologie der Schweiz* 14, 270–73; Fellmann, Rudolf 1999 Das Zink-Täfelchen vom Thormebodenwald auf der Engehalbinsel bei Bern und seine keltische Inschrift, *Archäologie im Kanton Bern* 4B, 133–75; Stüber, Karin 2005 *Schmied und Frau: Studien zur gallischen Epigraphik und Onomastik*, Series minor 19, Budapest: Archaeolingua 20–21.
42 Wyss, René 1976 Bern Engehalbinsel, *Reallexikon der germanischen Altertumskunde* II, edited by Henrich Beck, Herbert Jankuhn and Reinhard Wenskus, 2nd ed., Berlin: De Gruyter 284–88.
43 *Recueil des inscriptions gauloises* no. L–106.

may similarly represent an orthographic inadequacy. Yet Gallo-Greek inscriptions typically employ the usual Greek digraph for /u/, so such an interpretation would be quite unparalleled.[44]

More surprising for the discoverers of the Enge text, however, was the information suggested by the inscription. The figure Gobannos mentioned in the Berne dedication is known from several other ancient Alpine finds and seems to represent much the same figure as Irish Goibniu and Welsh Gofannon.[45] Yet the dative form *Dobnorēdo* which comes before the style *Goban(n)o* would be expected to represent the Helvetic god's theonym proper—the style Gobannos in the Berne inscription seems merely to represent a divine epithet 'the smith god'.[46]

The second part of the zinc text seems more revealing, however. The form *Bren(n)odor-* is evidently to be interpreted as an ablative (with understood final $-o < *-ū < *-ōd$?) 'from Brennoduron' (literally 'the lord's market'), seemingly the Celtic name of the city of Berne. This form presumably lays to rest the medieval folk etymology which explains that Berne received its name from the German word for 'bear'—that the founder of the medieval castle of Berne, Duke Berchtold V von Zähringen, named the site after a bear he killed there.[47] This etymology, encapsulated by the bear on the arms of the Canton of Berne, masks a Celtic origin for the ancient Helvetic town, the development of *Bern* < *Brenn-* presumably due to a metathesis comparable to that seen in (poetic) German *Born* 'fount' vs. (regular) German *Brunnen* 'well, source'. Indeed the ablative nature of the second part of the text seems to be assured by the final term *Nant-*

---

44 Cf. Stüber 29.
45 De Bernardo Stempel, Patrizia 2003 Die sprachliche Analyse keltischer Theonyme, *Zeitschrift für celtische Philologie* 53, 41–69: 49–50; Stüber 30–36.
46 Cf. De Bernardo Stempel, Patrizia 2008 More Names, Fewer Deities: Complex Theonymic Formulas and the Three Types of *interpretatio*, *Divindades indígenas em análise = Divinité pré-romaines—bilan et perspectives d'une recherche: Actas do VII workshop FERCAN, Cascais 25–27 mai 2006*, edited by José d'Encarnação, Coimbra: Centro de estudos Arqueològicos 65–73.
47 Studer, Gottlien, editor 1871 *Die Berner-Chronik des Conrad Justinger*, Berne: Wyss 8.

Figure 1.4 The Berne zinc tablet inscription. Drawing by Fellmann from Fellmann, Rudolf 1999 Das Zink-Täfelchen vom Thormebodenwald auf der Engehalbinsel bei Bern und seine keltische Inschrift, *Archäologie im Kanton Bern* 4B, 133–75, fig. 3.

aror-, the inscription clearly featuring the Old Celtic word for valley (*nant-*) as well as what seems to have been the original Celtic form of the ancient name of the river that flows about the Enge peninsular which is also attested in ancient epigraphic expressions such as *Aruranci* and *Arure(nsis)*.[48]

---

48   *Corpus Inscriptionum Latinarum* XIII nos 5096 and 5161; Greule, Albrecht 2014 *Deutsches Gewässernamenbuch: Etymologie der Gewässernamen und der dazugehörigen Gebiets-, Siedlungs- und Flurnamen*, Berlin: De Gruyter 22.

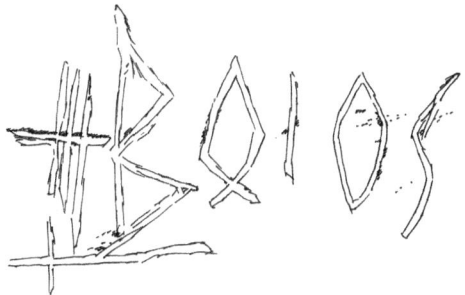

Figure 1.5 The Manching Boios inscription. Drawing by Bernard Mees.

The Liddes text shares both the indication of morphological datives with an -*o* rather than a -*u* and the appearance of a Latinate *r* with the Berne dedication. The alternation between omicron and omega in the Berne inscription also suggests that the characteristically 'footed' *o* from the Liddes inscription may represent the influence of a Greek omega. Moreover this 'footed' *o* from Liddes is also attested in one of the Manching inscriptions, in the Celtic anthroponym Boios.[49]

Excavated in 1972, the Manching inscriptions date to the second or last century BC and the *Boios* inscription varies a 'footed' *o* in its first syllable with a more regular *o* in the thematic suffix. In this way, the spelling employed at Manching is reminiscent of the variation seen on the Berne tablet in forms such as BRENOΔΩR, where the omega is used to represent etymological /u/. Rather than indicate that

---

49   Krämer, Werner 1982 Graffiti auf Spätlatènekeramik aus Manching, *Germania* 60, 489–99; Bammesberger, Alfred 1997 Celtic *BOIOS*, *Festschrift for Eric P. Hamp*, edited by Douglas Q. Adams, Journal of Indo-European Studies Monograph 23, 2 vols, Washington DC: Institute for the Study of Man I.60–66; Bammesberger, Alfred 1997 Vergleichende Sprachwissenschaft: ortsgebunden und weltoffen; Aufgaben—Methoden—Perspektiven, *Wozu Wissenschaft Heute: Ringvorlesung zu Ehren von Roland Hagenbüchle*, edited by Hans Hunfeld, Tübingen: Narr 9–24.

the Manching form should be understood as *Buios*, however, the appearance of 'footed' *o* in the Manching *Boios* inscription suggests how the similarly shaped character in the Liddes text developed.

Indeed such 'alphabet-switching' has been compared to second-language learning, as if the intrusions of Gallo-Latin epigraphic letterforms represent some kind of orthographic carry-over or 'substratum'.[50] The late La Tène and Julio-Claudian periods witness the production of several mixed and bilingual Roman/North Etruscan inscriptions, and a number of late North Etruscan texts from the eastern Alps appear to feature some amount of graphematic Romanisation, while the reverse is attested in others.[51] The geographically isolated inscription from Ptuj, Slovenian Styria, for example, appears to feature a Roman *b*, and a Roman *q* equally seems to have intruded into an otherwise graphematically North Etruscan text from Cadore, Belluno.[52] The bilingual inscription from Voltino, Brescia, similarly features a North Etruscan *ś* in its onomastic sequence *Saśadis* and comparable intrusions are attested in Roman texts from the Veneto.[53] The appearance of Roman letterforms in texts such as the Berne and Liddes dedications is an expected feature of Romanisation,

---

50 Adams 70–76.
51 Stifter, David 2009 Neue Inschriften in norditalischer Schrift aus Österreich, *Die Sprache* 48, 233–40; Eska, Joseph F. and Wallace, Rex E. 2011 Script and Language at Ancient Voltino, *Alessandria* 5, 93–113; Marchesini, Simona 2011 Identità multiple o *ethic change* durante la romanizzazione: il territorio attorno al Garda, *Identità e autonomie nel mondo romano occidentale: Iberia-Italia, Italia-Iberia; III Convegno Internazionale di epigrafia e storia antica, Gargnano, 12–15 maggio 2010*, edited by Antonio Sartori and Alfredo Valvo, Epigrafia e antichità 29, Faenza: Fratelli Lega 435–54.
52 Eichner, Heiner 2006 Zu den Quellen und Übertragungswegen der germanischen Runenschrift: Ein Diskussionsbeitrag, *Das fuþark und seine einzelsprachlichen Weiterentwicklungen: Akten der Tagung in Eichstätt vom 20. bis 24. Juli 2003*, edited by Alfred Bammesberger and Gaby Waxenberger, Ergänzungsbände zum Reallexikon der germanischen Altertumskunde 51, Berlin: De Gruyter 101–8: 105; Prosdocimi, Aldo L. 2006 Luogo, ambiente e nascita delle rune: una proposta, *Lettura dell'Edda: poesia e prosa*, edited by Vittoria Dolcetti Corazza and Renato Gendre, Bibliotheca Germanica: Studi e testi 19, Alessandria: Orso 148–202: 184–86.
53 Mainardis, Fulvia 2009 Forme e modalità dell'acculturazione epigrafica tra diglossia e digrafia, *Aspetti e problemi della romanizzazione: Venetia, Histria e*

although the appearance of a 'footed' *o* in the Liddes text is a reminder that multiple influences on epichoric writing traditions may appear in late Celto-Etruscan inscriptions. Most of the texts that feature evidence of alphabet-switching appear only on the margins of the broader Celto-Etruscan area, however, suggesting that Romanisation of this kind was restricted to the periphery of the region where the most Lepontic inscriptions have been discovered.

Conclusion

Although it looks at first glance to be quite irregular, the many unexpected features of the Liddes inscription can all be paralleled in comparably dating texts. Not just a testimony of how late the use of North Etruscan characters was in the western Alps, the Liddes dedication is crucial evidence of the process of Romanisation. Offered to a native Celtic god also attested in the Val Brembana, the Liddes text is a dedicatory rather than a *votum* expression, even if it appears to feature some graphematic Romanisation. The Liddes inscription is not linguistically Romanised, but instead seems to reflect a form of alphabet switching. Like the Berne inscription, the Liddes text is a native Celtic record of life from a time in which vernacular traditions were still in use, albeit in one of the less accessible regions of the early empire.

arco alpino orientale, edited by Giuseppe Cuscito, Antichità Altoadriatiche 68, Trieste: Editreg 331–53; Eska and Wallace, Script and language.

2
Landscapes, Myth-Making and Memory: Ecclesiastical Landholding in Early Medieval Ireland

Tomás Ó Carragáin

In Ireland, as elsewhere in early medieval Europe, land grants from kings and nobles were essential to the development of major ecclesiastical sites. For example, in the case of the kingdom of Fir Maige, Co. Cork, for which textual sources are relatively rich, it has been estimated that about fifteen percent of land, including some of the most fertile, was granted to its three principal church sites; and when the interests of lesser churches are taken into account, at least a third of the kingdom had strong ecclesiastical associations.[1] As there is no reason to suspect this was unusual, ecclesiastical landholding is clearly vital to an understanding, not only of ecclesiastical organisation, but of the character of early medieval polities. This chapter considers the phenomenon from an archaeological perspective. Focussing on the core lands of substantial (rather than lesser) churches, I will consider how earlier settlements, monuments and burial grounds were treated when land became ecclesiastical and will suggest that this can reveal a lot about attitudes to the past and how clerics sought to shape perceptions of their newly acquired landholdings.

---

1 Ó Carragáin, T. 2014 The Archaeology of Ecclesiastical Estates in Early Medieval Ireland: A Case Study of the Kingdom of Fir Maige, *Peritia* 24–25, 266–74: 272–73; MacCotter, P. 2012 Túath, Manor and Parish: Kingdom of Fir Maige, Cantred of Fermoy, *Peritia* 22, 211–48.

Pastoral Care and Farming

Before turning to this theme, let me briefly outline current trends in the study of ecclesiastical landholding. The passages in legal tracts and hagiography relating to it have been analysed by Thomas Charles-Edwards, Donnchadh Ó Corráin and Colmán Etchingham among others.[2] Historians, however, have rarely looked in detail at specific examples on the ground. One of the aims of University College Cork's Making Christian Landscapes project was to see whether this was possible.[3] While we lack charters like those available to Anglo-Saxonists,[4] Paul MacCotter found that it is sometimes possible to map them using hagiography, topographical texts and later and post medieval sources outlining the extents of church lands.[5] Such reconstructions are approximate and must be used cautiously. Nevertheless, they open up the possibility of using landscape analysis to address some of the key questions raised by ecclesiastical landholding.

For example, it has been suggested that pastoral provision was largely restricted to those living on ecclesiastical land.[6] If so, one might

---

2 Charles-Edwards, T. 1984. The Church and Settlement, *Ireland and Europe: the Early Church*, edited by P. Ní Chatháin and M. Richter, Stuttgart: Klett Cotta 167–78; Etchingham, C. 1999 *Church Organisation in Ireland, AD 650–1000* Maynooth: Laigin, 363–454; Ó Corráin, D. 2010 The Church and Secular Society, *L'Irland e gli Irlandesi nell'alto medioevo, Settimane di Studio ... sull'alto medioevo* 57, 261–322.
3 For an introduction to the project see Ó Carragáin, T. and Turner, S. 2016. Making Christian Landscapes in the Early Medieval Atlantic World, *Making Christian Landscapes in Atlantic Europe*, edited by T. Ó Carragáin and S. Turner, Cork University Press, 1–20.
4 Doherty, C. 1982 Some Aspects of Hagiography as a Source for Irish Economic History, *Peritia* 1, 300–28: 307.
5 For example, MacCotter 2012, 238–46; MacCotter, P. 2016 Reconstructing the Territorial Framework for Ecclesiastical and Secular Power Structures: a Case Study of the Kingdom of Uí Fáeláin, *Making Christian Landscapes in Atlantic Europe*, edited by T. Ó Carragáin and S. Turner, Cork University Press, 55–74.
6 Etchingham, C. 2006 Pastoral Provision in the First Millennium: a Two-Tier Service? *The Parish in Medieval and Post-Medieval Ireland*, edited by E. FitzPatrick and R. Gillespie, Dublin: Wordwell 79–90: 85.

expect ecclesiastical landholdings to have a far higher density of lesser churches than surrounding 'secular' territories, but this is rarely if ever the case. Thus, landscape archaeology seems to support the idea that a wider range of people had access to churches,[7] though we should not assume that pastoral provision was comprehensive or centrally organised. Another theory is that those interred in burial grounds without churches had limited engagement with Christianity in contrast to 'committed Christians' buried at church sites.[8] In some cases, it might be argued that this is supported by burial rites like cremation and horse burial, but many of those buried at such sites were probably considered Christian.[9] This seems especially likely in the case of burial grounds on church land. For example, roadway excavations uncovered an impressive settlement in Camlin on the lands of Monaincha.[10] It was established in the sixth century but in the seventh century occupation intensified and a burial ground was added that continued in use until the eleventh century. More women were interred there than men (1.4:1),[11] raising the possibility that some of the former became monks and were buried at Monaincha. In any case, sites such as this show that it was perfectly acceptable for Christians to be buried away from church sites. The incremental shift to churchyard burial is not a straightforward

---

7   As argued by Sharpe, R. 1992 Churches and Communities in Early Medieval Ireland: Towards a Pastoral Model, *Pastoral Care Before the Parish*, edited by J. Blair and R. Sharpe, Leicester University Press, 81–109; Swift, C. 2010 Early Irish Priests and their Areas of Ministry, *Parishes in Transition,* edited by E. Duffy, Dublin: Columba Press 20–46.
8   Etchingham 2006, 86–88.
9   O'Brien, E. and Bhreathnach, E. 2011 Irish Boundary *Ferta*, their Physical Manifestation and Historical Context, *Tome: Studies in Medieval Celtic History and Law in Honour of Thomas Charles-Edwards*, edited by Fiona Edmonds and Paul Russell, Woodbridge: Boydell 53–64.
10 Connon, A. and Ó Carragáin, T. 2009 Identifying and Characterising Ecclesiastical Sites in the Mag Réta Study Area, *The Making Christian Landscapes Project. Report for the Heritage Council*, edited by T. Ó Carragáin and J. Sheehan, Kilkenny, 311–440: 425; MacCotter, P. 2013 The M7 Motorway Historical Landscape: Studies in the History of Ikerrin and Elyocarroll, *Tipperary Historical Journal*, 25–57: 30; C. Flynn 2011 Camlin 3 Final Report. Unpublished Report by V. J. Keeley Ltd.
11 Flynn 2011, 637.

expression of conversion. Rather, along with other things, it reflects changes over the course of the period in what being Christian entailed.[12]

Another important question, which can only be touched upon here, is whether the character and scale of ecclesiastical landholding led to new methods of agricultural and craft production. Some ecclesiastical estates have distinctive settlement patterns. For example, on the estate of Brigown, Co. Cork, there are relatively few settlements but they are regularly spaced and a substantial proportion of them are lesser church sites with large enclosures. In contrast, neighbouring 'secular' territories have a higher density of smaller enclosures—mainly raths—representing largely self-sufficient family farmsteads. Perhaps instead, on the ecclesiastical estate, there was a planned network designed to harness the resources of the estate primarily on behalf of Brigown itself.[13] One does not find such marked contrasts in all cases, however, and in general there is little evidence to suggest a sharp dichotomy between the agricultural economies of ecclesiastical and secular lands. This is not surprising considering the textual evidence that, in addition to monks and labourers, a significant, though variable, proportion of those living on ecclesiastical estates were freeholders with hereditary rights over the lands they farmed. Clearly, there is considerable potential to use landscape analysis to explore the varying socio-economic strategies pursued by major church sites on their estates.

Monuments and Memory Work

Many of the subsidiary monuments dotted around complexes such as Armagh, Clonmacnoise and Inishmurray—from crosses to holy wells to lesser churches—were, it seems, intended to preserve memories

---

12 See, for example, Ó Carragáin, T. 2010a From Family Cemeteries to Community Cemeteries in Viking Age Ireland? *Death and Burial in Early Medieval Ireland in the Light of Recent Excavations,* edited by C. Corlett and M. Potterton, Dublin: Wordwell 217–26.

13 Ó Carragáin 2014, 276–81.

about the exemplary life of the founding saint.[14] Rings of monuments on the edges of the complex, sometimes on the line of its large curvilinear enclosures, facilitated circumambulatory processions around the complex impressing upon residents and visitors alike a sense of the site as a sacred centre.[15] Very rarely are prehistoric monuments found at these complexes. One example is at Armagh which of course was probably a centre for pre-Christian ritual. This is conveniently forgotten in Patrician hagiography, but at least one prehistoric monument seems to have been preserved at the site, namely a stone circle that stood in Gooseberry Gardens until the nineteenth century. It stood immediately outside the outer ecclesiastical enclosure and, if the street layout is any indication, seems to have been skirted by a notable kink in this enclosure, almost as if those laying out the site wished to emphasise its sanctity by consciously preserving this pagan monument only in order to exclude it.[16] This could be read in wholly negative terms, like a gargoyle at the exterior of a Gothic cathedral, but there are sometimes hints from both archaeology and hagiography of nuances and ambiguities in attitudes to pagan monuments, as we shall see. While particular interpretations of both pagan and Christian monuments sometimes found their way into saints' lives and other texts, most people experienced the cult of a saint primarily by engaging with landscapes and monuments directly, through movement, touch and speech.[17] While oral traditions are of course highly mutable, regular and formalised movement between and around monuments was a particularly effective way of shaping and conveying social

---

14 For an overview and some examples see Ó Carragáin, T. 2010b *Churches in Early Medieval Ireland. Architecture, Ritual and Memory,* New Haven: Yale 72–77, 156–58, 210–11, 215–25, 268–70. See also Manning, C. 2003 'Some early masonry churches and the round tower at Clonmacnoise', *Clonmacnoise Studies II,* edited by H. King, Dublin: Stationery Office 63–95: 71–72.

15 See for example O'Sullivan, J. and Ó Carragáin, T. 2008 *Inishmurray. Monks and Pilgrims in an Atlantic Landscape,* Cork: Collins Press 318–37.

16 Aitchison, N. B. 1994 *Armagh and the Royal Centres in Early Medieval Ireland,* Woodbridge: Boydell and Brewer for the Cruithne Press 222; Ó Carragáin 2010b, 157.

17 See, for example, Gosden, C. and Lock, G. 1998 Prehistoric Histories, *World Archaeology* 30, 2–12.

memory and preserving it over the long term.[18] For example, excavations on Inishmurray showed that the rituals carried out there until the 1970s on St Molaise's feastday probably preserved some aspects of a circumambulatory procession around the island devised about a millennium before, though the social context had changed dramatically.[19]

Now that whole ecclesiastical estates have been delimited, we have much larger canvases on which to consider this theme, often several kilometres across. In some cases, there is evidence that the ecclesiastical enclosure around the complex itself is augmented at a greater remove by an additional ring, or partial ring, of monuments. For example, on the lands of Brigown, several monuments are positioned on the banks of the River Gradoge, which encircles the site on three sides and which is identified as a boundary feature in the twelfth-century Life of Findchú.[20] Another is Inis Úasal, Co. Kerry where the establishment of the ecclesiastical estate meant a reordering of the landscape so that it was focused on the 'noble island' (Inis Úasal) itself, the exclusivity and sacredness of which was underscored not only by the waters of the lake in which it lies, but by a constellation of four evenly positioned lesser church sites in the area north of the lake delimited by the Coumduff ridge, and by several crosses positioned along this low but visually prominent ridge, one of them incised on what may possibly have been a pre-existing standing stone.[21] In neither case is the ring of monuments on the boundary of the estate itself. Rather, they are within the estate and represent an intermediate stage of ingress between the estate boundary on the one hand and the ecclesiastical enclosure on the other, amplifying the sacredness of the inner sanctum.

One does find monuments on the boundaries of estates, both new ones such as cross-slabs, and prehistoric monuments that may have been invested with new meanings, but usually they are modest in number and

---

18 See, for example, Connerton, P. 1989 *How Societies Remember*, Cambridge University Press; Coleman, S. M. and Elsner, J. 1994 The Pilgrim's Progress: Art, Architecture and Ritual Movement at Sinai, *World Archaeology* 26, 73–89.
19 O'Sullivan and Ó Carragáin 2008, 318–37.
20 Ó Carragáin 2014, 276.
21 Ó Carragáin, T., forthcoming, *Churches in the Irish Landscape, c.400–1100*.

tend to be at points of entry, rather than regularly spaced to mark out the extents of the estate.[22] Indeed, to date the most convincing examples of ecclesiastical foci placed at reasonably regular intervals on a boundary relate, not to those of ecclesiastical estates, but to the 'secular' territories—including local districts/*túatha* and larger-scale regional kingdoms—that contained such estates.[23] In these cases the foci in question are lesser ecclesiastical settlements rather than simply monuments like cross-slabs, and it seems they were placed on boundaries as assertions of dominion. These territories are too large, and the church sites on their boundaries too far apart, to envisage processions between them. Though definitive evidence is lacking, the partial rings of monuments *within* ecclesiastical estates, but at a remove from the complex itself, might more plausibly have been used in this way. After all, the routes they describe are comparable in length to the well-documented procession around the island of Inishmurray referred to above, which provides a good precedent for such rituals beyond the ecclesiastical enclosure. There is little textual or archaeological evidence for processions around whole ecclesiastical estates, however; indeed, it seems unlikely that these were common given the distances involved and the often-inhospitable terrain of estate boundaries.[24] As we shall now see, a more feasible scenario is a linear procession through the estate.

Re-envisioning the Past on the Lands of Inis Labrainne

Inis Labrainne, now Inch Co. Kerry, was one of the principal churches of the regional kingdom of Corcu Duibne. Its founder, Mochellóc, may have flourished in the seventh century and was reputedly related to the kings of Áes Irruis Tuascirt, one of the three sub-kingdoms of Corcu Duibne, comprising most of the Dingle

---

22 Ó Carragáin, forthcoming; Ó Carragáin 2014, 291.
23 Ó Carragáin 2014, 288–93; Connon, A. 2016 Territoriality and the Cult of Saint Ciarán of Saigir, *Making Christian Landscapes in Atlantic Europe,* edited by T. Ó Carragáin and S. Turner, Cork University Press, 109–157.
24 John Blair is also sceptical about the idea of *processions* on the boundaries of Anglo-Saxon ecclesiastical estates. Blair, J. 2005 *The Church in Anglo-Saxon Society,* Oxford University Press 479–88.

peninsula.[25] The later medieval parish centre of Inch is probably on the site of the early church, though no early archaeology is now evident. According to Paul MacCotter its estate comprised a substantial block of land running west from Inch, and a detached portion at the west end of the peninsula incorporating Fahan and the Blasket Islands, one of which, Inisvickillane, is named for Mochellóc.[26] There is a good deal of archaeological evidence to corroborate the identification of this detached portion as ecclesiastical land, including a tall cross marking an important point of entry on the eastern boundary of Fahan, and the greatest concentration in Ireland of ringforts (mainly cashels) with cross-sculpture.[27] There are also hints that both parts of the estate were granted by kings. Here I will focus on the distribution of cross-sculpture on the main portion of the estate around Inch itself.

One piece of sculpture, a Latin cross with expanded terminals, is inscribed on a standing stone near the northern boundary of the estate in Emlagh.[28] It stands in a prominent location at the far side of a narrow break in the hills that represents the only point of access to Inch from the north and the cross is carved on its north face. This is surely a boundary marker, signalling to people coming from the north that they are entering an ecclesiastical territory. Otherwise, however, instead of forming an arc around the site most of the sculpture is distributed in a linear fashion to either side of the most important routeway running through the estate, and the most important east–west road on the Dingle peninsula. This makes sense given the shape of the estate: long and narrow with the principal church at one end rather than positioned centrally like Inis Úasal and Brigown. There are eight inscribed crosses near the routeway and another route-side monument, a bullaun stone,

---

25   Ó Corráin, D. 2004 To Chellóc mac Oíbléni: Saint and Places, *Cin Chille Cuile: Texts, Saints and Places*, edited by J. Carey, K. Murray, M. Herbert, Aberystwyth: Celtic Studies Publications 258–67.
26   MacCotter, Paul, forthcoming, Ecclesiastical and Royal Estates of Corcu Duibne, *Churches in the Irish Landscape, 400–1100*, edited by T. Ó Carragáin.
27   Ó Carragáin, forthcoming.
28   Cuppage, J. 1986 *Corca Dhuibhne. Dingle Peninsula Archaeological Survey*, Ballyferriter: Oidhreacht Chorca Dhuibne, no. 102.

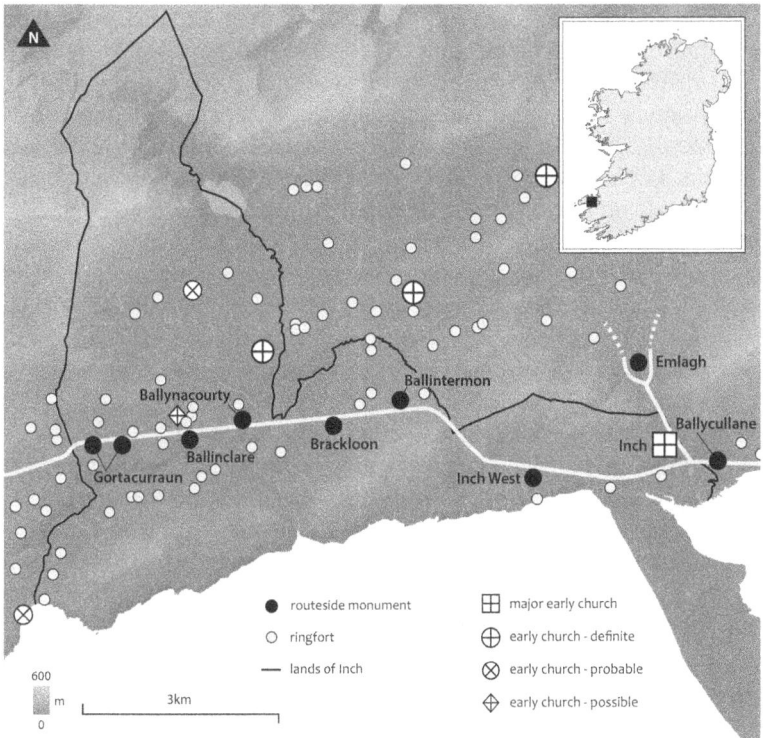

Figure 2.1 The core estate of Inch Labhrainne showing early medieval settlements and route-side monuments. Map by Nick Hogan and Tomás Ó Carragáin.

a short distance east of Inch.[29] Most of the crosses are very similar in form and size and their style suggests that they represent a single project. They have expanded terminals, a feature missing from crosses in Corcu Duibne that probably date to the fifth century. This supports the possibility that they were inscribed in the late sixth or seventh century when Inch and its estate was established, though a later date cannot be ruled out.

---

29 Cuppage, no. 963.

In addition to the Emlagh cross, three of the others, in Ballintermon, Brackloon and Ballynacourty, are on monuments classified as standing stones.[30] Unlike stone pairs and alignments, which are generally considered to date to the Bronze Age, one cannot assume that single standing stones are prehistoric; some could be early medieval. Thus, while the Dingle Archaeological Survey states that the crosses on those under discussion here were added to them 'at a later period,' we cannot be certain of this.[31] In particular, it is quite possible that those on the relatively small stones with broad faces at Emlagh and Ballynacourty are primary features of these monuments. In contrast, the massive, irregular examples in Ballintermon (3.9 m high) and Brackloon (3.25 m high) are reminiscent of stones in monuments of undoubtedly prehistoric date. Whether or not they are prehistoric, it seems clear that their diminutive crosses are additions.

Proximity to the routeway was clearly a factor when selecting which pre-extant monuments to inscribe, but it was not the only one. In the case of the two standing stones most likely to be prehistoric, there is evidence to suggest they had already been reactivated and reinterpreted by people in the more recent past. Excavations in 1991 showed that the Brackloon standing stone, and a nearby outcropping boulder with prehistoric rock art, had been chosen as foci for burial.[32] Two graves are known, but only one was excavated to modern standards and a radiocarbon date is not available. It was an extended inhumation so was probably early medieval, either pre-dating or contemporary with the Inch estate. At Ballintermon (from *termonn* meaning church land), the standing stone also has pre-550 ogham inscription, indisputable evidence for early medieval engagement with the monument before the establishment of Inch.[33] The individual commemorated may well have been buried nearby, and in any case, the inscription claimed the area for his descendants. Later, a substantial portion of it was removed by levering away a large spall. There is no evidence for comparable

---

30 Cuppage, nos. 77, 86, 163.
31 Cuppage 38.
32 Moore, F. 1991 [1991:067] Brackloon, Kerry, www.excavations.ie/report/1991/Kerry/0001126/.
33 McManus, D. 1991 *A Guide to Ogam,* Maynooth: Dept of Old Irish 94.

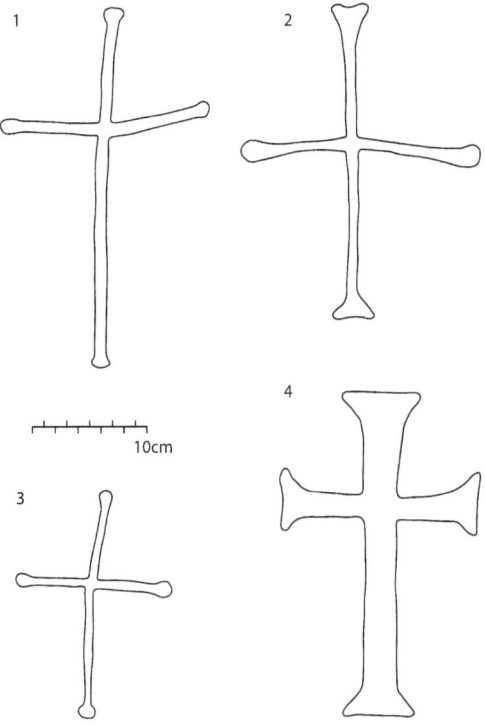

Figure 2.2 Crosses inscribed into standing stones at Emlagh, Brackloon, Ballintermon and Ballynacourty. Drawing by Nick Hogan and Tomás Ó Carragáin.

damage elsewhere on the monument and this has all the appearance of deliberate defacement, probably contemporary with the cross which is placed just beside it. Surely, this represents a new claim: that of Inch. Though probably carved on newly selected slabs, some of the other route-side crosses may also have been intended to overlay new meanings upon existing sacred foci: one is associated with a mound, possibly for burial,[34] while three of the others are at holy wells.[35] While it can never be assumed, there is always the possibility that particular

Figure 2.3 Standing stone in Brackloon with nearby rock outcrop decorated with prehistoric rock-art. At least two interments took place between these two monuments in the early medieval period and, perhaps later still, the standing stone was incised with a cross. Photo by Tomás Ó Carragáin.

wells were already considered sacred at the beginning of the early medieval period or even before.

Though sited on both sides of it, the crosses all face the routeway, reinforcing their association with it. However, while the larger standing stones are clearly visible from it, the crosses themselves would hardly have been, even if painted, for they are usually at least 100 m away. The estates of some church sites, like Portmahomack on the Tarbat Peninsula in north-eastern Scotland, feature highly impressive cross-slabs with complex iconography representing investment of

---

34   Cuppage, no. 842 (Gortacurraun).
35   Cuppage, nos. 913 (Gortacurraun), 939 (Ballinclare), 941 (Inch West).

considerable time, resources, artistic skill and learning. These are not directly analogous to the Inch crosses, for they are not simply wayside markers standing isolated in the landscape, but were probably at lesser church sites. Nevertheless, they also served to delimit the peninsula and Carver suggests they were designed to be visible on the horizon from the sea and that they were probably painted.[36] In contrast, on the Inch estate we see small, simple crosses some apparently added to pre-existing monuments. Their message was not one that could readily be appreciated by anyone who happened to pass through the estate, so how was it conveyed to the community of Inch, its patrons, tenants and neighbours? Perhaps we should envisage a public 'foundation' ritual during which the crosses were carved. Their very simplicity, and slight irregularities, support such an interpretation: it suggests they may have been carved quickly during such a ceremony. These crosses are too similar in size, design, positioning and execution to have been carved at different times as expressions of individual devotional impulses. There seems little doubt that their execution was co-ordinated to convey a unified message. Like the simple crosses carved on the (most likely wooden) church at Inch during its consecration,[37] perhaps their purpose was to (re)consecrate the wider landscape, thereby symbolically re-centring it on that church and claiming it for Mochellóc.

A version of this ritual, though not the act of carving, may have been re-iterated occasionally, perhaps annually, as has been proposed for circumambulatory rituals delimiting ecclesiastical sites. Here, then, we have tentative evidence for a linear procession of almost 10 km along the main road through an estate, presumably beginning in the east to culminate at Inch. Similar suggestions have been made regarding linear arrangements of crosses on routeways radiating from ecclesiastical sites in Cornwall, Brittany and Scotland.[38] Alternatively,

---

36 Carver, M., Garner-Lahire, J. and Spall, C. 2016 *Portmahomack on Tarbat Ness,* Edinburgh: Society of Antiquaries of Scotland 246–56.
37 Ó Carragáin 2010b 168–9.
38 Tanguy, B. 1984 La troménie de Gousnou, *Annales de Bretagne* 91, 9–25; Blair 479–80; O'Neill, P. 2005 Boundaries, Routes and Sculptured Stones in Early Medieval Scotland, *Exile and Homecoming. Papers from the Fifth Australian*

or in addition, some of the monuments might have been visited individually at different times of year, as indeed the three at holy wells were until recently. Whatever form it took, the character of the monuments and the crosses incised on them strongly suggest it was through ritual that the significance of this 'consecration' of the landscape was disseminated.

It is important to emphasise that Inch and its estate were not established in a pagan landscape. As Catherine Swift has shown, this peninsula has some of the earliest evidence for Christianity in Ireland, including fifth-century ogham stones with a version of the Christian HIC IACET formula.[39] So the defacement of the Ballintermon ogham stone probably did not take place in a missionary situation; it is not comparable, for example, to Boniface cutting down the pagan oak in Hessia. Rather, to some extent the message may have been more mundane: the overwriting of one claim of ownership by another. Assuming it was erected in the prehistoric period, the first early medieval claimants probably saw this impressive pre-extant monument as a source of kudos. They may have sought to control, and even solicit, rather than to neutralise, its lingering power. The same may have been true of their ecclesiastical successors, notwithstanding the social and religious changes in the intervening period. After all, it was the previous claim represented by the ogham inscription that they defaced, not the monument itself. Even in much later hagiography standing stones are not always depicted in wholly negative terms. For example, in *The Expulsion of Mochuda from Rahan*, St Mochuda orders Satan to: 'Be off . . . into the standing stone to the south of the church, and do no harm there to any one, except to those who come to attack the church': the monument is a focus for evil forces, but these are harnessed to help protect the site.[40] In earlier centuries one can well imagine an even greater degree of creative ambiguity when it came to interpreting

---

Conference of Celtic Studies, University of Sydney, July 2004, edited by P. O'Neill, University of Sydney: Sydney Series in Celtic Studies 276–88.

39 Swift, C. 1997 *Ogam Stones and the Earliest Irish Christians*, Maynooth: Dept of Old Irish 102–5.
40 Plummer, C. 1922 *Bethada Náem nÉrenn*, Oxford University Press II.294. Other hagiographical evidence for varying perceptions of pre-Christian monuments is discussed in Ó Carragáin, forthcoming.

Figure 2.4 Standing stone in Ballintermon showing fifth-century ogham inscription deliberately damaged by the removal of a large spall beside which a cross with expanded terminals was added. Photo by Tomás Ó Carragáin.

monuments like this. In early Irish literature ancient burial monuments, especially mounds, were portals to an otherworld which seems to have existed, in the minds of many, in parallel with the Christian heaven.[41] Such monuments could accommodate multiple meanings whose apparent contradictions were not problematic for medieval audiences. In the case of the Ballintermon standing stone, it is notable that the ogham inscription was not erased entirely. Traces of it were left as a reminder of the changing biography of the monument and the landscape to which it belonged. Rather than wiping the slate clean, ancient monuments, which may have retained some of their earlier associations, seem also to have been given prominent roles in a new narrative of ecclesiastical estate formation, the hero of which was undoubtedly St Mochellóc. No hagiography of Mochellóc survives so we do not know whether this narrative was ever written down. Perhaps instead it was developed and perpetuated solely through oral tradition and ritual, which as we have seen could be very effective at perpetuating memories over the long term, while also potentially accommodating differences in emphasis and interpretation.

Conclusion

Ecclesiastical landholdings are an important but under-studied phenomenon. Never before had so much land been given in perpetuity to undying institutions, and the potential of this to lead to new ways of settling, farming, managing and perceiving the landscape was considerable. As illustrated here by the example of Inch Labhrainne, studying them can provide insights into the complex process whereby perceptions of particular landscapes were altered through selective remembering, myth-making and ritualised movement. While this process had of course begun long before the establishment of ecclesiastical estates, indeed long before the advent of Christianity, not surprisingly it seems to have played out in distinctive ways on tracts of land granted to church sites.

---

41 Carey, J. 1982 The Location of the Otherworld in Irish Tradition *Éigse* 19, 36–43; Huckins MacGugan, J. 2012 Landscape and Lamentation: Constructing Commemorated Space in Three Middle Irish Texts, *Proceedings of the Royal Irish Academy* 112C 189–217: 209.

Figure 2.5 Other cross sculpture on the lands of Inch Labhrainne in Gortacurraun (a and b), Ballinclare (c) and Inch West (d) (after Cuppage 1986).

Acknowledgments

This paper draws upon research undertaken as part of the Making Christian Landscapes project funded by the Heritage Council through the Irish National Strategic Archaeological Research (INSTAR) Programme. Thanks to Paul MacCotter for historical research on the lands of Inch and Nick Hogan who prepared the illustrations. Sincere thanks also to Jonathan Wooding and the other members of the organising committee for the opportunity to present this research at the Ninth Australian Conference of Celtic Studies.

3
Remembering and Forgetting Holy Men and their Places: An Inscription from Llanllŷr, Wales

Jonathan M. Wooding

An early medieval inscribed monument preserved at Llanllŷr House in Ceredigion has been briefly discussed on a number of recent occasions with respect to its language, sources of its terminology, and as evidence for the cults of Insular saints.[1] Since a study by Sir John Rhŷs in the 1890s, however, not so much has been said about its potential as a source for the history of religious landscapes, which is the intent of this contribution.[2] The inscription, which dates from around AD 800,

---

1 Russell, Paul 1990 *Celtic Word-Formation. The Velar Suffixes*, Dublin: Institute for Advanced Studies 114; Thomas, Charles 1994 *'And shall these mute stones speak?' Post-Roman Inscriptions in Western Britain*, Cardiff: University of Wales Press 100–101; Sims-Williams, Patrick 2002 The Five Languages of Wales in the pre-Norman Inscriptions, *Cambrian Medieval Celtic Studies* 44, 1–36: 31–2; Sims-Williams, Patrick 2003 *The Celtic Inscriptions of Britain: Phonology and Chronology, c. 400–1200*, Publications of the Philological Society 37, Oxford: Philological Society 69, 209; Wooding, Jonathan 2007 The Figure of David, *St David of Wales: Cult, Church and Nation*, edited by J. W. Evans and Jonathan M. Wooding, Woodbridge: Boydell 1–19: 13; Edwards, Nancy *et al.* 2010 *A Corpus of Early Medieval Inscribed Stones and Stone Sculpture in Wales*, vol. 2, Cardiff: University of Wales Press 166–9.
2 Rhŷs, John 1896 Epigraphic Notes, *Archaeologia Cambrensis*, fifth series 13, 98–128: 121–5. An important study by Mark Handley also makes some assessment of the landscape context: Handley, Mark 2001 Isidore of Seville and 'Hisperic Latin' in Early Medieval Wales: The Epigraphic Culture of

records a transaction in which a site, apparently named for a person called Ditoc, was given to a church, monastery or *familia* bearing the name of an historical Irish saint, Modomnóc. The monument is thus a rare witness to the acquisition of property for religious use in first millennium Wales. Though other comparable property records come down to us from this period, they are mostly preserved in later copies that we suspect were subject to redaction in the light of contemporary claims.[3] In the Llanllŷr inscription, a record indisputably written in the first millennium, we see glimpses of things that appear to have been forgotten in the second. The place-name given for the piece of land, *Tesquitus Ditoc*, incorporates a Latin topographic term, *tesquum*, that in antiquity was associated with sacred topography. If it ever was widely productive of place-names in early medieval Wales it is now undetectable in the landscape. The personal names on the stone, likewise, are no longer remembered in local toponymy, though Modomnóc's at least survives in hagiography from the region. The data here are unusual in their detail—albeit so singular that there is some risk of overburdening their interpretation. Data recorded in the first millennium are, however, of necessity rare and these data are of undoubted importance for directing us both to a probable site of monastic settlement and its otherwise unknown association with an Irish saint. Questions raised by this monument, if nothing else, also challenge us to reflect on assumptions that have often been made concerning the early British church and its inheritance from late-antique religious culture.

Llanllŷr and Llanddewi Brefi, *Roman, Runes and Ogham: Medieval Inscriptions in the Insular World and on the Continent*, edited by J. Higgitt, K. Forsyth and D. N. Parsons, Donington: Shaun Tyas 26–36: 26–30.

3   For example in the charters of the Book of Llandaff, see Davies, John R. 2003 *The Book of Llandaf and the Norman Church in Wales*, Woodbridge: Boydell 63–75.

The Inscription

The monument, an inscribed pillar-stone, now stands in the garden of Llanllŷr House. The stone is cut from the local bedrock and is the surviving half of a rectangular monument that has been split from top to bottom. The extant portion measures some 141 cm tall. The width of all the faces is 24 cm—but two of these faces are now only half their original width. Reports of the monument's discovery are contradictory. The first reference is to it being exhibited at a meeting of the Cambrian Archaeological Association in Cardigan 1859. On that occasion J. O. Westwood expressed the hope that it was 'not allowed, bearing as it did the symbol of Redemption, to be used as a gate-post'.[4] In 1863, however, Westwood claimed more directly that it *had* 'been used as a gate-post'.[5] In 1893 Colonel John Lewes (1828–1900) reported to Sir John Rhŷs that the stone had been recovered from the wall of the 'main building' of the old house—namely the Tudor-era house that preceded the present one (see below).[6] These reports leave unclear whether the pillar-stone was recovered from use as a gate-post or from the fabric of a demolished building. I will take the latter as the more probable, being the testimony of the landowner himself.[7]

On what used to be the main face of the stone there is the surviving half of an incised ring-cross. A motif nearer to the base shows that there was once an extension of the central cross-arm downward ending in an upward curl, but the extending arm itself has been lost in the line of fracture.[8] There is a smaller, complete, ring-cross of similar type (but lacking the curl motif) on one side of the stone. The inscribed text is below the cross-ring on the main face, in four lines reading

---

4   Anon. 1859 Cardigan Meeting Report, *Archaeologia Cambrensis* 320–52: 338.
5   Westwood, J. O. 1863 Broken Incised Stone from Llanllear, Cardiganshire, *Archaeologia Cambrensis*, third series 36, 258–9.
6   Rhŷs 123 and Lewes to Rhŷs, 20 November 1895 (NLW).
7   I note, however, that Colonel Lewes, who had lived on the estate in his childhood, took over the house on his marriage in 1858, so the stone may have been found in building work that occurred when he was not resident.
8   Rhŷs 119–125; Edwards *et al. Corpus* 166–9.

Figure 3.1 The Llanllŷr inscription. Photo by Jonathan Wooding.

vertically from top to bottom of the stone.[9] It is clear that the cross was already on the stone when the text was added, as the writer had to compress the lettering in the last lines to fit the space delineated by the (lost) extended arm of the cross.

The ring crosses are in a common local style which Nancy Edwards would date to the sixth or seventh century.[10] Monuments from Tregaron, 14 km to the north-east (now lost), and Abergwili, 36 km to the south, evince crosses comparable in form.[11] None of the dates is precise enough to allow for certainty, but the possibly different dates for sculpture (sixth-seventh century) and text (eighth-ninth century) make it likely that the inscription is not only secondary to the cross, but added at a significantly later date.[12]

The text, in rounded half-uncial script, has been the subject of a number of readings. Nancy Edwards, with the assistance of Helen McKee and Patrick Sims-Williams, most recently reads: TESQUITUS DITOC | MADOMNUACO | AON FILIUS ASA | ITGEN DEDIT—'Tesquitus Ditoc Madomnuaco Aon filius Asa Itgen dedit'.[13] V. E. Nash-Williams, and earlier Rhŷs, read alternatively: 'Tesquitus Ditoc Madomnuac Occon filius Asaitgen dedit'.[14] The new reading restores the dative *Madomonuaco* and proposes the name *Aon* for the earlier reading *Occon*; *Asa Itgen* is preferred by Sims-Williams for *Asaitgen*.[15]

---

9   Sims-Williams, *The Celtic Inscriptions* 69, 209; Sims-Williams, The Five Languages 31–2; Edwards *et al. Corpus* 166–9.

10 Edwards, Nancy 2001 Monuments in a Landscape: The Early Medieval Sculpture of St David's, *Image and Power in the Archaeology of Early Medieval Britain—Essays in Honour of Rosemary Cramp*, edited by Helena Hamerow and Arthur MacGregor, Oxford 53–77: 57–8. A stone at St Non's in Pembrokeshire carries probably the best-known example of this type. Edwards, Nancy 2001 Early Medieval Inscribed Stones and Stone Sculpture in Wales: Context and Function, *Medieval Archaeology* 45, 15–39: 31–2.

11 Edwards *et al. Corpus* 197, 201–2.

12 Compare another unusually discursive Latin inscription from Caldey Island, where the original slab is unarguably earlier than the Latin text: Edwards *et al. Corpus* 294–99.

13 Edwards *et al. Corpus*, 166–9

14 Cf. Nash-Williams, V. E. 1957 *Early Christian Monuments of Wales*, Cardiff: University of Wales Press 100 (No. 124).

15 Sims-Williams, *The Celtic Inscriptions* 69, 209.

The inscription can be broadly translated as: 'the *tesquitus* of Ditoc that Aon son of Asa Itgen gave to Madomnuac'.[16] What a *tesquitus* might have been we will consider further below.

Monuments were sometimes used to mark land-holdings, but the use of them to record land transactions in this way is rare.[17] Only one other inscription from the Celtic-speaking regions, from Kilnasaggart in Co. Armagh, appears to record a gift of land while commemorating a saint, in this case by one Ternóc son of Ciaran for the sake of Peter the Apostle—so in that case a Biblical rather than local saint.[18] If, as we may suspect, the Llanllŷr monument was an already existing monument when the inscription was made, the use here could be compared to the contemporary use made of Gospel manuscripts to host charters and memoranda, with the already holy character of the object being perceived to bind the transaction.[19]

Mark Handley suggests that the inscription may have been made by the (presumably secular) giver, Aon son of Asa Itgen, to secure title for his family in case the site later passed back into secular control. This leads him to conclude that the inscription 'may, in fact, record the foundation of a monastery', perhaps 'the gift of an anchoritic monastery for the purposes of founding a coenobitic monastery on the site'.[20] My suggestion will also be that it is a gift of land to a monastery, but probably of a small site external to an already existing one.

---

16   Gwyn Thomas, in 1994, read *Qua Domnuaco* here, and his interpretation is followed by Wmffre, but no other recent scholar: Thomas, W. Gwyn 1994 A Catalogue of Inscribed Stones, *Cardiganshire County History*, vol. 1, edited by J. L. Davies and D. P. Kirby, Cardiff: University of Wales Press 412–420: 415–6; Wmffre, Iwan 2004 *The Place-Names of Cardiganshire*, BAR British Series 379, Oxford II.426–8.
17   See also Tomás Ó Carragáin, *supra*.
18   Macalister, R. A. S. 1927 The Sculptured Stones of Cardiganshire, *Transactions of the Cardiganshire Antiquarian Society* 5, 7–20: 10–11. The word for the gift used at Kilnasaggart is Old Irish *do-immna* 'entrusts'.
19   Charles-Edwards, Thomas 1993 *Celtic and Anglo-Saxon Kinship*, Oxford University Press 417–18; Jenkins, Dafydd and Owen, Morfydd E. 1983–84 The Welsh Marginalia in the Lichfield Gospels, Part Two, *Cambridge Medieval Celtic Studies* 7, 91–120.
20   Handley, Isidore of Seville 34, 35.

Figure 3.2 The flood-plain of Llanllŷr, looking north, with the house in the centre and Trichrug behind it. Photo by Jonathan Wooding.

The Site and Its Setting

As the Llanllŷr inscription incorporates what is arguably a topographic term (*tesquitus*) we should give a brief account of the most pertinent features of the landscape context. This is quite distinctive and so could offer some potential for interpretation in the light of the terminology of the inscription. The site is located on a flood-plain in a bend of the River Aeron (SN 5434 5588). This notably flat area contrasts significantly with the steep sides of the valley, the northern and western of which comprise the prominent hill Trichrug. The main site on the flood-plain is Llanllŷr House (68 m above sea-level), a mansion built c. 1830–72.

The sequence of settlement here is impressive. As we have already noted, the present house is the successor to a Tudor-era house of the same name. This stood around 150 m to the north-west and was demolished around 1840.[21] This Tudor-era house had itself succeeded

---

21 Lloyd, T., Orbach, J., Scourfield, R. 2006 *Carmarthenshire and Ceredigion*, Pevsner Architectural Guides: Buildings of Wales, New Haven CT: Yale

a medieval Cistercian nunnery, also named Llanllŷr.[22] The nunnery was founded in the late-twelfth century by Lord Rhys ap Gruffydd, Prince of Deheubarth (d. 1197) and it was dissolved in 1537. It is referred to by John Leland (c. 1540), only just after the Dissolution, as a 'cell' of the major Cistercian monastery at Strata Florida, which lies 23 km to the north-east of Llanllŷr; the association between these two foundations is supported by circumstantial evidence from medieval sources.[23] The nunnery and its lands passed fully into lay ownership in the 1550s and the estate was most recently sold in 1720 to one John Lewes (1680–1742), whose descendants remain in occupation.[24]

It was reported to Sir John Rhŷs by Colonel Lewes that the Tudor-era house incorporated parts of the former nunnery, retaining some medieval fabric until its demolition in the mid-1800s. Re-use of monastic buildings at the Dissolution was very common, so this is likely to be correct. A covered drain of probable Cistercian provenance commences from a point around 20 m north of the modern house and discharges into the field to the north-west of the old house—further evidence that the nunnery was on the site of the Tudor-era house.[25] As the early medieval pillar-stone is said to have been found in the vicinity of the old house it is usually inferred that the nunnery was itself the successor to a first-millennium religious house on or near the same site.

University Press 594; Lewes, J. H. 1971 Llanllŷr, 1180–1980, *Ceredigion* 6, 341–9: 342; Jones, Francis 2000 Llanllŷr, Lanfihangel Ystrad, *Historic Cardiganshire Homes and their Families,* Newport, Pembs.: Brawdy Books 173–6; Loveday Lewes Gee, *pers. comm.* Col. John Lewis [Lewes] to Sir John Rhŷs, 11 November 1895, cited in Rhŷs 123.

22 Wmffre, II.426 and Williams, David H. 1975 Cistercian Nunneries in Medieval Wales, *Cîteaux* 3, 155–74: 164.

23 Toulmin Smith, L. 1907–8 *The Itinerary of John Leland in or about the Years 1535–1543,* London: Bell 51; Williams, Cistercian Nunneries 164; Williams, David H. 2001 *The Welsh Cistercians,* Leominster: Gracewing 37.

24 Wmffre II.426–7; Williams, *The Welsh Cistercians* 85–7, 89; Lloyd, J. E. 1911 *A History of Wales,* London: Longman II.603; Dugdale, William 1825 *Monasticon Anglicanum,* London 32; Llysnewydd and Llanllŷr Estate Records (GB 0211 LLYSNEWYDD), Carmarthenshire Archives Service; Welsh National Monuments Record http://www.coflein.gov.uk/pdf/CPG146/.

25 Loveday Lewes Gee, *pers. comm.*; cf. Williams, *The Welsh Cistercians* pl. VIIA for a possibly comparable example from Strata Marcella.

This is a very probable sequence, as adoption of earlier religious sites by the reformed orders is an observable pattern in Britain and Ireland.[26] So the site of the Tudor-era house is probably a monastic site occupied from the Early Middle Ages up to the Dissolution.

Floors from the surrounds of the Tudor-era house remained identifiable into the twentieth century and were recently re-examined in excavations commencing in 2014.[27] These excavations, which also extended into the field to the north-east of the old house, identified stone walls and some apparent traces of burials. Timbers of medieval date were also recovered from nearby fishponds.[28]

A cross symbol with the legend 'Chapel (*Site of*)' is also marked on the 1891 Ordnance Survey (25" sheet) in the vicinity of the old house. This rather vague reference is probably based on Samuel Meyrick's brief report (1808) that a lead coffin had been dug up from the 'garden of Llanllear'.[29] Meyrick's 'garden' I presume to have been the walled garden to the east of the Tudor house, marked on an estate map of 1768. In 1895 Colonel Lewes observed, however, that

> Of the chapel and church I never saw a vestige & beyond the fact of a burial ground having been often pointed out to me I was not aware of any church or chapel.[30]

---

26   Known Welsh examples include Caldey, St Dogmaels (Tironensian), Beddgelert, Enlli, Flatholm, Penmon and Ynys Tudwal (Augustinian); also see Carville, Geraldine 1982 *The Occupation of Celtic Sites in Ireland by the Canons Regular of St Augustine and the Cistercians*, Kalamazoo: Cistercian Publications; Stöber, K. and Austin, D. 2013 Culdees to Canons: The Augustinian Houses of North Wales, *Monastic Wales, New Approaches*, edited by J. Burton and K. Stöber, Cardiff: University of Wales Press 39–54.

27   Jemma Bezant *pers. comm.* And site-visits by the author June 2014 and July 2015; Murphy, F. and Wilson, H. 2015 *Llanllyr, Ceredigion, Archaeological Evaluation 2014: Interim Report*, Llandeilo.

28   Jemma Bezant *pers comm*. Murphy and Wilson 1. Also see National Monuments Record NPRN 400436 and discussion by Wmffre 247.

29   Meyrick, Samuel 1808 *Cardiganshire*, London 242. This burial is probably best equated with the period of the nunnery. The cemetery would not have been used for burials after the Dissolution.

30   Col. John Lewes to Sir John Rhŷs, 20 November 1895 (NLW, Rhŷs Correspondence).

He also recalled the existence, in his own youth (i.e. c. 1830s–40s) of the foundations of a round 'tower' in the same vicinity, but this may have been a dovecote or similar structure.[31] Any supposed chapel, along with the ground-plan of the nunnery itself, remains elusive.

Turning now to the wider environs, we can observe that fields exempted from tithe should indicate which were the former monastic lands, as these were extra-parochial and their tithe exemption carried over to into secular ownership.[32] The old line of the River Aeron—which was moved northward in the mid-1600s—appears to mark the northern limit of the home estate of the religious house.[33] The low-lying village of Talsarn (68 m) is just over the river. It was the site of two fairs in the early modern period, which may have been located there on account of the adjacency of the boundary of the monastic lands, which is also a parochial boundary.[34] Talsarn's status as an early settlement centre is ambiguous, as Trefilan (90 m), higher up into in the foothills of Trichrug, is clearly the main medieval secular centre. Its place-name is attested from the thirteenth century and there is a motte there built by Lord Rhys' son Maelgwn (d. 1230), as well as the parish church.[35]

The identifiable pre-twentieth century farms around Llanllŷr mostly appear, like Trefilan, to be located above the 70 m contour,[36]

---

31 Lewes, Llanllyr 345; Colonel John Lewes to Sir John Rhŷs, 11 and 26 November 1895, in Rhŷs 122–4 (the original is missing from Rhŷs correspondence in NLW).
32 Tithe apportionment (1900) Parish of Llanfihangel Ystrad 4, National Library of Wales.
33 The fields explicitly labelled 'tithe exempt' are around 62 hectares in extent. The map provided by David Williams (*The Welsh Cistercians* 8) includes the area labeled 'Llanllyr Meadows', the area between the old and new river beds, as part of the monastic home estate, but I suspect only those fields numbered 48 and 49 in the apportionment mark the original monastic home estate. John Hext Lewes (1903–1992) also states that the land over the river was only acquired in the 1600s: [Hext] Lewes 345. I have not yet examined the early-modern estate records which might shed further light on this.
34 Wmffre II.661 (AD 1631); Johnson, R. 1776 *The New Gazetteer: Or, Geographical Companion*, London: Dilly and Baldwin, *s.v.* Talsarne, fairs on 8 September and 7 November.
35 Wmffre II.661–2.
36 Adjacent farmhouses with available data are: Felindre Isaf (80.43 m); Hendrelas (76.80 m); Cross Inn (73.76 m). Heights above sea-level calculated

at some remove from the flood-plain. This pattern—the status of the ambiguous Talsarn excepted—seems to make a distinct separation of secular and religious space, with the latter, either by intent or by default, mostly taking in the lower-lying land, possibly chiming with the monastic interest in occupying 'waste' or 'desert' spaces.[37] In connection with the toponym Llanllŷr, it is pertinent to note Oliver Padel's comment that *lann* sites in Cornwall are located 'especially in the bottoms of valleys and on the shores of creeks and estuaries', with secular farmsteads of the same period 'located on the sides of valleys'.[38]

There is a further report of a religious site in the valley linked to Llanllŷr. Meyrick gives an account of a reputed chapel on the nearby farm of Lloyd Jack, which he says was linked by a 'covered way' to Llanllŷr.[39] Lloyd Jack is a farm around 1.2 km to the west, but the *lands* of the two houses meet around 700 m to the north-west of Llanllŷr, near the end of an avenue of trees marked on the 1768 estate map—which might be the 'covered way' of Meyrick's report, for what that is worth.

In summary on the landscape context, the site of Llanllŷr offers an impressive sequence of monastic settlement, spanning the first into the second millennium. There is evidence to potentially identify landscape spaces which had distinct religious use. Recent discussion of the inscription has mostly focused on linguistic questions, uncoupled from the specific landscape context—with Handley's study an exception, though ultimately concerned with a theory of literary influence on local inscriptions.[40] In their investigation of the monument and site in the 1890s, described in published and unpublished correspondence, Sir

---

from datum-points on 1887 Ordnance Survey 6" sheet (Cardiganshire XXV SE) and Landranger sheet for Lampeter and Llandovery. Wmffre II.421, 423–5.

37 McGinn, Bernard 1994 Ocean and Desert as Symbols of Mystical Absorption in the Christian Tradition, *Journal of Religion* 74, 155–181: 160–6; Le Goff, J. 1988 *The Medieval Imagination*, University of Chicago 50–51.

38 Padel, Oliver forthcoming Brittonic *lann* in Place-names, *Essays in memory of Duncan Probert*, edited by S. Bassett and A. Spedding, Donington: Shaun Tyas. I would like to thank Dr Padel for kindly sending me this item in advance of publication.

39 Meyrick 242.

40 Handley, Isidore of Seville 26–36.

John Rhŷs and Colonel Lewes had made thoughtful attempts to relate the evidence of the inscription to the local topography and toponymy.[41] Their discussion retains considerable interest and I am inclined to attempt to reassess the evidence along some of the same lines.

Modomnóc, Ditoc, and Llŷr: Forgetting Saints in the Landscape

It is of significant interest that at least one of the named persons, *Madomnuac*, can be identified. The stem here is *domn-*, to which is affixed a prefix *ma-* and a suffix *-uac*: either Irish *-óc*, or Old Welsh *-auc*, here rendered as *-uac*. *Ma-* is a known variant of Old Irish *mo-* ('my') and this type of name of a saint (hagionym), with the addition of possessive prefix and diminutive suffix, is a common 'hypocoristic' form ('my/dear little X') showing veneration of a saint.[42] Our *Madomnuac* should be identified with St Modomnóc, commemorated at 13 February in the Tallaght Martyrologies,[43] as he has a known cult in Wales. He is an Irish saint, his main cult based in Leinster, centring on Tipperaghney, Co. Kilkenny. The primary text of the martyrology *Félire Óengusso* (c. 830) reports a legend that Modomnóc brought bees to Ireland and this story also features in Rhygyfarch's *Vita S. David* (c. 1080), as well as in the *Topographica Hiberniae* of Giraldus Cambrensis (c. 1190).[44] Rhygyfarch presents Modomnōc as one of number of Irish

---

41 I would like to thank Siân Bowyer and Wyn Thomas of National Library of Wales for their kind assistance in accessing Rhŷs' letters concerning Llanllŷr.
42 On hypocorism see: Russell, Paul 2001 Patterns of Hypocorism in early Irish Hagiography, *Studies in Irish Hagiography*, edited by John Carey, Máire Herbert and Pádraig Ó Riain, Dublin: Four Courts Press 237–49; also, Ó Riain, Pádraig 1982 Towards a Methodology in early Irish Hagiography, *Peritia* 1, 146–159; and for a recent case study from Wales, Jacobs, Nicolas 2017 Non, Nonna, Nonnita: Confusions of Gender in Brythonic Hagionymy, *Transactions of the Honourable Society of Cymmrodorian* 23, 19–33: 20.
43 Ó Riain, Pádraig 2011 *Dictionary of Irish Saints*, Dublin 477–8; Best, R. I. and Lawlor, H. J. editors 1931 *Martyrology of Tallaght*, London: Henry Bradshaw Society 16; Stokes, Whitley, editor 1905 *Félire Óengusso*, London: Henry Bradshaw Society 60, 75, 113.
44 Stokes 60; *Vita S. David* chs 41 and 43, Sharpe, Richard and Davies, John Reuben 2007 *Vita S. David*, St David of Wales: Cult, Church and Nation,

followers of St David (d. 589). As it is often the case that saints are connected up retrospectively, we cannot take this later source as proof that Modomnóc was a contemporary of David, but he is likely to have been a saint from much closer to the time of David than that of the inscription.

The gift is thus made to a saint, whose (hypocoristic) name is used as a metonym for, presumably, one of the following: a religious house, a network of religious houses (*familia*) that followed his rule, or a church on the site dedicated to him. We can compare the 'Idnert' inscription from Llanddewibrefi, 12 km to the east, where a man is commemorated (c. 800) as having been killed 'on account of the plunder of St David' (*propter predam Sancti David*).[45] Here the long dead St David also appears to be a metonym for the property of a church or cult. In this case the church on the site is still dedicated to the same saint, in contrast to Llanllŷr.

The name Ditoc in our inscription is not confidently identified. If, as we will see below, *tesquitus* is likely to be a term denoting specifically a sacred space, then Ditoc should be presumed to be a religious person of some sort. His name might be hypocoristic, with the prefix *ty-*, generally used in preference to *mo-* in British saints' names, but for the terminal we might the expect the form *-auc* (if British), or *-uac* again (if Irish *-óc*). Accordingly, Sims-Williams, comparing the name ITOCUS from an inscription at Llanboydy, offers the alternative of the *-oc* here having been formerly a medial *-oc-* made terminal through loss of the final syllable.[46] For this reason it is impossible to say for certain that this is a hypocoristic name. Rhŷs suggested that Ditoc might be the same name as the eponym (Dudoch) of *Llandudoch*, the Welsh name for St Dogmaels, around 50 km to the south-west of Llanllŷr.[47] This is possible, but as there is no other obvious connection

---

edited by J. Wyn Evans and J. M. Wooding, Woodbridge: Boydell 107-55: 136-9; Giraldus, see *Topographica Hiberniae* I.6.
45 Edwards *et al. Corpus* 152.
46 Sims-Williams, *The Celtic Inscriptions* 69.
47 Rhŷs 121; Edwards *et al. Corpus* 166. It is unclear whether Dogmael is derived from Dudoch or is a separate name, see Charles, B. G. 1992 *The Place-names of Pembrokeshire*, Aberystwyth: National Library of Wales 177-9.

between St Dogmaels and Llanllŷr I will not pursue the matter further here.[48]

Whether or not he was an identifiable historical figure, the now obscurity of Ditoc at Llanllŷr is consistent with our most recent model for the development of the cult of saints in early medieval Wales. In a comprehensive study of the spread of cults of saints in Celtic Britain, Richard Sharpe rightly rejects the older model of John Fisher, E. G. Bowen and others that sought the origins of the early medieval churches in a process of 'secondary mission' to Celtic Britain, with its leaders commemorated in the dedications of their own early monastic foundations.[49] Sharpe, however, posits instead that the promotion of new cults was a periodic process that came to obscure the names of earlier saints and founders, as new visions of the deeds of saints came into fashion—to the extent that names were forgotten and earlier place-name elements made redundant as they ceased to be productive.[50] This is an observable pattern on the Continent in the same period and Sharpe sees no reason to imagine that it was very different in Britain.

I would suggest that the text of the Llanllŷr monument may be a rare sidelight onto this process as it was occurring. What could be concurrently existing 'dedications' to holy people are found at Llanllŷr in the last quarter of the first millennium. The name Llanllŷr, first recorded in 1291 (*Taxatio*), is *not* found in the inscription, but Padel suggests that *llan-* was widely used in Wales as early as the seventh or

---

48 The two sites are close enough (40 km) that it is at least conceivable the transaction could be the gift of the one site to the other. I also note here, though I suspect they are irrelevant, two seventeenth-century references to *Llanlleere* as an alternative name for St Dogmaels, which Bertie Charles assumes to be a corrupt form of *Llandre*: Charles 178–9.

49 Chadwick, Owen 1954 The Evidence of Dedications in the Early History of the Welsh Church, *Studies in Early British History*, edited by Nora K. Chadwick, Cambridge University Press 173–88.

50 Sharpe, Richard 2002 Martyrs and Local Saints in Late Antique Britain, *Local Saints and Local Churches in the Early Medieval West*, edited by Alan Thacker and Richard Sharpe, Oxford University Press 75–154: 136–153. Also recent discussion in Parsons, David N. 2013 *Martyrs and Memorials: Merthyr Place-names in Early Wales,* Abertyswyth: Centre for Advanced Welsh and Celtic Studies.

even sixth century,[51] so the dedication to Llŷr could have co-existed on the site with the other names commemorated on the stone.[52] The inscription suggests that a religious house or *familia* (?) named for Modomnóc, perhaps settled on an older *llan*, acquired a site named for a person named Ditoc. Ditoc and his toponym appear to have been wholly forgotten, while the Irish saint, associated with the powerful cult of St David, at least remained visible in the historical record. The monument, a chance survival, is our only record of this past diversity at Llanllŷr. The case of nearby Llanddewibrefi, noted above, where an early inscription and the extant dedication record the same saint (David), offers an interesting contrast to the situation at Llanllŷr, prompting us to reflect on what different processes of memory were in action at these two religious sites.

Tesquitus: Tenuous Memories of a Word

The term *tesquitus* is the most challenging feature of the inscription. Its role here is open to a number of interpretations. We should first ask whether the toponynm *Tesquitus Ditoc* was an actual name used locally

---

51   See Padel, Brittonic *lann*; Padel, O. J. 1985 *Cornish Place-Name Elements*, Nottingham: Place Names Society 142–5; Sharpe, Martyrs 148; Davies, The Saints 393–5.
52   The -*llŷr* here is usually associated with Llŷr Forwen (Llŷr the Virgin), a female saint recorded in some calendars at 21 October, but who may be a doublet of Llŷr Marini/Merini, a mythical (male) ancestor of kings of Gwent. Whether traditions associating the site with the cult—real or imagined—of a Welsh virgin had any role to play in the choice of site for a house of female Cistercians (an order whose houses were ubiquitously co-dedicated to the Holy Mother) must remain at the moment an open question. Bartrum, P. C. 1993 *A Welsh Classical Dictionary*, Aberystwyth: National Library of Wales 421–2; Baring-Gould, S. and Fisher, John 1907–13 *The Lives of the British Saints. The Saints of Wales and Cornwall and such Irish saints as have Dedications in Britain*, London: Cymmrodorian Society I.74, III.386–7; Ó Riain, Pádraig 1994 The Saints of Cardiganshire, *Cardiganshire County History*, vol. 1, 378–396: 383; Wmffre II.427. I also note here Patrick Sims-Williams' suggestion (*pers. comm.*) that the *llŷr* element may be topographical (from *llyr* 'sea' or 'watercourse', *Geiriadaur Prifysgol Cymru* s.v. *llŷr*), rather than a dedication.

or was it a calque of British name-elements? One notes here the regular use of Latin *podum* to substitute for *llan-* in putatively early charters from the Book of Llandaff.[53] Does *tesquitus* likewise mask a particular British term? This seems probable, but no obvious counterpart springs to mind. In light of the semantics we will identify for *tesquum* below we can say that any underlying British word is at least unlikely to be *llan*.

Llanllŷr's *tesquitus* appears mostly assumed, following Rhŷs, to be a diminutive—the exception being Handley, who identifies it as an adjectival suffix.[54] It appears to be a wholly unique coinage from *tesquum*. The Oxford Latin Dictionary defines *tesquum* as:

> An augural term of uncertain sense; assoc. w. *templum* and perhaps synonymous; by non technical writers interpreted as a tract of waste or desolate land.

To cite some classical uses: Horace (d. 8 BC) describes *tesqua* as places in the country that the townsman perceives as *deserta et inhospita* (empty and unwelcoming), but which to the countryman have potential fertility.[55] Such a sense is also found in the *Pharsalia* of Lucan (d. AD 65).[56] Varro (d. AD 27), in *De Lingua Latina,* perceives *tesqua* as places in the country: 'quod loca quaedam agrestia, quae alicuius dei sunt, dicuntur tesca' (certain places in the country, which are the property of some god, are called *tesca*).[57] His further discussion is mainly in the context of its use as a religious term—including the comment cited from Ennius that 'temples shall be tesca' (*templa ut sint tesca*), which gives rise to the *OLD*'s claim that these words are synonymous.[58] The

---

53   Padel, Brittonic *lann*.
54   Handley, Isidore of Seville, 29, n. 18; cf. on *turrita*, below n. 78.
55   Horace, *Epistles* I.14, edited by Fairclough, R. 1926 Horace, *Odes and Epistles,* Cambridge MA: Harvard University Press 338–41.
56   Lucan, *Pharsalia,* line 426, edited by Duff, J. 1928 Lucan, Cambridge MA: Harvard University Press 88–9.
57   Varro, *De lingua Latina* VII.10, edited by Kent, R. 1938 Varro, *De lingua Latina,* Cambridge MA: Harvard University Press 276–7.
58   Varro, *De lingua Latina* VII.10, Kent 276–7; also Goldberg, S. and Manuwald, G. editors 2018 *Fragmentary Republican Latin, Volume II: Ennius, Dramatic Fragments. Minor Works,* Cambridge MA: Harvard University Press 194–5

sense of *tesquum* as a perceived rugged and uncultivated terrain, as Handley observes, converges in the monastic context with the idea of a 'desert' (which in the monastic context may be an empty, but not necessarily arid, space).[59]

The term *tesquum* was always fairly rare—and very rare in the post-Roman period. The most recent use previous to our monument appears to be by Isidore of Seville (d. 636) in his *Etymologiae* (XX), where he defines *tesquum*: 'for some, it is a *tugurium*, for others it is a rugged and harsh terrain' (quidam putant esse tuguria, quidam loca praerupta et aspera).[60] The equation of *tugurium,* a rural hut, with *tesquum* appears singular to Isidore; other definitions of the term all seem to make it topographic. *Tugurium,* as *tegorium/-olum,* is used in Hiberno-Latin sources to describe secular (St Patrick) and monastic (Adomnán) buildings, so a writer seeking a synonym might have taken *tesquum* from Isidore, whose *Etymologiae* were known in early medieval Ireland by at least the late-seventh century.[61] Handley identifies Sidonius Apollinaris (d. 489), the fifth-century bishop of Clermont, as another late-antique writer who uses *tesqua*. He does so three times, ranging across a number of different contexts: once in a panegyric to Majorian, once in a poem of thanksgiving to his friend Faustus of Riez, and once as a metaphor in a discussion of the metrics of the poetry of his friend Claudianus (I will term these, respectively, 'Sidonius 1, 2 and 3'). Sidonius's (1) panegyric to Majorian has the Goddess Africa, speaking from beyond the sea, urge Majorian (emperor 457–61) to move against Gaiseric, the Vandal ruler in Africa who waits in Carthage: 'velut hispidus alta sus prope tesqua iacet' (as

---

    (where it is noted that this passage of Ennius was epitomised by the Carolingian Paul the Deacon).
59 Handley, Isidore of Seville 28–9 and see McGinn, Ocean and Desert 160–1.
60 Barney, S. A., Lewis, W. J., Beach, J. A., Berghof, Oliver, editors and translators 2006 *The Etymologies of Isidore of Seville,* Cambridge University Press 314.
61 Smyth, Marina 2017 Isidorian Texts in Seventh-Century Ireland, *Isidore of Seville and his Reception in the Early Middle Ages,* edited by A. Fear and J. Wood, Amsterdam: E. J. Brill 111–30.

a shaggy boar lies low on the edge of the wild).[62] In his (2) poem to Faustus, the latter is exhorted in his pursuit of the monastic life

> Seu te flammatae Syrtes et inhospita tesqua seu caeno viridante palus seu nigra recess incultum mage saxa ...
> Whether thou dost tarry roughly garbed in a cheerless wilderness by the sun-fired Syrtes or choosest rather a marsh full of green slime or the dark recesses of rocks ...[63]

Tesqua is thus used here to reference North-African deserts in contrast to marshes or caves (the latter characteristic of early hermits in Britain).[64] Sidonius' other (3) use of *tesquum* is to make a simile of his friend Claudianus' poetic expression, which, when confined by traditional metrics, thrives 'intra spatii sui terminum' (within the limits of its space), but breaks out like a powerful horse 'inter tesqua vel confraga' (amid wild and broken country).[65] Subsequent to our period, the Norman historian William of Poitiers (d. 1090) uses *tesqua* as one type of place in which people in Normandy were able to graze their flocks safely 'seu campestria, seu tesqua' (whether in fields or on waste).[66]

From the above we can identify a number of possible meanings of *tesquum*:

---

[62] Anderson, W. B. editor and translator 1936 and 1965 *Sidonius Apollinaris: Poems and Letters,* Cambridge MA: Harvard University Press I.68–9.
[63] Anderson I.250–1.
[64] This Annick Stoehr-Monjou would place amongst a number of references in this poem to Horace's *Epistles*, in this case contrasting of Faustus' contentment with the desert with the discontent of a steward with country living, Stoehr-Monjou, Annick 2013 Sidonius and Horace: The Art of Memory, *New Approaches to Sidonius Apollinaris,* edited by J. A. van Waarden and G. Kelly, Leuven: Peeters 133–69: 159. This is convincing, but the other uses of *tesqua* by Sidonius are not necessarily from Horace. On caves see Gildas, *De excidio Britanniae* 34.2.
[65] Sidonius, Epistle IV.3.8–9, Anderson II.76–7.
[66] *Gesta Guillelmi,* II.45, edited by Davis, R. H. C. and Chibnall, M. 1998 *The Gesta Guillelmi of William of Poiters,* Oxford University Press 180.

1. A rugged, waste space (Horace, Lucan, Sidonius 2, Isidore), contrasted or juxtaposed with level fields (William of Poitiers), urban terrain (Horace) or enclosed spaces (Sidonius 3).
2. A (pagan) religious space in the countryside (Varro).
3. A hut (Isidore).

The wide range of detail in Varro concerning *templum* and *tesquum* is difficult to reconcile, as it is a commentary on religious conceptions that were probably by his time archaic and subject to different reinterpretations.[67] Classical scholars suggest nuances to the use of the term in the civic context of Rome, which include a liminal sense of *tesqua* as spaces outside the boundary of the consecrated or inaugurated area and boundary of the urbs.[68] Jerzy Linderski sees the *tesquum* as a rugged external space, complementary to the consecrated space of the *templum*: 'a *tescum* was not a *templum*, but at the same time it was a necessary complement of a *templum*'.[69] He also interprets Varro's conception of the *tesquum* as indicating a place of a god in the countryside, spontaneously created, without a process of dedication: '*tescum* was a place spontaneously occupied by a deity, without any intervention on the part of the people, i.e. without the ceremony of *dedicatio* and *consecratio*'.[70] Although these terms appear to have uses specific to different periods and contexts, in his view the *tesqua* are, generally, unconsecrated extramural spaces. So we might add to our possible definitions of *tesquum* above the further sense of an unconsecrated sacred space juxtaposed with a consecrated one. In the Christian context this might be applied to, say, the extramural cell of a hermit or a natural sacred space such as a holy well.

---

67 See discussion in Palmer, L. R. 1954 *Outline History of the Latin Language*, London: Faber 64–6.
68 Linderski, Jerzy 1986 The Augural Law, *Aufstieg und Niedergang der römischen Welt II*, Band 2.16.3, Berlin: De Gruyter 2146–2312: especially 2256–2263; Ziolkowski, Adam 1993 Between Geese and the *Auguraculum*: the Origin of the Cult of Juno on the Arx, *Classical Philology* 88.3, 206–219; Lipka, M. 2009 *Roman Gods: A Conceptual Approach*, Amsterdam: E. J. Brill 15–16.
69 Linderski 2259, n. 444.
70 Linderski 2259, n. 444.

There is not sufficient space to adequately deconstruct the complex arguments here—nor am I really qualified to attempt this—but we will observe that the theorising of *tesqua* as spaces liminal to the boundary of consecrated spaces would have synergies with Sidonius' usages. It is also interesting that Linderski places the term amongst a set of 'three different types of *loca* in which the gods could be worshipped' (*templum, sedes* and *tesquum*).[71] A fuller study of the influence of all these terms in the Insular context would be interesting—the word *sedes,* for example, is used a number of times in Insular Latin texts to describe *loci* on hilltops or coasts from which saints are given visions of distant, sometimes mystical, lands.[72] David Jenkins, in a very important recent study, has identified a central concern of Insular theologians as being with the delineation of space in the ground-plan of the monastery and its exegesis in terms of imagery of the 'temple'.[73] In his study he focuses more closely on imagery of the Biblical temple than the Classical, but he lays out a context of Latin terminology in which *tesquum* could have found a role, for example in describing spaces relative to a monastery that is itself identified with the *templum*.[74] One could also note here Sidonius' (3) juxtaposition of *tesqua* with *termini; terminus* (Irish *termonn*) is a term used in Insular writings to describe the larger enclosed space around a monastery.[75]

Handley is inclined to see *tesquitus* as evidence of 'Hisperic' usage—a style of showy Latin usage found in Insular writings—and drawing upon Isidore for the word *tesquum* itself. So he sees the word used here as a choice out of an intellectual context and used imprecisely as a synonym for 'monastery' or 'hermitage' with 'little regard for its root word'.[76] The inscription certainly conforms to some proposed

---

71 Linderski 2259, n. 444.
72 See Wooding, Jonathan 2005 The Munster Element in *Nauigatio Sancti Brendani Abbatis, Journal of the Cork Historical and Archaeological Society* 110, 33–47: 59–60. *Sedes* is found in Welsh toponymy in Rhygyfarch's *Vita S. David,* chapter 3. The likely convergence of this term with the cognate native term *síd* also would warrant further investigation.
73 Jenkins, D. H. 2010 *'Holy, Holier, Holiest': The Sacred Topography of the Early Medieval Irish Church,* Turnhout: Brepols 186–8, for summary, and 95–9.
74 Jenkins 128–44, Sharpe 145.
75 Jenkins 87–92.
76 Handley, Isidore of Seville 26–32.

criteria for 'Hisperic' diction that he sets out: namely a propensity to use suffixes to coin neologisms and to use obscure terms as synonyms.[77] Some circumstantial support could also be found for his thesis in Hisperic literature.[78] It is worth saying that in his interpretation Handley might be influenced by the *OLD*'s suggestion that *tesquum* was possibly a word that was generally indistinct in meaning, which, as we have seen above, is probably an error on the basis of Varro.[79] Handley is also guardedly inclined to accept David Howlett's contention that there is a metrical quality to the nearby Llanddewibrefi inscription—albeit he is sceptical concerning Howlett's wider thesis concerning 'Biblical Style'.[80] Howlett's arguments for styles inherent in Insular texts are difficult to evaluate, however, and we should be cautious of their use as premises for further interpretations.[81]

We also should be wary of assuming narrow paths of arrival for this word, notwithstanding its rarity. Handley himself has noted that, unlike in the Irish church, Latin in the British church was a living language inherited from the Roman period; he has on this basis questioned the older, isolationist, theories in which British inscriptional formulae were explained by singular connections to particular provinces of Gaul.[82]

---

77   Handley, Isidore of Seville 30.
78   In *Hisperica Famina* are described what may be small huts in fields that surround the great city: 'in quibus turrita multiformi compage astunt tuguria' (in which there are round houses of varied construction): *Hisperica Famina*, line 454, edited and translated in Herren, Michael 1974 *Hisperica Famina* I, Toronto: Pontifical Institute of Medieval Studies 100–101 and notes on lines 221 and 454. The qualification of *tugurium* here with *turrita* (round or tower-*like*), formed with the suffix *-itus,* might be significant, though the *tesquitus* of the inscription is apparently used as a noun. Herren translates *turrita* as 'round', following Isidore and making an explicit comparison with Irish 'beehive' monastic cells. *Tesquum* is not, however, used here.
79   Handley, Isidore of Seville 26–7.
80   Handley, M. 2000 Review of Charles Thomas, *Christian Celts*, Britannia, 31, 463–464.
81   McKee, H. and McKee, J. 2006 Chance or Design? David Howlett's *Insular Inscriptions* and the Problem of Coincidence, *Cambrian Medieval Celtic Studies* 51, 83–101; also the general comments of Clancy, T. 200 Review of C. Thomas, *Christian Celts: Messages and Images*, Innes Review 51, 85–8.
82   Handley, Mark 2001 The Origins of Christian Commemoration in Britain, *Early Medieval Europe* 10, 177-99: 189–90; we should, in the light of the

More recently, Anthony Harvey, on the basis of an examination of the Latin lexis of the British inscriptions, has argued that the early medieval British were the inheritors of an 'unbroken, still-functioning Latin tradition' perhaps even up to the ninth or tenth century.[83] When a term is so singular in its use as *tesquitus* here, Occam's Razor *might* suggest a singular borrowing is the easiest explanation, but it is also quite possible that the word also had a meaning remembered in local Latin usage. The term may also have been brought into Britain in a monastic vocabulary of sacred space.[84] My suggestion is that, while this was undoubtedly a rare term, we should interpret it on the assumption that it was already known in British Latin and used here on the basis of one or other of its established meanings.

Conclusion

Though this has been a close look at only a very small amount of evidence, the case of Llanllŷr is impressive. The site shows continuity of monastic use from the first millennium into the second. So rare is any evidence that can point us to the site of a first-millennium monastery in Wales that this alone makes it significant. The unusual reference by an inscription to a saint's name in hypocoristic form, to a property transaction, and use of the unusual place-name element *tesquitus*, is evidence certainly worthy of holistic assessment. In reassessing Handley's analysis I am moved to differ from some of its premises,

---

above discussion, also note Handley's own explicit rejection of the isolationist thesis in Handley, M. 2000 The British Isles and the Mediterranean World: Contact and Exchange, *Origins and Revivals: Proceedings of the First Australian Conference of Celtic Studies,* edited by Evans, G. *et al.,* Sydney Series in Celtic Studies 159–85: 166.

83 Harvey, Anthony 2018 Philological Considerations Set in Stone: Looking Again at the Early Medieval Inscriptions of Wales, *Epigraphy in an Intermedial Context*, edited by Alessia Bauer, Elise Kleivane and Terje Spurkland, Dublin: Four Courts Press 18–30: 24–5.

84 Sidonius' writings show no sign of having been known in early medieval Britain, but the monastic culture of southern France was probably influential in Britain, even if its influence has sometimes been overstated—see Sharpe 98–102.

but not to disagree with the broad conclusion that *Tesquitus Ditoc* was a site given to a larger community. In the light of the foregoing discussion, however, I would be inclined to seek an explanation that takes account of the diversity of holy people commemorated at Llanllŷr, the rugged and liminal senses of *tesquum,* and assume (*pace* Handley) that Modomnóc's cult might not have been, in effect, replacing Ditoc's on the same spot. If we take account of William of Poitiers' contrast of *tesqua* with *campestria,* which might suggest a flat field, we could be looking for a more rugged terrain than the flood-plain and this would fit with the Classical usages as well.[85]

If the *tesquitus* is presumed not to be Llanllŷr itself, where might we look for it? We might first ask how large a 'little' *tesquum* might be—but how long is a piece of string? Paul Russell has observed that whilst diminutives are used in hypocoristic names for saints, there is no reason to assume by extension that diminutives used to describe inanimate objects associated with saints (monasteries, boats etc.) are anything other than actual diminutives.[86] So Ditoc's 'little' hermitage is likely to indeed have been just that, *little*.[87] The *tesquitus* is likely to have been a space outside the monastic estate, perhaps across the river or over some other boundary. Perhaps it was the cell of a hermit, living outwith the main estate in a space not formally consecrated, but having an association with the monastery, whose cell was later donated into the monastery and its separate identity forgotten. Such a model indeed could also be seen as a metaphor for the modern heritage of the early Welsh church, where the removal of many monuments inside the boundaries of churchyards and into the interiors of church buildings

---

85 Lewis and Short, *s.v. campester*. But I also note *Dictionary of Medieval Latin from British Sources, s.v. tesquum,* which suggests a possible later-medieval meaning of 'marshland' for *tesquum*.
86 Russell, Patterns 239.
87 Though Oliver Padel and Lynette Olson have both drawn to my attention the gift of in 960 of the quite large estate of Tywarnhayle, where it is still described as *portiuncula* 'a little portion', a description Padel sees as 'conventional modesty': Padel, O. J. 2014 The Boundary of Tywarnhayle (Perranzabuloe) in AD 960, *Journal of the Royal Institution of Cornwall,* 69–92: 71.

now makes it harder to remember that saints were once often found commemorated in the wider landscape.[88]

Appendix

Rhŷs and Lewes were also inclined to seek *Tesquitus Ditoc* outside the boundary of the monastic estate. In a letter of 16 November 1895 to Rhŷs, Colonel Lewes drew attention to a site lying to the north-west of the house, across the old river bed, that was partly exempted from tithe.[89] This was a small, irregularly shaped, field known as 'Caedegwm', in which he speculated might be found a corruption of the name *Ditoc*. Lewes' theory of the name is not probable; *degwm* means 'tithe', hence *cae degwm* 'tithe field' and there is another field with the same generic name in the parish of Llanbadarn Fawr around 20 km to the north.[90] This site is nonetheless of more than passing interest, as a tithe-ambiguous space adjacent to a boundary of a larger religious site.[91]

---

88   Versions of this chapter were presented at the Conference of the Australasian Early Medieval Association and at a Colloquium on the Letters of Sir John Rhŷs at the National Library of Wales. The kind interest of the Lewes family, especially Dr Loveday Lewes Gee, inspired my initial investigation. I would also like to thank Jemma Bezant, Siân Bowyer, Anthony Harvey, Joseph Flahive, Karen Jankulak, Gerald Morgan, Lynette Olson, Oliver Padel, Paul Russell, Wyn Thomas, Patrick Sims-Williams and the reviewers for helpful comments and advice. All opinions and errors remain my responsibility.
89   In 1841 it was listed (field No. 20) as a possession of the Lewes family and the rector of Trefilan, with the coda that 'Only the hay from No. 20 belongs to the rector'.
90   RCAHMW Tithe Map Database, Llanbadarn Fawr Field Number D70.
91   It is also near the end of the avenue of trees that we have identified as possibly that described by Meyrick (above), though Caedegwm is not on the land of Lloyd Jack.

4
Early Irish *Peregrinatio* as Salvation History

Meredith D. Cutrer

The colorful lives of Irish *peregrini*—the intrepid monks who sailed in search of their *herimus in ociano*[1]—have long attracted the attention of those interested in Irish monasticism. The origin of the Irish enthusiasm for *peregrinatio*, defined in a clerical context as exile from one's native land or people for religious reasons, has been the subject of several excellent studies and arose, at least in part, from native elements in Irish society.[2] However, less attention has been given to the manner in which the journeys of the *peregrini* were framed in order to situate

---

1   *Vita S. Columbae* (Life of St Columba) 1.6.
2   There have been several important studies done on Irish *peregrinatio* that consider its social, historical, and legal contexts. Johnston, Elva 2016 Exiles from the Edge? The Irish Contexts of *Peregrinatio*, *The Irish in Early Medieval Europe: Identity, Culture and Religion*, edited by Roy Flechner and Sven Meeder, Basingstoke: Palgrave Macmillan 38–52; Charles-Edwards, Thomas 1976 The Social Background to Irish *peregrinatio*, *Celtica* 11, 43–59; Stancliffe, Clare 1982 Red, White and Blue Martyrdom in Ireland, *Early Medieval Europe: Studies in Memory of Kathleen Hughes*, edited by Dorothy Whitelock, Rosamond McKitterick, and David Dumville, Cambridge: Cambridge University Press 21–46; O'Hara, Alexander 2013 *Patria, Peregrinatio, and Paenitentia*: Identities of Alienation in the Seventh Century, *Post-Roman Transitions: Christian and Barbarian Identities in the Early Medieval West*, edited by Walter Pohl and Gerda Heydemann, Turnhout: Brepols 89–124.

them within Christian salvation history. In examining a few striking theological themes and literary motifs found in Biblical sources which are then appropriated in the literature about the Desert Fathers and Irish *peregrini* it becomes clear that a number of prominent pieces of literature about or by the *peregrini* did not perceive *peregrinatio* as a unique expression of Christian identity or outside the bounds of orthodox Christian expressions of piety. Rather, several key sources intentionally positioned the Irish practice of *peregrinatio* within a well-established tradition of Christian exile thus legitimising the Irish *peregrinus'* role as part of a larger narrative of Christian salvation history wherein the *peregrini* participated as active contributors in the unfolding of God's redemptive plan.

One of the recurring themes that unifies the Old and New Testaments esteemed by many early Irish *peregrini* is the alienation and dispossession of God's people who are often portrayed as exiles either from a physical or spiritual home. Those who long for their homeland, particularly a spiritual homeland, find validation in Sacred Scripture which takes great care to emphasise the transient nature of the Christians' earthly dwelling. The Apostle Paul teaches, 'For we know that if the tent that is our earthly home is destroyed, we have a building from God, a house not made with hands, eternal in the heavens. For in this tent we groan, longing to put on our heavenly dwelling …' (2 Cor 5:1–2) and later, 'We know that while we are at home in the body we are away from the Lord.' (2 Cor 5:6). The state of being a foreigner, whether through physical exile as in the case of Adam and Eve (Gen 3:23–24), Abraham (Gen 12:1–2), and the Israelites (Dan 1–6, Jer 39–43, 2 Kings 17: 6–41) or spiritual exile as described by Paul, Peter and the author of Hebrews (1 Pet 1:1, 2:11; Heb 11), is a motif woven through the Bible from Genesis to Revelation. As a result, exile, whether penitential or ascetic in nature, becomes a significant part of the theology shaping early Christian monastic communities and enjoys a long and rich history of practice in the deserts of Egypt and the Middle East, particularly in the lives of the Desert Fathers.

Scholars have long noted the connections between the Desert Fathers and the Christian communities in Europe through the teachings of such theologians including John Cassian, Eucherius and others from the abbey of Lérins, whose founder Saint Honoratus, had studied with Christians in Egypt.[3] The retreat into the desert by early monastic communities is in part due to the prominence of the wilderness in the Biblical narrative. In the Bible, many of God's most extraordinary interactions with his people occur in the wilderness—a place outside the bounds of the inhabited world where humans are required to confront the vulnerabilities of their mortal condition with particular urgency. It also serves as the backdrop to the lives of some of the Bible's holiest figures: Moses, Elijah, Elisha and John the Baptist. The Desert Fathers take note and retreat into the desert in order to pursue sanctification and divine interaction following several Biblical *exempla*. With a similar awareness of the desert's role in salvation history, the Irish *peregrini* likewise seek the wilderness highlighting a striking theological continuity in the traditions from the Egyptian to the Irish monastic communities. In undertaking their journeys, the Irish *peregrini* situate themselves as part of the unfolding Biblical narrative in the same traditions as holy figures who had come before.

The early Irish found inspiration in Egyptian monasticism which thrived from the fourth century onwards.[4] Egypt witnessed the flourishing of a form of monasticism that had a profound impact on monastic practices in Western Europe. Drawing upon the lives of several Biblical figures, the Egyptian Desert Fathers taught a theology notably eschatological in orientation which in turn gave rise to rigorous ascetic practices that simultaneously served as preparation for Judgment Day and a foretaste of Heaven. A number of prominent

---

3   O'Loughlin, Thomas 1995 The Symbol Gives Life: Eucherius of Lyon's Formula for Exegesis, *Scriptural Interpretation*, edited by Thomas Finan and Vincent Twomey, Portland: Four Courts Press 221–252; Lawrence, C.H. 2015 *Medieval Monasticism: Forms of Religious Life in Western Europe in the Middle Ages*, New York: Routledge 10–15.

4   Dunn, Marilyn 2003 *The Emergence of Monasticism: From the Desert Fathers to the Early Middle Ages*, Oxford: Blackwell Publishing 138–146; Albeit from a somewhat later date than the *peregrini* discussed below, Colleen Thomas argues persuasively that the frequent inclusion of Antony and Paul on the Irish high crosses highlights the fact that early Irish monks saw themselves in the same tradition as their Egyptian predecessors. See Thomas, Colleen M. 2013 Missing Models: Visual Narrative in the Insular Paul and Antony Panels, *Making Histories: Proceedings of the Sixth International Conference on Insular Art*, edited by Jane Hawkes, Donington: Shaun Tyas 77–89.

monastic leaders residing in continental Europe, taught by these same Desert Fathers directly or through the writings of their disciples, incorporated this eschatologically driven asceticism into their monastic practices and modified it for their geographical context and cultural milieu.[5] During this theological transmission, distinctive localised features in the practice of exile emerged. Nevertheless, there are several significant motifs that highlight the continuity of tradition from the Biblical narrative through the Egyptian Desert Fathers into the Irish context including the centrality of the wilderness as the optimal locus for divine interaction, the liminality of the people of God who resided between 'the world' and the Promised Land or Heaven, and the eschatologically oriented pursuit of an earthly foretaste of Heaven.

To understand how Scripture shaped Egyptian and Irish asceticism, it is important to recognise how the ascetics interpreted the Biblical texts. For the Desert Fathers, Scripture is a multivalent work. John Cassian, a student of the Desert Fathers, writes about the four levels of interpreting Scripture that demonstrates the manner in which many early medieval Christian communities spiritualised Biblical events and figures. This allows for an interpretation of Scripture in which post-apostolic Christians can participate in the Biblical narrative. Cassian writes:

> one and the same Jerusalem can be taken in four senses: historically as the city of the Jews; allegorically as Church of Christ, anagogically as the heavenly city of God 'which is the mother of us all,' tropologically, as the soul of man ... [6]

This type of interpretation fosters a remarkable diversity in ascetic praxis. The four-fold method of Scripture interpretation encourages the monastic communities to view traditional Biblical accounts such as the Israelites' escape from Egypt as types that have a direct application

---

5   Le Goff, Jacques 1988 The Wilderness in the Medieval West, *The Medieval Imagination*, translated by Arthur Goldhammer, Chicago: University of Chicago Press 50–52; O'Loughlin, Thomas 2000 Island Monasteries, *The Encyclopedia of Monasticism*.
6   Cassian, John, *Conferences* 14.8, edited by Edgar C. S. Gibson 1894 *A Select Library of Nicene and Post-Nicene Fathers of the Christian Church,* second series, volume 11, Buffalo: The Christian Literature Company.

to their own lives. Through the teachings of Cassian, the four-fold model of interpretation gained widespread usage in the medieval era.[7] The early Irish, in turn, interpreted Sacred Scripture as a dynamic text having various modes and levels of interpretative meaning which allowed them to be active participants in the unfolding narrative of God's plan for salvation.[8]

The Irish, like Cassian, understood that the Biblical account of the Israelites' enslavement, miraculous liberation, and journey through the desert to the Promised Land was a particularly powerful image which later generations of Christians interpreted as both a type and a model of their own spiritual journey.[9] The Biblical Egypt was an enormously wealthy and powerful country but also the source of bondage for God's people (Ex 1:8–14). To receive the fulfillment of God's blessing, the Israelites left Egypt and traversed through the wilderness to receive that which God had promised to them—a land of tremendous resources. However, after the Israelites left Egypt, their faith in God wavered when confronting the Amorites and they began to grumble and disobey. Due

---

7   Leithard, Peter J. 2008 The Quadriga or Something Like It: A Biblical and Pastoral Defense, *Ancient Faith for the Church's Future*, edited by Mark Husbands and Jeffrey Greenman, Downers Grove IL: InterVarsity Press 114. The nature of Irish exegesis needs more study, but a good overview is McNamara, Martin 1996 The Irish Tradition of Biblical Exegesis, A.D. 550–800, *Iohannes Scottus Eriugena: The Bible and Hermeneutics*, edited by Gerd van Riel, Carlos Steel, and James McEvoy, Leuven: Leuven University Press 25–54, particularly his note on Cassian and Eucherius 29, 32–34 and 42–45. While it is presently unclear that the Irish adopted Cassian's four-fold exegesis at an early stage, it is undeniable that Irish exegetes did see Scripture imbued with more than one level of meaning.
8   Thomas O'Loughlin notes, for instance, how Patrick understands his missionising work on the edge of the known world as participating in part of salvation history wherein the Gospel will spread from Jerusalem outwards to 'the ends of the earth' before the End Times (Acts 1:8). O'Loughlin, Thomas 2001 Patrick on the Margins of Space and Time, *Eklogai: Studies in Honour of Thomas Finan and Gerard Watson*, edited by Kieran McGroarty, Maynooth: Cardinal Press 44–58.
9   O'Reilly, Jennifer 2017 The Bible as Map, On Seeing God and Finding the Way: Pilgrimage and Exegesis in Adomnán and Bede, *Place and Space in the Medieval World*, edited by Meg Boulton, Jane Hawkes, and Heidi Stoner, New York: Routledge 210–226.

to their disobedience, God did not allow that generation of Israelites to enter the Promised Land (Deut 1:19–45). They were destined to live in the Egyptian wilderness until they died.

Their time in the desert, however, was not strictly punitive. Rather, the desert journey also featured some of the most impressive and regular displays of providential power and interaction since Adam and Eve's expulsion from the Garden of Eden. In the wilderness, God's presence manifested in the daily provision of manna (Ex 16), regular divine revelations (Ex 20: 18–21; Deut 5), and a number of miraculous occurrences (Ex 13: 14–6; 14: 21, 31; Lev 9:23–24; Num 16:31–35; Num 16:42–45). Addressing the Israelites, God spoke through Moses saying,

> God has led you these forty years in the wilderness, that he might humble you, testing you to know what was in your heart … Your clothing did not wear out on you and your foot did not swell these forty years … For the Lord your God is bringing you into a good land, a land of brooks of water, of fountains and springs, flowing out in the valleys and hills, a land of wheat and barley, of vines and fig trees and pomegranates, a land of olive trees and honey, a land in which you will eat bread without scarcity … (Deut 8: 2–9 ESV)

Deuteronomy made clear that the time in the wilderness was a time of testing, refinement, and miraculous provision in preparation for and in expectancy of a future promised land. For later monastic communities, the narrative of Israel in the wilderness served as a type in which monks, too, participated in the wilderness experience. The spiritualisation of the wilderness as a place to encounter God in anticipation of a promised land influenced several prominent early Irish *peregrini* to pursue the wilderness as they sought their own heavenly Promised Land.[10]

The centrality of the wilderness as a locus of divine interaction is a feature throughout both the Old and New Testaments.[11] While

---

10 For instance, see the voyages of Báetán and Cormac Ua Liatháin (*Vita S. Columbae* I.20 and I.6, II.42 respectively).
11 Ex 16:10: 'And as soon as Aaron spoke to the whole congregation of the people of Israel, they looked toward the wilderness, and behold, the glory of

the lives of John the Baptist and Jesus show the importance of the wilderness in their ministries, Hebrews 11 is particularly illuminating for understanding the theology of the *peregrinus* and highlights some important themes in the *Navigatio S. Brendani* (*Voyage of Saint Brendan*). Hebrews 11 selects heroes of the Christian faith who all share two characteristics: faith in God characterised their life on Earth and none of them actually received what they longed for (i.e. the Promised Land) while on earth. The author of Hebrews notes that when they died, 'they had not received the things promised, but having seen them and greeted them from afar … [they] acknowledged that they were strangers and exiles (*peregrini et hospites*) on the earth' (Heb 11:13). These *peregrini* can only anticipate from a distance what God had promised them. Their life on earth is marked by this tension—they are in the world as *peregrini* but look forward to another world as their home. Hebrews 11 states that while dwelling in the earthly Promised Land (*terra repromissionis*) Abraham lived in a tent which, as Bede points out, is not permanent but is used in journeys and signals Abraham's transience.[12] The Hebrews author makes clear that what Abraham seeks is no earthly location.

The earthly Promised Land served as a type for an eschatological destiny. As Hebrews argued, Abraham sought a 'city that has foundations, whose designer and builder is God' (Heb 11:10). The theme of God's people being *peregrini* on earth continued throughout the chapter as Hebrews pointed out other Christians who were 'wandering about in deserts and mountains' (Heb 11: 38) looking forward to a land God had promised them, but dwelling in the Promised Land was not to be fulfilled while they were alive. God's people, in a spiritual sense, were in the same wilderness as the Israelites in Exodus. The wilderness, in the Bible and the post-apostolic Christian communities, served a crucial role in God's interaction with his people.

---

the Lord appeared in the cloud.' Hosea 2:14: God says of Israel, 'Therefore, behold, I will allure her, and bring her into the wilderness, and speak tenderly to her.' Isaiah 40:3: 'A voice of one calling: "In the wilderness prepare the way for the Lord; make straight in the desert a highway for our God."'

12 Bede, *On Genesis* 9.27, translated with an introduction and notes by Calvin B. Kendall 2008 Translated Texts for Historians 48, Liverpool: Liverpool University Press.

The wilderness was simultaneously an actual physical location situated in time and space and a spiritual landscape that was most conducive to a foretaste of the Promised Land. A number of Desert Fathers, following the model of several prominent Biblical figures, sought the wilderness in part in order to achieve the foretaste of the Promised Land that God has promised to his faithful, a theme that would be addressed in several early Irish texts about *peregrinatio*.

The influential theologian Cassian, through the figures of Abbas Paphnutius, Serapion, and Theonas, wrote that his contemporary monks were the spiritual equivalent to the Israelites. Abba Serapion, in cautioning against the excesses of extreme asceticism, warned that human weakness would cause an imprudent monk 'to return again to the land of Egypt, i.e. to our former greed and carnal lust which we forsook when we made our renunciation of this world. And this has happened in a figure, in those who after having gone forth into the desert of virtue again hanker after the flesh pots over which they sat in Egypt.'[13] In this passage, Abba Serapion noted that the Israelite escape from Egypt was a type for later monks and thereby situated both himself and his monastic counterparts as part of the Biblical Exodus narrative in a spiritual sense. What happened in Exodus, while history, also served as a spiritual example for the monk who sought Heaven.

To Cassian, Egypt represented the sinful and enslaving yet alluring, wealthy and powerful entrapments offered by the world. The distractions of Egypt were antithetical to the quest for holiness, and the writings of both the Desert and Patristic Fathers were rife with admonitions about succumbing to the lure of the 'spiritual Egypt'[14] and characterised monks who were drawn back to their previous life as having 'returned in heart to Egypt.'[15] Having established the world that the monks left behind as a spiritual Egypt, the Desert Fathers envisaged themselves as the spiritual Israel. Abba Theonas taught, 'The Egyptians formerly oppressed the children of Israel with grievous afflictions, so now also the spiritual Egyptians try to bow down the true Israel, i.e.

---

13   Cassian, *Conferences* 5.18.
14   Cassian, *Conferences* 5.22.
15   Cassian, *Conferences* 3.7.

the monastic folk, with hard and vile tasks ... '[16] The interpretation of monks as the new Israel would find great support in continental Europe through the pupils of the Desert Fathers.

Equating the Biblical account of Israel in the desert with the contemporary monk was a motif found in the writings of some theologians living in continental Europe. Eucherius was Cassian's associate and quoted by Columbanus and likely known on Iona.[17] In his *Formulae*, he sought to explain the spiritual meaning of common words and themes in the Bible. He posited that 'Egypt is this world,'[18] which affirmed that he, like Cassian and the Desert Fathers, viewed the Exodus account as a spiritual type. In explaining Psalm 80:8 he teaches, 'the vineyard is the church or the people of Israel' whom, he notes, God has 'brought out ... from Egypt.'[19] Eucherius explicates this interpretation in his work *In Praise of the Desert* where he asserted,

> You are now the true Israel ... who has just been freed from the dark Egypt of this world ... Because you keep company with Israel in the desert, you will certainly enter the Promised Land with Jesus.[20]

Eucherius explicitly connects the monk's spiritual journey to the heavenly Promised Land with the Israelites' time in the desert before their admittance to the physical Promised Land providing a symbolically rich picture.

The Insular sources likewise viewed themselves as the new Israel. St Samson of Dol, a monk in the same tradition as the celebrated

---

16 Cassian, *Conferences* 21.28.
17 Lake, Stephen 2011 Usage of the Writings of John Cassian is some early British and Irish writings, *Journal of the Australian Early Medieval Association* (Vol. 7) 107. Eucherius is possibly echoed in other early Irish works. See McNamara The Irish Tradition of Biblical Exegesis 29 and O'Loughlin, Thomas 2001 Monasteries and Manuscripts: The Transmission of Latin Learning in Early Medieval Ireland, *Information, Media and Power Through the Ages*, edited by Hiram Morgan, Dublin: University College Dublin Press 49, 55–56, 58.
18 Eucherius and Mandolfo, Carmela 2004 *Evcherii Lvgdvnensis: Formvlae Spiritalis Intelligentiae*, Turnhout: Brepols book IX, line 1128, page 69.
19 Eucherius and Mandolfo, Carmela 2004 *Evcherii Lvgdvnensis: Formvlae Spiritalis Intelligentiae*, Turnhout: Brepols book III, lines 286–288, page 17.
20 Vivian, Tim, Vivian, Kim and Russell, Jeffrey Burton 1999 *The Lives of the Jura Fathers*, Kalamazoo: Cistercian Publications 44.

Irish *peregrini* Brendan and Columbanus,[21] when urged to visit his ailing father, refused citing that he had 'already left Egypt.'[22] Samson viewed Egypt in a spiritual sense as his former life that he had fled in pursuit of the Promised Land. Similarly, the *Vita S. Columbani* (*Life of St Columbanus*) contains a number of allusions to Exodus.[23] In one scene, Columbanus retreated to the wilderness to seek the will of God when he ran out of food. He and two disciples went in search of food and found some fish which Jonas called 'manna' that God had prepared for them.[24] During a similar time of starvation later in the *Vita*, Jonas reported that 'as great a number of birds appeared as the quails that covered the camp of the Israelites.'[25] In another episode, Columbanus lived alone in the wilderness when his young assistant complained of the exhausting efforts required to fetch water. Columbanus bade him to be 'mindful that the Lord caused water to pour from rock for the people of Israel.'[26] Columbanus then prayed and water miraculously began flowing from the rock in a scene alluding to Exodus 17. Jonas described Columbanus' *peregrinatio* in Gaul with language and miracles that reflected the Israelites' journey in the wilderness. Jonas intentionally placed Columbanus in the same tradition as Moses thereby situating Columbanus in broader Christian history.[27] Several prominent early Irish *peregrini* and their hagiographers, far from viewing their exiles

---

21 The *Vita S. Samsonis* is datable to c. 680–707. For a fuller discussion of *peregrinatio* in the *Life of St Samson*, see Wooding, Jonathan M. 2017 The Representation of Early British Monasticism and *Peregrinatio* in *Vita Prima S. Samsonis*, *St Samson of Dol and the Earliest History of Brittany, Cornwall and Wales*, edited by Lynette Olson, Woodbridge: Boydell 137–161.
22 *Life of Saint Samson of Dol* 1.24, translated by Taylor, Thomas 1925 London: Macmillan.
23 The *Vita S. Columbani* was written ca. 639–642.
24 Jonas, *Vita S. Columbani* I.11, translated by O'Hara, Alexander and Wood, Ian 2017 *Jonas of Bobbio: Life of Columbanus, Life of John of Réomé, and Life of Vedast*, Translated Texts for Historians 64, Liverpool: Liverpool University Press; cf. Ex 16.
25 *Vita S. Columbani* I.27; cf. Ex 16:13.
26 *Vita S. Columbani* I.9; cf. Num 20:11.
27 For Jonas' use of the Bible, see O'Hara, Alexander 2018 *Jonas of Bobbio and the Legacy of Columbanus: Sanctity and Community in the Seventh Century*, New York: Oxford University Press 155–179.

as a localised or distinctive feature of the Church in Ireland, saw themselves as participating in a form of asceticism and expression of faith that shifted their place from the periphery of the known world to being placed alongside important figures including Moses, Joshua and Elijah in the unfolding narrative of salvation history.

The association between the Irish *peregrini* and their predecessors reveals, in addition to the incorporation of their exiles into the ongoing Christian story, other themes found in the Bible, the Desert Fathers, and the *peregrini* which offer an illuminating glimpse into the motivations that partly inspired the perilous journeys of the *peregrini*. In the book of Psalms, the psalmist writes, 'My heart says of you, "Seek his face!" Your face, Lord, I will seek … I will *see* the goodness of the Lord in the *land of the living*' (Ps 27:8,13, emphasis mine). The psalmist shows confidence that in pursuing the Lord, he will experience God while alive. This is not a hope to be fulfilled in the Eschaton as seen in Hebrews 11, but a promise to be fulfilled in the present. Jesus, in the Sermon on the Mount, clarifies who can see God when he teaches, 'Blessed are the *pure in heart*, for they will *see* God' (Matt 5:8, emphasis mine).[28] The monks believe that a vision of God is only attainable to those who are free from sin as sin separates people from God (Is 59:2). Seeing God while on earth is an anticipation of the Christians' heavenly blessing as described in Revelation where God's people in heaven 'will *see* his face' (Rev 22:3-4, emphasis mine). Many Desert Fathers and some notable Irish *peregrini* seek the wilderness as a more conducive location for cleansing sins and where, free from the disturbances of the world, they might see God while yet alive.

The Desert Fathers' retreat into the wilderness was in part to confront their sin which polluted their purity of heart. By overcoming sin through penance and ascesis, the monks received regular divine interaction in the form of miracles and ecstatic visions. Interestingly, many of these miracles and experiences have clear parallels to the physical Promised Land of the Israelites or to its heavenly spiritual

---

28 For a discussion of this verse, seeing God, and seeking paradise in Patristic theology, see Ladner, Gerhart B. 1959 *The Idea of Reform: Its Impact on Christian Thought and Action in the Age of the Fathers*, Cambridge: Harvard University Press 63-107.

counterpart described in Revelation. Cassian's *Conferences* offer some of the most revealing commentary from the Desert Fathers about both the goal and the earthly reward of the monastic life. Abba Moses, in extolling the benefits of purity of heart, observed that it was for the pursuit of purity of heart that Cassian and his companion left homeland and family and came to the holy men who were 'living in this wretched state in the desert.'[29] Abba Moses made clear that Cassian's own journey into the desert originated in Cassian's desire for purity of heart, which, as Jesus taught, allowed him to see God. Abba Isaac encouraged Cassian's quest for purity by telling him that he would receive a glimpse of his heavenly future while still on earth when he stated,

> For according to the measure of purity ... the mind ... can look with purest eyes on his Godhead ... while still living in the body ... [we] may manage in some degrees to adapt ourselves to some likeness of that bliss which is promised hereafter to the saints.[30]

Abba Isaac clearly connected a person's purity of heart—his or her freedom from sin—with a vision of God while still living on earth.

'Seeing' God while on earth is a theme found in the writings of the celebrated *peregrinus* Columbanus.[31] Columbanus writes a sermon instructing his disciples that God can 'at least in part be seen ... he [may] be partly seen by the pure heart'[32] emphasising the connection between purity of heart and a vision of God. This vision, Columbanus

---

29 Cassian, *Conferences* 1.2. Abba Moses repeats this same type of explanation several times in the first conference, highlighting its importance to the monastic vocation. See Cassian, *Conferences* 1.5, 1.17.
30 Cassian, *Conferences* 10.6.
31 For Cassian's *theoria* in Irish hagiography, see Follett, Westley 2006 Cassian, Contemplation, and Medieval Irish Hagiography, *Insignis Sophiae Arcator: Essays in Honour of Michael W. Herren on his 65th Birthday*, edited by Gernot Wieland, Carin Ruff, and Ross Arthur, Turnhout: Brepols 87–106.
32 Columbanus, Sermon 2, edited and translated by Walker, G. S. M. 1957 *Sancti Columbani Opera*, Scriptores Latinae Hiberniae 2, Dublin: Dublin Institute for Advanced Studies; for more detail on the writings and sermons of Columbanus, see Stancliffe, Clare 1997 The Thirteen Sermons Attributed to Columbanus and the Question of their Authorship, *Columbanus: Studies on*

notes, is in 'proportion to the deserts of our purity.'[33] The vision of God is an anticipation of an eschatological destiny promised to the faithful in the New Testament—a destiny that can be enjoyed, albeit imperfectly, while on Earth. Abba Isaac explains that purity of heart is the 'goal of a monk' so that a monk

> may deserve to possess in this life an image of future happiness and may have the beginnings of a foretaste in this body of that life and glory of heaven.[34]

The monastic quest for purity in expectation of a divine experience of Heaven serves as a unifying theme in both the writings of the Desert Fathers and several Irish *peregrini*.

Such language is employed in the *Navigatio S. Brendani*, a tale that describes Brendan's temporary experience in the Promised Land while still in his earthly body. After Barrind, who had recently returned from the Promised Land, finishes his description, Brendan praises God because he had blessed the monks 'with such a spiritual foretaste.'[35] Brendan then sets out on his own voyage seeking the Promised Land described by Barrind, saying, 'I have resolved in my heart if it is God's will ... to go in search of the Promised Land of the Saints'[36] which the author calls *terra repromissionis sanctorum*. This is an allusion to Hebrews 11:9 and describes the Promised Land that God promises to Abraham and his descendants. Hebrews 11 is the only time that the particular phrase is used in the Vulgate and it is a definitively eschatological land, thus highlighting that the land Barrind reaches and Brendan seeks is a spiritual one.[37] The author of the *Navigatio*

---

    the Latin Writings, Studies in Celtic History 17, edited by M. Lapidge, Woodbridge: Boydell 93–202.
33 Columbanus, Sermon 8.
34 Cassian, *Conferences* 10.7.
35 *Navigatio S. Brendani* 1, translated by O'Meara, John J. 2002 The Voyage of Saint Brendan: The Latin Version, *The Voyage of Saint Brendan*, edited by W. R. J. Barron and Glyn S. Burgess, Exeter: University of Exeter Press 28.
36 *Navigatio S. Brendani* 2, O'Meara 28.
37 O'Loughlin, Thomas 1999 Distant Islands: The Topography of Holiness in the *Nauigatio Sancti Brendani*, *The Medieval Mystical Tradition in England*,

S. Brendani spiritualises the land promised to Abraham and his seed, Israel, a family and inheritance into which the monastic communities consider themselves adopted (see Eph 1:5). By echoing the language of the Bible, the Irish author of the *Navigatio S. Brendani* places Barrind and Brendan within a broader and well-established tradition of Biblical exile.[38] Brendan's *peregrinatio*, rather than distinguishing him from the community of saints, actually places him firmly within the universal Christian tradition.

The earthly foretaste of a Promised Land is a theme found in Biblical literature. The first generation of Israelites was unable to enjoy the Promised Land because they had sinned (Num 14:20–23). Even Moses, their leader, was forbidden to enter because of his sin (Num 20:12). However, while living in the wilderness, Moses sent twelve spies to scout the Promised Land who brought back proof of the land's abundance including grapes, pomegranates, and figs (Num 13:23–26). This same fruit was offered as evidence when certain holy monks experienced a foretaste of their Promised Land to come. Patermuthius experienced a vision in the desert that transported him into Paradise where he saw 'all the good things that await those who are true monks ...'[39] There he gathered a fig from the paradisal fruit to take back to his brethren. Another Desert Father, Apollo, prayed and immediately at the entrance to his cave, complete strangers appeared who brought food with obvious ties to the bounty brought by the twelve spies: grapes, figs, pomegranates, milk, honeycombs, and honey.[40] As the Israelites in the desert before them, the Desert Fathers enjoyed the abundance of the Promised Land by foretaste while living in the desert.

Ireland, and Wales: Exeter Symposium VI, edited by Marion Glasscoe, Cambridge: Brewer 9–10.

38 For a discussion on the link between the Desert Fathers and Brendan, see Wooding, Jonathan (forthcoming) *Saints and the Sea in the Celtic Lands*, Cardiff: University of Wales Press; Fagnoni, Anna Maria 2006 Oriental Eremitical Motifs in the *Navigatio Sancti Brendani*, *The Brendan Legend: Texts and Versions*, edited by Glyn Burges and Clara Strijbosch, Leiden: Brill 53–79.

39 Russell, Norman 1980 *Lives of the Desert Fathers*, Kalamazoo: Cistercian Publications, Patermuthius 10.20.

40 Russell *Lives of the Desert Fathers*, Apollo 8.38; Num 13:23–26.

In the *Navigatio S. Brendani*, the author also utilised the same motif of bringing fruit back from the Promised Land of Saints. When Brendan visited the Promised Land of Saints, his spiritual guide told him he might only enjoy part of the land right now, but encouraged him to take 'some of the fruit of the land.'[41] Brendan's time in the Promised Land of Saints finds clear precedent in Biblical and early Christian literature where holy men journey temporarily to the Promised Land and collect fruit to bring back to their brethren so that they could enjoy the land by foretaste. None of these holy men were able to enjoy their experiences indefinitely. Residence in this land was not available until death which explained Brendan's inability to cross the river in the Promised Land of Saints. He could, just as the Israelites and Desert Fathers before him, only enjoy part of the land then. He received a foretaste of what was to come, or as Hebrews 11 put it, he was looking forward to his home whose architect is God (Heb 11:10). Ultimately, Brendan sought a spiritual Promised Land with the Israelites' Promised Land serving as a type. The author of the *Navigatio S. Brendani*, like Jonas of Bobbio for Columbanus, placed his *peregrinus* in the Biblical and monastic tradition of salvation history.

The Irish *peregrini* embrace their demanding voyages with enthusiasm. From an examination of the literature about some of the well-known *peregrini* it is clear that early Irish *peregrinatio* finds its theological origins in a well-established tradition of Christian exile based upon a multivalent interpretation of Sacred Scripture which sees the Biblical narrative as a type for later monks to follow. In undertaking *peregrinatio*, the *peregrini* or their hagiographers are situating themselves as part of the same narrative as God's people in the wilderness who await their Promised Land. However, as they wait on earth, they seek the wilderness in part in order to experience a foretaste of their Promised Land to come.

---

41   *Navigatio S. Brendani* 28; O'Meara 63.

5
Insular Influences on Carolingian and Ottonian Literature and Art

Penelope Nash

> Even if painting is dearer to you than all art, I ask you not to scorn the thankless labour of writing, the effort of singing and the fervour and ardour of reading. For writing is worth more than the vain shape of an image and gives the soul more beauty than the false painting which shows the form of things in an unfitting manner ... Writing reveals the truth by its countenance ... its words and its meaning. The picture sates the sight while it is still new but it palls once it is old, quickly loses its truth, and does not arouse faith.[1]

---

1   'Nam pictura tibi cum omni sit gratior arte, / Scribendi ingrate non spernas posco laborem. / Psallendi nisum, studium curamque legendi, / Plus quia gramma valet quam vana in imagine forma, / Plusque animae decoris praestat quam falsa colorum / Pictura ostentans rerum non rite figuras. / Nam scriptura pia norma est perfecta salutis, / Et magis in rebus valet, et magis utilis omni est, / Promtior est gustu, sensu perfectior atque / Sensibus humanis, facilis magis arte tenenda. / Auribus haec servit, labris, obtutibus atque, / Illa oculis tantum pauca solamina praestat. / Haec facie verum monstrat, et famine verum, / Et sensu verum, iucunda et tempore multo est, / Illa recens pascit visum, gravat atque vetusta, / Deficiet propere veri et non

Introducing Hraban Maur

In about AD 835 the respected scholar Hraban Maur, abbot of Fulda and archbishop of Mainz, wrote the letter whose poetic translation by Rosamond McKitterick is printed above.[2] Hraban Maur favoured text over art. In this article I examine selected works that found their way to or were created on the European continent towards the end of the first millennium. The focus of this chapter is how certain Insular motifs were expressed or re-formed in Carolingian derivatives and Ottonian re-imaginings. First, how and why ideas in earlier Insular texts might be remembered and incorporated in later Carolingian or Ottonian texts. Second, how aspects of Insular art appear and reappear transformed but recognisable in Carolingian and Ottonian art, particularly manuscript art. By Insular I mean works and items that were produced or illustrated in the British Isles.[3] We should note that such influences often resulted in complex and multi-faceted results. One example is the English adoption of the style of handwriting created by the Irish, Insular script.[4] I also survey the development of iconography in art that featured the Crucifixion. After what must be a compact discussion, I conclude by assessing Hraban Maur's real belief as opposed to his own statement that opens this article.

---

fide sequestra est.' Full text as in Hraban Maur, *Carmina* 38, edited by Ernst Dümmler 1884 *MGH Poetae Latini. Aevi Carolini* II.196 lines 1–19.

2   McKitterick, Rosamond 1995 Text and Image in the Carolingian World, *The Frankish Kings and Culture in the Early Middle Ages*, edited by Rosamond McKitterick, Aldershot: Variorum VIII.297–318: 297–298.

3   Olson, Lynette 2007 *The Early Middle Ages: The Birth of Europe*, Basingstoke: Palgrave Macmillan 1.

4   Olson 61. For an overview of Insular book production, see Duncan, Elizabeth 2016 The Irish and their Books, *The Irish in Early Medieval Europe: Identity, Culture and Religion*, edited by Roy Flechner and Sven Meeder, London: Palgrave 214–230. See also Brown, Michelle P. 2010 From Columba to Cormac: The Contribution of Irish Scribes to the Insular System of Scripts, *L'Irlanda e gli Irlandesi nell'alto medioevo: Spoleto, 16–21 aprile 2009*, Spoleto: Presso la Sede della Fondazione 623–649: 631–646.

Insular Motifs: Saints and Swine

The first of the interactions and influences that I examine comes from textual evidence, especially how the presence and activity of animals, specifically swine, so prevalent in the lives of Celtic saints in the early medieval Celtic world, might link to Ottonian histories.[5] Karen Jankulak in a detailed analysis sets out the importance of the activities of swine to Celtic saints in the selection of the sites of their foundation houses. In particular Jankulak links such saintly stories to the foundation myth of the town of Alba Longa, a precursor to Rome. Virgil reinforced the predictive myth that when a large white sow lay on the ground with her litter of thirty snow-white young, she selected the correct location for the site of the city.[6] In AD 852, nearly 900 years after Virgil composed his poem, Oda, the founder of the Liudolfing dynasty with her husband, Liudolf, established a female monastery, located initially at Brunshausen. In the late tenth century the canoness Hrotsvitha of Gandersheim wrote about the foundation in her *Primordia coenobii Gandeshemensis* (*The Establishment of the Monastery at Gandersheim*). Hrotsvitha recorded that shortly after the initial establishment brilliant lights in the sky at night foresaw a new site at Gandersheim near the existing monastery. Certain men, who

---

5   For a general discussion of animals and their symbolism in the Middle Ages, see Alexander, Dominic 2008 *Saints and Animals in the Middle Ages*, Woodbridge: Boydell. For a detailed examination of the symbolism of pigs, boars and swine in the Middle Ages, see Kearney, Milo 1991 *The Role of Swine Symbolism in Medieval Culture: Blanc Sanglier*, Studies in Mediaeval Literature, Lewiston: Edwin Mellen Press. For a list of saints who record the sighting of an animal leading to the location of a monastery as a sign of sanctity, see Bray, Dorothy Ann 1992 *A List of Motifs in the Lives of the Early Irish Saints*, Helsinki: Suomalainen Tiedeakatemia 132 and under the names of individual saints.

6   Jankulak, Karen 2003 Alba Longa in the Celtic Regions? Swine, Saints and Celtic Hagiography, *Celtic Hagiography and Saints' Cults*, edited by Jane Cartwright, Cardiff: University of Wales Press 271–284: 271, 273–274, 277–279. For discussion of Virgil's sometimes confusing inclusion of swine, Alba Longa and the foundation of Rome in *The Aeneid*, see especially Jankulak 278; Kearney 183; Fitzgerald, Robert, translator 1984 *The Aeneid*, New York: Alfred A. Knopf 3.79 line 529, 8.230 line 58, 8.231 line 64.

were caring for their swine (*porcos*) in enclosures at night, were singled out to observe and report on the phenomenon.⁷ Hrotsvitha always included information for a purpose. If she mentioned men minding swine it was no casual aside. For that reason the subtle association between swine and the foundation story has more meaning in her *Primordia* than might normally be inferred. The presence of swine as a symbol associated with *The Aeneid* imparts a special aura to the foundation story of Gandersheim, amounting to a prophecy. As well as the overt Biblical reference to the shepherds and their flocks, to whom the angels appeared, Celtic foundation stories and Virgilian memories and allusions have been combined in at least this one Ottonian text.⁸

If we concur that Hrotsvitha deliberately included in the *Primordia* an allusion to the foundation myth of Alba Longa (and by implication to Rome) or indeed to *The Aeneid*, albeit obliquely, we can note that this is not the only time that she introduces *The Aeneid* in her works. Her *Gesta Ottonis* (*Deeds of Otto*) details the rise of the Ottonian dynasty, just as *The Aeneid* is the story among other matters of the legitimisation of the Julio-Claudian dynasty. The analogy continues as Hrotsvitha writes about her difficulty in determining how to select and present appropriately all the illustrious achievements from among the many royal deeds as being like trying to find her path without a guide through a dark forest.⁹ This sentiment is reminiscent of the representation in

---

7   Hrotsvitha of Gandersheim *Primordia coenobii Gandeshemensis*, edited by Walter Berschin 2001 *Hrotsvit Opera omnia*, Munich: K. G. Sur, 306–329: 313 lines 189–192; translated by Thomas Head 2001 The Establishment of the Monastery of Gandersheim, *Medieval Hagiography: An Anthology*, New York: Routledge 237–254: 243, 246. For another English version of the first 66 lines of the *Primordia*, see Wilson, Katharina M. 1998 *Hrotsvit of Gandersheim: A Florilegium of Her Works*, Library of Medieval Women, Woodbridge: D. S. Brewer 108–110. See also Lees, Jay T. 2013 David *Rex Fidelis*? Otto the Great, the *Gesta Ottonis*, and the *Primordia coenobii Gandeshemensis*, *A Companion to Hrotsvit of Gandersheim (fl. 960): Contextual and Interpretive Approaches*, edited by Phyllis Rugg Brown and Stephen L. Wailes, Leiden: Brill 201–234: 225–233.

8   Hexter, Ralph and Townsend, David, editors 2012 *The Oxford Handbook of Medieval Latin Literature*, Oxford University Press 13.

9   Hrotsvitha of Gandersheim, *Gesta Ottonis*, edited by Berschin, *Hrotsvit Opera omnia*, 271–305: 271 lines 11–19, 272 lines 1–9; translated by Mary

The Aeneid of the forest as destitute, a prison, a maze and even a landscape of exile.[10] It is worth considering, albeit tentatively, whether there exist more links between Celtic and Ottonian foundation myths than is usually noted that could be explored in another study.

Insular Motifs Travel to the Continent with Eriugena and Others

The transfer of Insular motifs to the European continent in the early Middle Ages occurred because of the *peregrinatio* (ascetic self-exile) of men and women, who journeyed not only from Ireland but also from England. Many settled permanently in the new locations; some also were alerted to the possibilities of Carolingian patronage.[11] John Scotus

---

Bernardine Bergman in Hill, Boyd H. editor 1972 *Medieval Monarchy in Action: The German Empire from Henry I to Henry IV*, London: Allen and Unwin, 118-137: 119.

10   Saunders, Corinne J. 1993 *The Forest of Medieval Romance: Avernus, Broceliande, Arden*, Cambridge: D. S. Brewer, 26-29. For the *Gesta Ottonis* as an Ottonian *Aeneid*, see Stevenson, Jane 2005 *Women Latin Poets: Language, Gender, and Authority, from Antiquity to the Eighteenth Century*, Oxford University Press 6. For the *Gesta Ottonis* as an heroic epic that looked back to the *Waltharius*, see Ward, John O. 1993 After Rome: Medieval Epic, *Roman Epic*, edited by A. J. Boyle, London: Routledge 261-293: 285.

11   For a discussion of the processes of and problems faced by early medieval religious conversion, see Wickham, Chris 2016 The Comparative Method and Early Medieval Religious Conversion, *The Introduction of Christianity into the Early Medieval Insular World: Converting the Isles I*, edited by Roy Flechner, Máire Ní Mhaonaigh and Eric Cambridge, Turnhout: Brepols 13-37. See also Brito-Martins, Manuela 2004 The Concept of *Peregrinatio* in Saint Augustine and Its Influences, *Exile in the Middle Ages: Selected Proceedings from the International Medieval Congress, University of Leeds, 8-11 July, 2002*, edited by Laura Napran and Elisabeth M. C. van Houts, Turnhout: Brepols 83-94: 83-87; Johnston, Elva 2016 Exiles from the Edge? The Irish Contexts of *Peregrinatio*, *The Irish in Early Medieval Europe* 38-52: especially 39-40. For voyaging in Irish monastic literature, see Wooding, Jonathan M. 2000 Monastic Voyaging and the *Nauigatio*, *The Otherworld Voyage in Early Irish Literature: An Anthology of Criticism*, edited by Jonathan M. Wooding, Dublin: Four Courts Press 226-245: 232-244. For the first Insular *peregrinus*, see Wooding, Jonathan M. 2017 The Representation of Early British Monasticism and *Peregrinatio* in *Vita Prima S. Samsonis*, *St Samson of Dol*

Eriugena of Irish origin is recorded at the palace 'school' of Charles the Bald (youngest son of Louis the Pious by his wife Judith, grandson of Charlemagne, and ruler from 840 until 877) in the Laon region by 851.[12] Eriugena probably began as a teacher, from which he developed as a 'controversialist, a translator, a philosopher, and an exegete.'[13] He was one of several of Irish ancestry, who arrived in France and moved to Cambrai, Liège, Péronne, Soissons, Laon, Reims and elsewhere. He may even have been at the abbey of Saint-Médard at Soissons from 856/7.[14] We must also not forget the migrations of Willibrord,[15] Boniface,[16]

---

and the Earliest History of Brittany, Cornwall and Wales, edited by Lynette Olson, Woodbridge: Boydell 137–161: 137, 140–141, 154–156. See also the collections by Carver, M. O. H. 2003 *The Cross Goes North: Processes of Conversion in Northern Europe, AD 300–1300*, Woodbridge: Boydell and Brewer, and by Minnis, Alistair J. and Roberts, Jane, editors 2007 *Text, Image, Interpretation: Studies in Anglo-Saxon Literature and Its Insular Context in Honour of Éamonn Ó Carragáin*, Studies in the Early Middle Ages 18, Turnhout: Brepols.

12 For a map of locations, see Beckwith, John 1985 *Early Medieval Art: Carolingian, Ottonian, Romanesque*, World of Art, New York: Thames and Hudson 8. See also Nelson, Janet 1992 *Charles the Bald*, The Medieval World, London: Longman, esp. 16, 169 and the essays in Gibson, Margaret T. and Nelson, Janet L. editors 1990 *Charles the Bald: Court and Kingdom*, 2nd ed., Aldershot: Variorum, especially McKitterick, Rosamond 1990 The Palace School of Charles the Bald 326–339.

13 O'Meara, John J. 1988 *Eriugena*, Oxford: Clarendon Press 1, and for a summary of the life of Eriugena, see 1–21. Historians have placed Eriugena's origins variously in Scotland, England or the East (*ibid.* 1–3); however, his name clearly indicates that he was from Ireland. See Luhtala, Anneli 2003 A Priscian Commentary Attributed to Eriugena, *History of Linguistics 1999: Selected Papers from the Eighth International Conference on the History of the Language Sciences, 14–19 September 1999, Fontenay-St Cloud*, edited by Sylvain Auroux *et al.*, Amsterdam/Philadelphia: John Benjamins 19–30: 19; Carabine, Deirdre 2000 *John Scottus Eriugena*, Great Medieval Thinkers, Oxford University Press 13–14. For more on Eriugena's background see Byron, Mark S. 2014 *Ezra Pound's Eriugena*, Historicizing Modernism, London: Bloomsbury, 15.

14 Eriugena's best known work is *De divisione naturae* (*The Division of Nature*), which reviews the totality of all things. See Sheldon-Williams, I. P. *et al.* 1968–1995 *Johannis Scotti Eriugenae Periphyseon (De divisione naturae)*, 4 vols, Scriptores Latini Hiberniae 7, 9, 11, 13, Dublin: Dublin Institute for Advanced Studies. All Eriugena's works are recorded in Migne, *PL* 122. See

and the English nuns Thekla[17] and Leoba,[18] and others—those of Anglo-Saxon origin, who went as missionaries to the Continent.[19]

---

   also Contreni, John J. 1978 *The Cathedral School of Laon from 850 to 930: Its Manuscripts and Masters*, Münchener Beiträge zur Mediävistik und Renaissance-Forschung 29, Munich: Arbeo-Gesellschaft.
15 Willibrord was born in Northumbria, the son of a Saxon. Hen, Yitzhak 1997 The Liturgy of St Willibrord, *Anglo-Saxon England* 26, 41–62: 41–47. See Hen's useful references: Bede, *Historia ecclesiastica*, III.13 and 27, V.9–11 translated by Bertram Colgrave and R. A. B. Mynors 1969 *Bede's Ecclesiastical History of the English People*, Oxford Medieval Texts, Oxford: Clarendon Press 252–255, 310–315, 454–487; *The Calendar of St Willibrord*, edited by H. A. Wilson 1918 Henry Bradshaw Society 55, London: Harrison and Sons, esp. the marginal note on 39v; Alcuin, *Vita Willibrordi*, edited by W. Levison 1951 *MGH, SS rer. Merov. 7*, Hanover 81–141. See also Wood, I. N. 1994 *The Merovingian Kingdoms 450–751*, London: Longman, especially 317–321.
16 Boniface was born in Wessex. For an overview of his life, see Levison, Wilhelm 1946 *England and the Continent in the Eighth Century*, Oxford: Clarendon Press 70–86.
17 The English Thekla (Thecla, Tecla) should not be confused with the earlier Thekla. (The life of the earlier Thekla was written in about AD 470 at Seleukeia-on-the-Kalykadnos, located on the southern coast of current-day Turkey. See Davis, Stephen J. 2001 *The Cult of Saint Thecla: A Tradition of Women's Piety in Late Antiquity*, Oxford Early Christian Studies, Oxford University Press 2–10.) For the English Thekla, see Lifshitz, Felice 2014 *Religious Women in Early Carolingian Francia: A Study of Manuscript Transmission and Monastic Culture*, Fordham Series in Medieval Studies, New York: Fordham University Press 22, 83; Farmer, David Hugh 1980 *Benedict's Disciples*, Leominster: Fowler Wright 17, 108; Farmer, David Hugh 1996 *Oxford Dictionary of Saints*, 3rd ed., Oxford University Press, *s.v.* 'Tecla'.
18 For the Latin text, see *Vita Leobae*, edited by Waitz, G. 1887 *MGH, SS* 15.1, Hanover 118–131. For extracts from the Life of Leoba (Liobgytha) written by Rudolf of Fulda, a pupil of Hraban Maur, see Talbot, C. H. 1954 *The Anglo-Saxon Missionaries in Germany*, Makers of Christendom, London: Sheed and Ward 205–228. For recent analysis, see Talbot, C. H. 1995 The Life of Saint Leoba, *Soldiers of Christ: Saints and Saints Lives from Late Antiquity and the Early Middle Ages*, edited by Thomas F. X. Noble and Thomas Head, University Park: Pennsylvania State University Press 255–277; Lifshitz, *Religious Women* 17, 21, 22; McKitterick, Anglo-Saxon Missionaries in Germany: Personal Connections, *The Frankish Kings*, I.1–40: 11, 13–14, 15–16; Farmer, *Oxford Dictionary of Saints, s.v.* 'Lioba'.
19 For a brief history of the settlement, see Levison, *England and the Continent* 45–69. For the origin of the words 'mission' and 'missionaries' and for early

I do not propose to examine Eriugena's written works in detail here. Initially I want to select some of the locations in France where he and others visited or settled as jumping off points for an examination of the inclusion of Insular motifs in Carolingian artistic works.[20] However, we should note J. David McGee's comments about Eriugena's influence on art. He argues persuasively that Eriugena influenced iconography and iconology of Carolingian art during his life. Eriugena was responsible for a noticeable increase in the number of angels in illuminations (because he advocated their closeness to God) and for a change in the details of depictions of the Crucifixion, especially in the location and appearance of the moon and the sun. Eriugena also made post-iconoclastic Byzantine art more comprehensible to the later Ottonian artists because his Greek aesthetic philosophy educated them in the Eastern way of thinking.[21] Later in this article I examine the influence of Eriugena on artwork created at the Court of Charles the Bald.

Insular Objects and Insular-Influenced Objects

To identify Insular influences in Carolingian and Ottonian art initially appears straightforward, although much about dates, origins and models is contested.[22] This section is concerned primarily with Insular

---

Irish missions, see Wood, Ian N. 2016 What is a Mission? *The Introduction of Christianity into the Early Medieval Insular World*, Turnout: Brepols 135–156, esp. 135–143.

20 The Carolingian period was named after Charles Martel (d. 741). After the death of his grandson Charlemagne in 814, the empire fragmented and is generally considered to have terminated with the coronation of Hugh Capet (d. 996), who was the first of the Capetians.

21 McGee, J. David 1988 Reflections of the Thought of John Scotus Erigena in some Carolingian and Ottonian Illuminations, *Mediaevistik* 1, 125–143: 125–126. See how Byzantine art influenced Carolingian and Ottonian art more generally in Nash, Penelope 2011 Demonstrations of *Imperium*: Byzantine Influences in the Late Eighth and Tenth Centuries in the West, *Basileia: Essays on Imperium and Culture in Honour of E. M. and M. J. Jeffreys*. Byzantina Australiensia 17, 159–172.

22 See, for example, Ó Cróinín, Dáibhí 1984 Rath Melsigi, Willibrord and the Earliest Echternach Manuscripts, *Peritia* 3, 17–49: 17–20. For appraisal of the

and Insular-influenced objects and documented transitions, out of which come Carolingian derivatives. We will start with a purely Insular example. The gold buckle from Sutton Hoo and one of the carpet pages from the Book of Durrow appear to have common origins. The buckle originated in East Anglia, or perhaps Sweden, and is dated to after AD 625. Two serpents occupy the two half circles, where the tongue is attached. The body of the buckle shows snakes intertwining with other snakes and with quadrupeds.[23] The Book of Durrow, created in about AD 680 in Ireland, Northumbria or perhaps at Iona or at another monastery in Dalriada, contains carpet pages and Evangelist initials and symbol pages. It is the earliest of the surviving fully decorated Gospel books. The decoration on the carpet page is inspired by a source similar to the buckle. The page is filled with plait work of multi-coloured ribbons that picks up the motif of intertwining animals and biting quadrupeds and includes a central disc or circular medallion, like a shield boss, with a cross in the middle.[24]

---

    art and imagery of the Insular Gospel books in their historical context, see Henderson, George 1987 *From Durrow to Kells: The Insular Gospel-Books, 650–800*, London: Thames and Hudson. For an overview of Carolingian art, see Nees, Lawrence 1995 Art and Architecture, *The New Cambridge Medieval History*, edited by Rosamond McKitterick, Cambridge University Press 809–844: 839–844. See also the studies edited in the magnificent volume on art, one of three issued on the 800th anniversary of Charlemagne's death: van den Brink, Peter and Ayooghi, Sarvenaz 2014 *Karl der Grosse = Charlemagne: Karls Kunst*, Dresden: Sandstein. For an overview of Ottonian art, see Cohen, Adam S. 2010 Vigentennial Views on Ottonian Art History, *Peregrinations: International Society for the Study of Pilgrimage Art* 3, 1–7.

23 Nees, Lawrence 2002 *Early Medieval Art*, Oxford History of Art, Oxford University Press 110–111. For the Sutton Hoo treasures see Bruce-Mitford, Rupert Leo Scott and Evans, Angela Care 1975–1983 *The Sutton Hoo Ship-Burial*, 3 vols, London: British Museum Publications.

24 Carpet Page. Book of Durrow, Iona (?), seventh century. Dublin: Trinity College Library, MS 57 (A.IV.5) fol. 192v. See illustration in Nordenfalk, Carl 1995 *Book Illumination: Early Middle Ages*, Geneva: Skira 28. See also Werner, Martin 1990 The Cross-Carpet Page in the Book of Durrow: The Cult of the True Cross, Adomnan, and Iona, *The Art Bulletin* 72, 174–223: 174–176, 179–180; Netzer, Nancy 2011 New Finds Versus the Beginning of the Narrative on Insular Gospel Books, *Insular and Anglo-Saxon Art and Thought in the Early Medieval Period*, edited by Colum Hourihane, Index of

The link between the British Isles and the Carolingian world is clear in the Echternach Gospels of St Willibrord, an Englishman, who went to Ireland and from there to the Continent.[25] Produced in the late seventh century, the Gospels were possibly given to Willibrord before his journey to convert the heathen Frisians or else created at his foundation monastery at Echternach, located in modern-day Luxembourg.[26] Two pages are of interest. The first shows an energetic lion of Mark, presented without wings and with the feet of the lion cutting into the borders and with heraldic qualities. Such transgression of the borders is not obviously associated with Insular influences. Why is this apparently dissonant lion included in a Gospel so infused with Insular iconography? Nancy Netzer provides one answer. She asserts that full-length lions, in profile, with open jaws and extended tongues originated with the Book of Durrow, and influenced other Insular manuscripts. Although there is no precedent in contemporary Continental manuscripts, she links the Willibrord lion to the Trier Gospels. An initial *I*, shaped like a lion of Insular and Merovingian

---

Christian Art Occasional Papers 13, University Park PA: Pennsylvania State University Press 3–13: 6–7.

25 Bede wrote the history of Egbert, a monk of Northumbria, who intended to leave Ireland for the Continent; his 'mission' to convert the heathens. However, a monk told Egbert that he had dreamed that Egbert's ship would encounter a storm and be wrecked. A storm did indeed sink Egbert's ship. Therefore God did not mean him to go, and it was God's will that Willibrord should go instead and achieve success, which he did. *Historia ecclesiastica* 5.9–5.10, Colgrave and Mynors 474–481. For the importance of the spiritual authority of dreams and visions especially in early Christianity, see Moreira, Isabel 2000 *Dreams, Visions, and Spiritual Authority in Merovingian Gaul*, Ithaca NY: Cornell University Press. For an understanding of the scale of Willibrord's mission, see Wood, What is a Mission? 142–143.

26 The Lion, Symbol of Saint Mark. Gospels of St Willibrord, Echternach, c. 690. Paris: Bibliothèque Nationale, MS lat. 9389, fol. 75v. For discussion and an illustration of the lion, see Nordenfalk, *Book Illumination* 30–32; Nordenfalk, Carl 1977 *Celtic and Anglo-Saxon Painting: Book Illumination in the British Isles, 600–800*, London: Chatto and Windus 52 and 51 plate 10. See also Ó Cróinín 17–49. For background about Echternach, see Wagner, Stephen 2010 Establishing a Connection to Illuminated Manuscripts made at Echternach in the Eighth and Eleventh Centuries and Issues of Patronage, Monastic Reform and Splendor, *Journal of Medieval Art and Architecture* 3, 49–82.

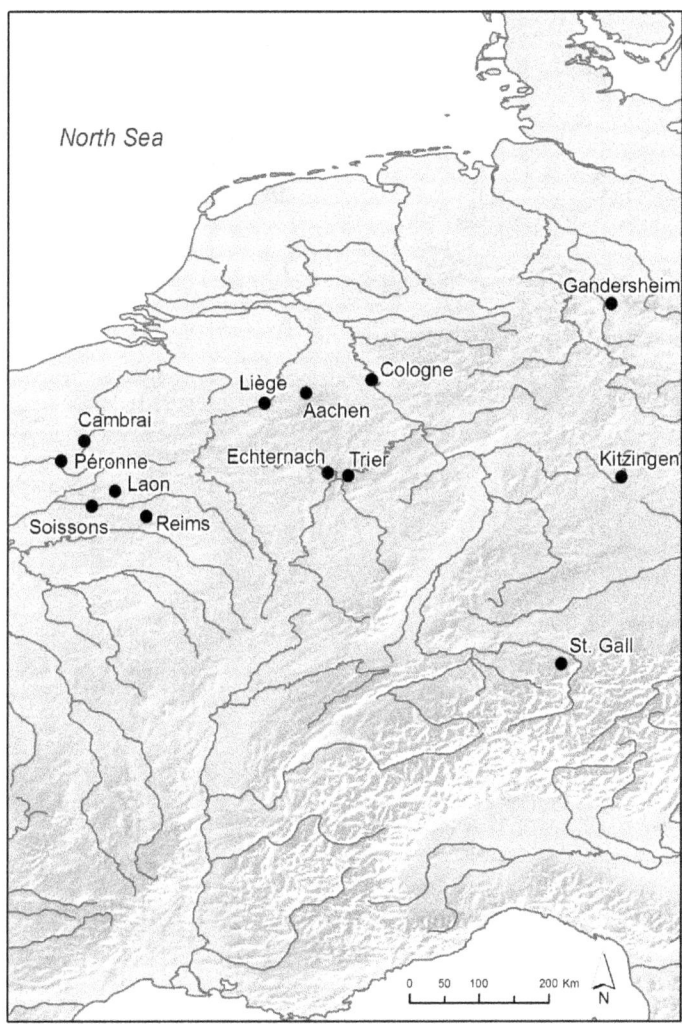

Figure 5.1 Map of Europe showing places mentioned in the text. © Penelope Nash.

Figure 5.2 Carpet page, Book of Durrow. Source: The Yorck Project 2002 *10.000 Meisterwerke der Malerei* (DVD-ROM), distributed by DIRECTMEDIA Publishing GmbH. https://bit.ly/2ryZK2Q

inspiration, and debased lions in other initials *F, E, C* and *E* appear in the Trier Gospels (AD 700–750);[27] the lions are of uncertain origin but may have been created in Echternach Abbey.[28] Even if Netzer's argument can be refuted, there is no doubt that the fancy displacement and the whole conception of the display script, page and layout is Insular and not found in Merovingian Gaul. The second page of interest in the Echternach Gospels is the initial page in the Gospel of St Mark. The first word is *Initium* and the first two letters of the 'I' and the first vertical stroke of the 'N' are united in a double stem. The initials and the decorative capitals obey the 'diminuendo effect' of Insular book decoration, that is the stepping down in size of the letters.[29] I analyse the diminuendo effect in more detail later in this paper in the paragraph that discusses the Coronation Gospels of Charlemagne. The two pages of the Echternach Gospels discussed here illustrate that artistic items with otherwise strong Insular influences did not always obviously present as such within one text.

A Gospel Book from the ninth century, currently located at Arras, clearly shows Insular and classicising influences in a Carolingian context. The manuscript comes from the Anglo-Frankish or Franco-Insular school (also known as the Franco-Saxon school).[30] The lettering

---

27 Trier Gospels. Trier: Cathedral Treasury, MS 61, fols 180v, 141v, 171v, 203v, 172v.
28 Netzer, Nancy 1994 *Cultural Interplay in the Eighth Century: The Trier Gospels and the Making of a Scriptorium at Echternach*, Cambridge Studies in Palaeography and Codicology 3, Cambridge University Press 2–3, 52–53, 97–98. See also de Vegvar, Carol Neuman 1997 The Echternach Lion: A Leap of Faith, *The Insular Tradition*, edited by Catherine D. Karkov *et al.*, Albany NY: State University of New York Press 167–188: 167–172; Henderson, Isabel 1982 Pictish Art and the Book of Kells, *Ireland in Early Mediaeval Europe: Studies in Memory of Kathleen Hughes*, edited by Dorothy Whitelock *et al.*, Cambridge University Press 79–105: 80, 82.
29 Initial Ini(tium), Saint Mark. Echternach Gospels of St Willibrord, Ireland(?), Echternach, c. 690. Paris: Bibliothèque Nationale, MS lat. 9389, fol. 76r. See illustration in Nordenfalk, *Book Illumination* 31; Rollason, D. W. 2003 *Northumbria 500–1100: Creation and Destruction of a Kingdom*, Cambridge University Press 155–157, esp. 156; Duncan 215.
30 Nordenfalk distinguishes between the Anglo-Frankish/Franco-Insular school and the Franco-Saxon school. The former nomenclature is more correct. The latter description should apply only to the manuscripts that are Frankish in

is clearly Insular-influenced with diminuendo use of the letters and scroll work, but the images of the Evangelists set within square frames are strongly classical, as is shown by the flexible forms for the figures, who wear flowing and floating robes.[31]

Carolingian Derivatives: Setting the Scene

Let us now set the scene more firmly in the Carolingian context. Carolingian art continued to be nurtured by a court culture encouraged particularly by Charlemagne, who 'loved foreigners'.[32] After he became sole ruler of the Frankish kingdom in 771, he supported the development of an intellectual court, the geographical focus of which from 788 and especially in his later years was at Aachen.[33] On Christmas Day in AD 800 he was crowned emperor in Rome by the pope. Charlemagne's elephant lived and travelled with him on his campaigns in the same period that he and his court-sponsored schools were producing the Evangelistary by the scribe Godescalc[34] and the gospel of St Médard at Soissons.[35] Neither the figure of Christ in the Godescalc Evangelistary nor the figure of Mark from the Gospel of

style with their origins in Saxony, but that distinction is rarely drawn. Nordenfalk, *Book Illumination* 75.
31 Initial Page with Figured Frame. Gospel Book, Franco-Saxon School, second half of ninth century. Arras: Bibliothèque Municipale, MS 233 (1045), fol. 8. See illustration in Nordenfalk, *Book Illumination* 74.
32 Einhard, *Vita Karoli* 21, edited by Waitz, George 1911 *MGH SS rer. Ger.* 25, Hanover; translated by Lewis G. M. Thorpe 1969 *Two Lives of Charlemagne*, Harmondsworth: Penguin 76.
33 Nelson, Janet L. 2007 Aachen as a Place of Power, *Courts, Elites, and Gendered Power in the Early Middle Ages: Charlemagne and Others*, Aldershot: Variorum XIV.1–23: 1–16. For an overview of the international scene at Charlemagne's court, see Meeder, Sven 2016 Irish Scholars and Carolingian Learning, *The Irish in Early Medieval Europe* 179–194: 180–86.
34 Christ. Godescalc Evangelistary, Court School of Charlemagne, between 781 and 783. Paris: Bibliothèque Nationale, MS nouv. acq. lat. 1203, fol. 3r. See discussion and illustration in Mütherich, Florentine and Gaehde, Joachim E. 1977 *Carolingian Painting*, London: Chatto and Windus 24, 32, 33 plate 1.
35 Saint Mark. Gospels of Saint-Médard of Soissons, Court School of Charlemagne, between 781 and 783. Paris: Bibliothèque Nationale, MS lat.

St Médard displays strong Insular influences, although the interlace borders do for the Evangelistary and the wings of the lion do in the Gospel.[36] The Carolingian influences can be seen in the plant ornaments, the seated figure and architectural background of the former and in the depiction of an Ancient cameo at the top of the arch in the latter. They show the development of a Merovingian-Carolingian-Insular hybrid that had its origins in an Insular background combined here probably with Italian inspirations.

Carolingian Derivatives

In the first of three case studies the Book of Durrow can profitably be compared with the Coronation Gospels of Charlemagne. Each displays elaborate decoration for the opening page of the Gospel of St Mark that have elements in common and that demonstrate Insular influences. By tradition the German emperors took their coronation oaths on the Coronation Gospels, also known as the Vienna Coronation Gospels, created in about AD 800. The Gospels were reputedly rediscovered in AD 1000 when Emperor Otto III ordered that Charlemagne's tomb be opened and examined.[37] In the long 'I' on the Gospel page of St Mark we can see patterns of interlace that have their origins 'in ancient Celtic art' and possibly 'enamelled metalwork' in red at the top and bottom of the letter.[38] Here also is the Insular

---

8850, fol. 81v. See discussion and illustration in Mütherich and Gaehde 24, 44, 42 plate 6. For Charlemagne's elephant, see Einhard 16.

36 Brown, Michelle P. 1996 *The Book of Cerne: Prayer, Patronage, and Power in Ninth-Century England*, The British Library Studies in Medieval Culture, University of Toronto Press 78–80, 88–91.

37 There are five roughly contemporaneous accounts of the opening—the *Lamberti Annales, Annales Hildesheimenses*, the *Chronicon* of Thietmar of Merseburg, the *Historianum* of Ademar of Chabannes, and the *Chronicon Novaliciense*. These were compiled (though they may have been written earlier) in 1077, 1120, between 1013 and 1018, in 1030, and in the second quarter of the eleventh century, respectively.

38 Gospel Page of Saint Mark. Coronation Gospels of Charlemagne, c. 800. Vienna: Schatzkammer, fol. 77r. For discussion and illustration, see Mütherich and Gaehde 24, 47 plate 9; Olson 2.

Figure 5.3 The Lion, symbol of Saint Mark, Echternach Gospels of St Willibrord. Source: The Yorck Project 2002 *10.000 Meisterwerke der Malerei* (DVD-ROM), distributed by DIRECTMEDIA Publishing GmbH. https://bit.ly/2qK4Dps

Figure 5.4 Gospel Book, initial page with figured frame. Franco-Saxon School.
Source: The Yorck Project 2002 *10.000 Meisterwerke der Malerei* (DVD-ROM), distributed by DIRECTMEDIA Publishing GmbH. https://bit.ly/2rDeAFB

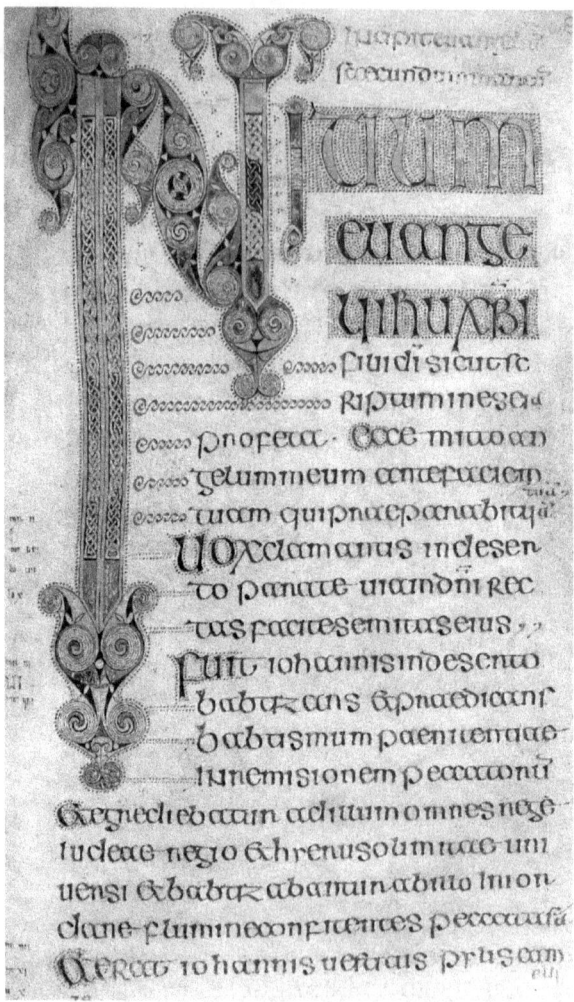

Figure 5.5 Initial Ini(tium), St Mark, Book of Durrow. Source: The Yorck Project 2002 *10.000 Meisterwerke der Malerei* (DVD-ROM), distributed by DIRECTMEDIA Publishing GmbH. https://bit.ly/2ryZK2Q

'diminuendo effect'. In the two examples, the first word *Initium* steps down from the 'I' to the 'N', then from the 'N' to the remainder of the word '-itium', then from '-itium' to the rest of the text (although there is an extra step down from the 'i' to the 'u' for the Durrow page).[39] In the Coronation Gospels we also see Roman influences. Gold ink on purple parchment recalls the imperial Roman colour scheme that was adopted in early medieval Christian and in Carolingian art.[40] Other Roman influences occur in the formations of the letters. The 'rustic capital script' in the very top line and the large square capitals in the next line below are both ancient Roman ways of writing. However, the rest of the letters, more rounded, are in uncial script, which appeared in the later Roman empire and continued into early medieval use.[41] The Coronation Gospels follow the same layout as the Book of Durrow, which is an Insular one, yet for the Coronation Gospels the overall impression is Roman. We see in the Coronation Gospels a combination of those influences to produce a very beautiful image.

After Charlemagne's death in 814 the centre of Carolingian manuscript painting moved to Reims, the seat of Bishop Ebo (816–835, 840–845). A second case study involves the Ebo Gospels, which represented a new epoch while still drawing on Insular traditions. On the first page of the Gospel of St Matthew, the evangelist is depicted showing intense emotion, religious fervour and energy, not at all reminiscent of Insular influences, but rather of 'an original development of medieval influences'.[42] Nevertheless the presentation of

---

39 Initial Page of Mark. Book of Durrow, Iona(?), seventh century. Dublin: Trinity College Library, MS 57 (A.IV.5) fol. 86r. See discussion and illustration in Nordenfalk, *Celtic and Anglo-Saxon Painting* 40, 41 plate 5; Alexander, J. J. G. 1978 *Insular Manuscripts, 6th to the 9th Century*, A Survey of Manuscripts Illuminated in the British Isles, vol. 1, London: Harvey Miller 30–32 and illus. 18. See also Netzer 6.
40 See, for example, Gospel Book, Reims, third quarter of ninth century. Reims: Bibliothèque Municipale, MS 11, fol. 133r, discussed and illustrated in Hamburger, Jeffrey F. 2014 *Script as Image*, Corpus of Illuminated Manuscripts, Paris: Peeters 20, 22, 21 fig. 12.
41 Olson 1–2. I am grateful to Dr Olson for reminding me of the importance of the Coronation Gospels and for her fine analysis of the page from St Mark, which I have summarised here.
42 Lynette Olson, pers. comm. 23 March 2017.

the initial 'I' located opposite the image of Matthew still repeats Insular motifs that can be seen in the intertwining of the symbols and the 'diminuendo effect' as in the Initial Page in the Gospels of St Willibrord. In the Ebo Gospels the intersecting letters 'L' and 'I' contribute to the word *Incipit* as well as to the word *Liber* at the start of the text.[43] The artist here is being clever in playing with the letter form.

A third case study concerns a Franco-Saxon Psalter, produced under King Louis the German (r. 826–876), which does not contain miniatures.[44] These 'Franco-Saxon' manuscripts were produced over half a century, mostly in northern France. Florence Mütherich and Joachim E. Gaehde propose that Insular motifs took priority over ornamental motifs of Mediterranean derivation. The beginning page for Psalm 1 in the Psalter of King Louis displays the initial B, executed in gold, with its interlace pendants and its tail of birds' heads. The four corners depict Insular bird and dragon heads.[45] Another Franco-Saxon book has an initial page for the Gospel of St Luke that displays the word *Quoniam* with the Q at the beginning of the word enclosing the M at the end. Monks from Saint-Vaast in Prague created this book in the late ninth century.[46] I have included it here because it contains elaborate intertwined beasts and is not dissimilar in splendour from the contemporary work of the Court of Charles the Bald. Note that his so-called Second Bible displays Insular-derived heads of beasts and birds and the use of red dotted lines around the letters on the page decorating the initial to Genesis.[47]

---

43   Saint Matthew. Ebo Gospels, Reims, between 816 and 835. Épernay: Bibliothèque Municipale, MS 1, 18v, 19r. For discussion and illustration, see Mütherich and Gaehde 13–15, 58–62, 61 plates 14, 15.
44   For Louis' interest in liturgical manuscripts and other writings, see Goldberg, Eric Joseph 2006 *Struggle for Empire: Kingship and Conflict under Louis the German, 817–876*, Conjunctions of Religion and Power in the Medieval Past, Ithaca NY: Cornell University Press, esp. 19, 37–39.
45   Beginning to Psalm 1. Psalter of King Louis (the German), St Bertin, second quarter of the ninth century. Berlin: Stiftung Preußischer Kulturbesitz, Staatsbibliothek, MS theol. lat. fol. 58, fol. 3r. For discussion and illustration, see Mütherich and Gaehde 25, 66, 67 plate 17.
46   Initial to the Gospel of Saint Luke. Gospels, Saint-Vaast, late ninth century. Prague: Kapitulni Knihovna, Cim. 2, fol. 127r. For discussion and illustration, see Mütherich and Gaehde 27, 112, 113 plate 41.

Carolingian Derivatives and Ottonian Re-Imaginings: Crucifixions

Before we look at Crucifixion depictions, it is useful to consider the figure of St Mark in the St Gall Gospels (eighth century). The Gospels were probably made in Ireland and brought to the Continent at a later date, although they may have been composed by monks on the Continent. A figure, probably of Mark, appears static and unrealistic, as do the surrounding evangelists.[48] Mark has a cloak that is tightly wound around him in a very formal depiction-structure, a presentation that becomes significant later in this paper.

A crucified Christ showing no pain has models in other Insular work such as the frontispiece for the Pauline Epistles from Kitzingen.[49] Located in the Main River valley near Würzburg, Kitzingen is the place where Boniface founded a new women's monastery for Thekla in 741. Crucifixion miniatures, which may have had an Insular model, were only just becoming common when the Kitzingen theologian-artist was active. The figure on the cross in the Pauline Epistles is fully clothed in a tunic (the *colobium*). Felice Lifshitz suggests that the fabric folds in the frontispiece for the Pauline epistles derive from carved wooden monumental Crucifixions, based on earlier versions that were like the later *Volto Santo*, a carving displayed in the Cathedral of St Martin in Lucca, dated to the late twelfth or early thirteenth century. The author posits that the Latin transitional version of the *Visio Pauli*, the consecration rite for virgins, and Origen's twenty-fourth homily on the Book of Numbers were influential on the female community at Kitzingen.[50] In brief the women pictured themselves as one with Christ/ Paul on the cross.

---

47   Initial to Genesis. Bible of Charles the Bald [so-called Second Bible of Charles the Bald], Saint-Amand, between 871 and 873. Paris: Bibliothèque Nationale, lat. 2, fol. 11r. For discussion and illustration, see Mütherich and Gaehde 28, 125–126, 127 plate 48.
48   Saint Mark and the Four Evangelist Symbols. St Gall. St Gall: Stiftsbibliothek, Cod. 51, fol. 78. For illustration, see Nordenfalk, *Book Illumination* 26.
49   Kitzingen Crucifixion Miniature. St Paul, Epistles, Germany, late eighth century. Würzburg: Universitätsbibliothek. Cod. M.p.th.f. 69, fol. 7r. For discussion and illustration, see Alexander, *Insular Manuscripts* 78 and illus. 265.

Kurt Weitzmann warns us about failing to distinguish between stylistic and iconographic influences in his examination of another Crucifixion image from the St Gall Gospels, the history of which I addressed briefly above.[51] Stylistically this Crucifixion miniature 'is thoroughly rooted in the Irish tradition; ... the dissolution of the organic structure of the human bodies and the strongly patterned garment of Christ ... [recall] a mummy shroud.'[52] Iconographically Weitzmann agrees with Lifshitz in tracing Christ's sleeveless garment in the St Gall Crucifixion image back to the *colobium*. He perceives a likeness to the Syrian representations of the Crucifixion in the Rabbula Codex of AD 586, originally created in Zagba in Mesopotamia.[53] The imperial purple colour appears and the spear bearer and the sponge bearer hold similar positions in the two images.[54] If Weitzmann is correct, the iconographical peculiarities show how the Irish miniature of St Gall has been influenced, in this case, by East Christian influences. We should note that Christ's head is tipped in the St Gall crucifixion image and in the *Volto Santo* carving (and in the Gero Cross, discussed

---

50 Lifshitz, *Religious Women* 21, 66–67, 77, 80, and plates 4 and 10; Croenen, Godfried and Ainsworth, Peter F. 2006 *Patrons, Authors and Workshops: Books and Book Production in Paris around 1400*, Synthema, Louvain: Peeters 94–95, for the *colobium* on the *Volto Santo*.

51 Crucifixion. St Gall. St Gall: Stiftsbibliothek, Cod. 51, fol. 266. For discussion and illustration, see Alexander, *Insular Manuscripts* 66–67 and illus. 203.

52 Weitzmann, Kurt 1966 Various Aspects of Byzantine Influence on the Latin Countries from the Sixth to the Twelfth Century, *Dumbarton Oaks Papers* 20, 1–24: 5.

53 Crucifixion. Rabbula Gospels, St John of Zagba, Syria 586. Florence: Biblioteca Medicea Laurenziana, fol. 13r.

54 Weitzmann 5. See also Coatsworth, Elizabeth 2000 The 'Robed Christ' in Pre-Conquest Sculptures of the Crucifixion, *Anglo-Saxon England* 29, 153–176: 155, 162; Wright, David H. 1973 The Date and Arrangement of the Illustrations in the Rabbula Gospels, *Dumbarton Oaks Papers* 27, 197–208: 201, 208; Cecchelli, C., G. Furlani and Salmi, M. 1959 *The Rabula Gospels*, Olten-Lausanne (not available to me). For Bishop Rabbula's life, see Drijvers, Han J. W. 1999 Rabbula, Bishop of Edessa: Spiritual Authority and Secular Power, *Portraits of Spiritual Authority: Religious Power in Early Christianity, Byzantium and the Christian Orient*, edited by Jan Willem Drijvers and John Watt, Leiden: Brill 139–154: 141–152.

Figure 5.6 Crucifixion, St Gall Gospels. Source: https://bit.ly/38qqKlJ

later), but neither in the St Gall figure of Christ nor in the Pauline Epistles.

The style of the Reims School still shows through in my next Crucifixion example—the reliefs on the front cover of the Lindau Gospels, which date to the third quarter of the ninth century, about a hundred years later than the Pauline Epistles.[55] Horst Janson observes that the Celtic-Germanic metalwork tradition was adapted splendidly to the Carolingian revival. The semiprecious stones are raised on claw feet, allowing the light to penetrate from beneath. According to Janson, the crucified Jesus seems to stand rather than to hang, his arms spread out in what I perceive as an all-encompassing gesture. Janson states that 'to endow him with the signs of human suffering was not yet conceivable [for the Carolingian artists]' despite the fact that the eight figures that surround him clearly express grief.[56] However, the more equivocal Jeanne-Marie Musto detects elements of suffering in Christ's 'protruding ribs, inclined head, and (slightly) twisting body'.[57] We might even go further and determine that the position of the head is less an inclination than a twist, like the body. We should note too that part of a binding made at the court workshop of Charles the Bald was used in the early rebinding of the Lindau Gospels at St Gall, the important centre of influence for Ottonian art as well as Carolingian art as discussed above.[58]

With the Gero Cross, the last Crucifixion example, thought to have been commissioned by Archbishop Gero of Cologne in about 975, we enter the Ottonian period of rule.[59] The Ottonian empire,

---

55 Front Cover. Lindau Gospels. New York: The Pierpont Morgan. MS M. 1. For illustration, see Cole, Bruce and Gealt, Adelheid M. 1989 *Art of the Western World: From Ancient Greece to Post-Modernism*, New York: Summit Books 39. For a detailed discussion of the front cover of the Lindau Gospels, see Musto, Jeanne-Marie 2001 John Scottus Eriugena and the Upper Cover of the Lindau Gospels, *Gesta* 40, 1–18: 1–3, 6, 7 and plate 1.
56 Janson, H. W. and Janson, Anthony F. 1997 *History of Art*, 5th ed., New York: Harry N. Abrams 282.
57 Musto 9.
58 Nordenfalk, *Book Illumination* 75.
59 The Ottonian period encompassed the reigns of King Henry I (d. 936) and Emperors Otto I (d. 973), Otto II (d. 983), Otto III (d. 1002) and

with its power base in what was the eastern part of the Carolingian empire, arose out of the division of Charlemagne's empire into three for his surviving grandsons at the Treaty of Verdun in 843.[60] (The eastern part eventually became Germany.) The Gero Cross, one of the few works of sculpture to survive from that time, is over two metres tall and is currently displayed in Cologne Cathedral. Christ no longer endures stoically and perhaps rather impassively as in the Gospel Book of St Gall, but is now shown as suffering. The Gero Cross appears to owe nothing to Insular influences but is included here to show the dramatic shift in Crucifixion iconography and style. The vigorously alive Christ (St Gall) has changed to the undoubtedly dead Saviour by the later tenth century, when the Ottonians dominated the empire.[61] Nevertheless Insular influences can clearly be seen in other categories of Ottonian art.

Ottonian Re-Imaginings: Manuscripts

We now turn to Ottonian manuscript production. Henry Mayr-Harting asserts that manuscript illumination was rated of less importance among the arts than was metalwork during the tenth and eleventh centuries in the West; consequently, we have little detail about the art that existed inside the book covers in the German treasure lists of the Middle Ages.[62] The book cover of the Gospel Book of Otto III,

---

Henry II (d. 1024). See also McKitterick, Rosamund, Continuity and Innovation in Tenth-Century Ottonian Culture, *The Frankish Kings* XII.15–24.

60 Stasavage, David 2011 *States of Credit: Size, Power, and the Development of European Polities*, The Princeton Economic History of the Western World, Princeton University Press 96–99.
61 Jensen, Robin M. 2017 *The Cross: History, Art, and Controversy*, Cambridge MA: Harvard University Press 151, 163.
62 Mayr-Harting, Henry 1991 *Ottonian Book Illumination: An Historical Study*, 2 vols, London: Oxford University Press 1.48–49. However, see the variety of Ottonian manuscript art in Klemm, Elisabeth 2012 Anfänge und Blütezeit der ottonischen Buchmalerei, *Pracht auf Pergament: Schätze der Buchmalerei von 780 bis 1180*, edited by Christiane Lange and Claudia Fabian, Munich: Hirmer 90–97.

showing the ivory panel executed at Constantinople with Byzantine bloodstones in filigree on a gold background, owes little directly to Insular workmanship.[63] McKitterick has argued that we have no comparable evidence of royal patronage by the Ottonians as exercised by Carolingian rulers, whose benefaction included material rewards and scholarly recognition.[64] McGee observes that Ottonian art originated from a number of monastic centres rather than directly from the court.[65] Nevertheless we should note the cultural continuity from Carolingian to Ottonian art, while observing the focus on the Imperial presence especially in Ottonian manuscripts. Despite her reservations, McKitterick examines several surviving Ottonian manuscripts in detail. The one of interest here is a folio of the Saint-Gereon Gospels, produced in the Cologne school between 990 and 1000. The *Incipit* of St Matthew presents clockwise images of Emperor Otto III, his mother Empress Theophanu and his grandmother Empress Adelheid, with the lamb of God overseeing all, displayed with noticeable vestiges of Insular inspiration in the diminuendo effect of the letters L and I.[66] Such

---

63 Book Cover. Gospel Book of Otto III, 998–1001. Munich: Bayerische Staatsbibliothek, Clm. 4453. See discussion and illustration in Garrison, Eliza 2012 *Ottonian Imperial Art and Portraiture: The Artistic Patronage of Otto III and Henry II*, Farnham: Ashgate, 39, 46–51, 42 illus. 12. Garrison proposes that the Gospel Book may date from as early as 983, created in celebration of Otto III's coronation at the age of three. See also Mayr-Harting, *Ottonian Book Illumination* 1.156–178.

64 McKitterick, Rosamond 1995 Ottonian Intellectual Culture in the Tenth Century, *The Empress Theophano: Byzantium and the West at the Turn of the First Millennium*, edited by Adelbert Davids, Cambridge University Press 169–93: 171. See also McKitterick, Rosamund 1995 Women in the Ottonian Church: An Iconographic Perspective, *The Frankish Kings* XI.79–100: 85–86, 93.

65 McGee 128.

66 Adelheid, Theophanu, Otto III and Lamb of God. Initial Page, Matthew Evangelistary, Gospel of Saint-Gereon, c. 990–1000. Cologne: Historisches Archiv der Stadt Köln, Cod. W 312, fol. 22r. See illustration in Kahsnitz, Rainer 1991 Ein Bildnis der Theophanu? Zur Tradition der Münz- und Medaillon-Bildnisse in der karolingischen und ottonischen Buchmalerei, *Kaiserin Theophanu: Begegnung des Ostens und Westens um die Wende des ersten Jahrtausands*, edited by Anton von Euw and Peter Schreiner, 2 vols, Cologne: Schnütgen-Museum 2.101–134: 102 illus. 1. For the depiction of

inspiration where the 'I' cuts the 'L' over its lower stroke was first observed in the initial page to the Gospel of St Matthew in the Ebo Gospels (discussed earlier).[67] Lynette Olson notes that the top of the 'I' in the Coronation Gospels of Charlemagne (discussed earlier) is similar to the top of the 'L' here in the Ottonian Saint-Gereon Gospels and that the interlace shows Insular influence. However, she detects Eastern rather than Insular influence in the depiction of the bird with a plant scroll, except perhaps for the way it playfully nibbles the top of the L, 'as playfulness is a characteristic of Insular art.'[68] Several hundred years after the first Insular peregrinations to the Continent, imperial art work still exhibited traces of the Insular inspirations brought by those intrepid pilgrims.

Eriugena Returns

I will now revisit John Scotus Eriugena and unite him with a manuscript. Musto and Fabrizio Crivello have confirmed that the Codex Aureus of St Emmeran, created for the dedication of Charles the Bald's palatine chapel in about 877 and the most important work of the school of the court, contains verses attributed to Eriugena.[69] Musto associates many of the lines from Eriugena's poem about God's all-presence in time and place, the 'Aulae Sidereae', with the *tituli* of the illuminations in the Codex Aureus manuscript. Consequently, either the *tituli* influenced the manuscript or the manuscript

---

female rulers in the tenth century, see the discussion in Nash, Penelope 2017 *Empress Adelheid and Countess Matilda: Medieval Female Rulership and the Foundations of European Society, Queenship and Power*, Basingstoke: Palgrave Macmillan 155.

67 Initial Page to the Gospel of Saint Matthew. Ebo Gospels, Reims. Épernay: Bibliothèque Municipale, MS 1, fol. 19r. See discussion and illustration in Mütherich and Gaehde 25, 59, 61 plate 15.
68 Lynette Olson, pers. comm. 7 March 2017.
69 Christ in Majesty, the four evangelists, and scenes from the life of Christ. Book-cover (front). Codex Aureus of St Emmeran, Regensburg, 870. Munich: Bayerische Staatsbibliothek, MS Clm. 14000. For an image of the cover, see Musto 3 fig. 2.

Figure 5.7 Adelheid, Theophanu, Otto III and Lamb of God. Initial page, Matthew Evangelistary, Gospel of Saint-Gereon. © Raimond Spekking / CC BY-SA 3.0 (via Wikimedia Commons). https://bit.ly/2LFsWf

influenced the *tituli*. In addition the poet philosopher was involved in the production of the Codex Aureus, including the design of the elaborate jewelled cover, as well as its preparation.[70] We have now brought together text and image.

Full Circle

I began my article with Hraban Maur's plea for the primacy of text over image. I would like to conclude with quotations from two other writers. The first comes from *Topography of Ireland* written in 1187 by Gerald of Wales, who looks back in this passage to fifth/sixth-century Ireland:

> Among all the miracles of Kildare nothing seems to me more miraculous than that wonderful book which they say was written at the dictation of an angel during the lifetime of the virgin.[71]

He refers here to St Brigid, who was thought to have died in AD 523. He continues that the book contains a list of the main words in the four gospels, according to St Jerome's version. He is amazed that there are nearly as many drawings, mostly in colour, as there are number of pages.

---

70 Crivello, Fabrizio 2010 L'Irlanda e l'arte carolingia, *L'Irlanda e gli Irlandesi* 757-777: 767; Musto 9, 17 n. 56; Herren, M. W. 1987 Eriugena's 'Aulae Sidereae', the 'Codex Aureus' and the Palatine Church of St Mary at Compiègne, *Studi medievali* 28, 593-608: 593; McGinn, Bernard 2002 Eriugena Confronts the End, *History and Eschatology in John Scottus Eriugena and his Time*, edited by Michael Dunne and J. J. McEvoy, Leuven University Press 3-29: 14.

71 'Inter universa Kildariae miracula, nihil mihi miraculosius occurrit quam liber ille mirandus, tempore virginis, ut aiunt, angelo dictante conscriptus.' Giraldus, *Topographia Hibernica* 2.38, edited by J. S. Brewer 1867 *Giraldi Cambrensis opera*, vol. 5, Rerum Britannicarum medii aevi scriptores, London: Longmans, Green, Reader, and Dyer; translated by O'Meara, John J. 1982 *The History and Topography of Ireland*, rev. ed., Harmondsworth: Penguin Books 2.71.

> Here you can look upon the face of the divine majesty drawn in a miraculous way; here too upon the mystical representations of the Evangelists, now having six, now four, and now two, wings. Here you will see the eagle; there the calf. Here the face of a man; there that of a lion. And there are also innumerable other drawings.[72]

Continuing with a marvellous description of the images, Gerald of Wales asks the viewer to look closely at the images in order to see their intricacies and fresh colourings—the result of the work 'not of men, but of angels'.[73] Because we no longer have the book that Gerald describes, (ironically) we must rely on his verbal portrayal to visualise the images.

The second quotation comes from Patriarch Photios, who wrote about the main apse in Hagia Sophia in AD 867. The patriarch was a supporter of the visual over the auditory. 'Has the mind *seen*? Has it *grasped*? Has it *visualised*? *Then* it has effortlessly transmitted the forms to the memory. [my italics]'[74] According to Photios, what the viewer sees is remembered far better than what she or he hears.

Conclusion

I have taken a swift journey through the history of the influence of Insular art on art of the European continent in the Carolingian and Ottonian periods. The art that arose was a mixture of the memory of old styles incorporated into new ones. The courts of the Carolingians, the schools of Trier and St Gall and others, and the court of Charles the Bald especially shone as the result of coordinated patronage. Despite

---

72 'Hic Majestatis vultum videas divinitus impressum; hinc mysticas Evangelistarum formas, nunc senas, nunc quaternas, nunc binas alas habentes; hinc aquilam, inde vitulum, hinc hominis faciem, inde leonis; aliasque figuras fere infinitas' (*loc. cit.*).
73 'potius angelica quam humana' (*loc.cit.*).
74 Mango, Cyril 1958 *The Homilies of Photius, Patriarch of Constantinople*, Dumbarton Oaks Series 3, Cambridge, MA: Harvard University Press, Homily XVII, Image of the Virgin 5. I am indebted to McKitterick, Text and Image VIII.299, in which I first read this apt sermon by Photius. I hope I have included it here with a new insight.

the distance of the works of the Ottonian court in time and place, some traces of Insular influences can be seen in certain manuscripts, fewer in the paintings, and none in the Gero sculpture of the Crucifixion. Nevertheless there was in general cultural continuity and the remembrance of past symbols.

Epilogue: Hraban Maur has the Last Word, or Does He?

Hraban Maur, whose letter strongly favouring words over images introduced this article, wrote a poem that was included in a contemporary manuscript produced in dedication copies for Louis the Pious (r. 814–840), Pope Gregory IV, the Archbishop of Mainz, and others. *De laudibus sanctae crucis* (*In Praise of the Holy Cross*) was the first text embellished with miniatures and the first (preserved) manuscript portrayal of a Carolingian emperor. The manuscript contains seven coloured images. One is an awkward-looking Louis the Pious, portrayed as a Christian warrior with halo and holding a cross, placed within and overwritten by a Latin text.[75] Another similar in style is of Hraban kneeling before the Cross surrounded by the letters that spell out the words of his poem.[76] The poem is the twenty-eighth and the last of the poems in the manuscript. Hraban Maur believed twenty-eight to be a significant number as it is the sum of the numbers one to seven, the number of days God took to create the world.[77] Other parts of the manuscript deal primarily with numbers and text rather than focusing on images.

Mütherich and Gaehde assess the page showing Louis the Pious, and the manuscript in general, as: 'Hardly outstanding for its artistic merit ... [Its] claim to originality ... does not extend to the form of

---

75 Portrait of Louis the Pious. Hrabanus Maurus, *De laudibus sanctae crucis*, Fulda, c. 840. Rome: Bibliotheca Vaticana, Reg. lat. 124, fol. 4v. For discussion and illustration, see Mütherich and Gaehde 25, 55, 54 plate 12.
76 Hrabanus Maurus before the Cross. Hrabanus Maurus, *De laudibus sanctae crucis*, Fulda, c. 840. Rome: Bibliotheca Vaticana, Reg. lat. 124, fol. 33v. For discussion and illustration, see Musto 7, 10 fig. 9.
77 Hrabanus Maurus, *De laudibus sanctae crucis*, Louanges de la Sainte Croix, poeme XXVIII, http://expositions.bnf.fr/parole/grand/e113.htm.

either the text or the image.'[78] The text and style owe a debt to late antique origin and nothing to the grace and imagination of Insular or Carolingian artistry, and that is a pity. Was Hraban Maur adversely affected in his assessment of the worth of artistic endeavours by the mundane illustrations in this work or were these the result of his lack of interest in art? We do not know—but his writing persuades us less than it might do with better art.[79]

---

78 Mütherich and Gaehde 55.
79 I would like to thank The University of Sydney, Faculty of Arts and Social Sciences, School of Literature, Art and Media, The Medieval and Early Modern Centre, for support in the development of this article. Professor Jonathan Wooding, the late Professor Anders Ahlqvist, and especially Dr Lynette Olson contributed greatly to several of the ideas and to the structure of this article.

6

The *De xii abusivis saeculi* and Prophetic Tradition in Seventh-Century Ireland

Constant J. Mews

Of all the texts produced in Ireland in the seventh century, few were more widely copied than the *De xii abusivis saeculi* (On the Twelve Abuses of the Age).[1] Its ninth chapter, about a bad king, was attributed to Patrick in the *Collectio canonum Hibernensis* in around 700 and frequently quoted in subsequent manuals of government from the Carolingian period and beyond.[2] Julianna Grigg has provided an eloquent discussion of its model of just kingship as

---

1   Hellmann, Siegmund, editor 1909 *Ps.-Cyprianus. De xii abusiuis saeculi*, Texte und Untersuchungen zur Geschichte der altchristlichen Literatur 34, Leipzig; this improved on the editions included among the works of Cyprian, Migne, PL 4.869B–882B, and of Augustine, PL 40.1086–88.
2   *Collectio canonum Hibernensis* [CCH] 25.3–4, edited by Wasserschleben, Hermann 1885 *Die irische Kanonensammlung*, 2nd ed., Leipzig: Bernhard Tauchnitz [first edition, Giessen 1874] 91–92. See Anton, Hans Hubert 1982 Pseudo-Cyprian: *De duodecim abusivis saeculi* und sein Einfluss auf den Kontinent, insbesondere auf die karolingischen Fürstenspiegel, *Die Iren und Europa im früheren Mittelalter*, edited by Heinz Löwe, Stuttgart: Klette-Cotta, II.568–617; Meens, Rob 1998 Politics, Mirrors of Princes and the Bible: Sins, Kings and the Well-Being of the Realm, *Early Medieval Europe* 7, 345–57. There is only brief mention of *De xii abusivis* in Kershaw, Paul J. E. 2011 *Peaceful Kings: Peace, Power and the Early Medieval Political Imagination*, Oxford University Press, 72–73, 151–52.

working in harmony with the Church.³ By and large, however, the treatise has received little attention. The complexity of its manuscript tradition and literary debts was studied by the late Aidan Breen, who edited and translated the work in his 1988 doctoral thesis, but which remains unpublished.⁴ My concern here is not with Breen's analysis of the manuscript tradition, but with the way this work both draws on and transforms the prophetic tradition embodied by Gildas, who is so much concerned in the *De excidio* with the departure of both bishops and kings from the standard of justice. I support Breen's broader argument that it was written in the mid-seventh century in a circle which followed the Roman Easter.⁵ I would go further, however, in arguing that the Twelve Abuses demonstrates significant thematic connections with the Penitential of Cummian, most likely to be Cummianus Longus or Cuimine Fota (d. 662), one of the sages of seventh-century Ireland, about whom many legends are preserved.⁶

---

3   Grigg, Julianna 2010 The Just King and *De duodecim abusivis saeculi*, *Parergon*, 27(1), 27–52. Johnson, Maire 2012 has observed thematic connections with the earliest Life of Brigit in The *Vita I S. Brigitae* and *De duodecim abusiuis saeculi*, *Studia Celtica Fennica* 9, 22–35.
4   Breen, Aidan 1988 *De xii abusivis*. A Critical Edition with Translation and Introduction, PhD thesis, University of Dublin; the text (DDA) is referred to by the page of Breen's edition, along with the parallel reference to the column in PL 4.869B–882B. Its core conclusions are summarised in Breen 2002 *De xii abusiuis*: Text and Transmission, *Ireland and Europe in the early Middle Ages: Texts and Transmissions / Irland und Europa im früheren Mittelalter: Texte und Überlieferung*, edited by Próinséas Ní Chatháin and Michael Richter, Dublin: Four Courts Press 78–94. See also: Breen 1987 Pseudo-Cyprian *De duodecim abusivis* and the Bible, *Irland und die Christenheit: Bibelstudien und Mission*, edited by Próinséas Ní Chatháin and Michael Richter, Stuttgart: Klett-Cotta 230–45; Breen 1987 The Evidence of Antique Irish Exegesis in Pseudo-Cyprian, *De duodecim abusivis saeculi*, *Proceedings of the Royal Irish Academy* 87C, 71–101.
5   I am not persuaded by the suggestion of Breen (1988 *De xii abusivis* 222–25), not repeated in later publications, that it could have been written by a relatively little known computist, Mo-Curoc maccu Neth Semon (perhaps to be identified with Cronan of Roscrea), on the strength of a note in a Würzburg MS (M.p.th.f. 61) that he was 'described by the Romans as doctor of the whole world'. Breen draws on a text discussed by Ó Cróinín, Dáibhí 1982 Mo Sinnu moccu Min and the Computus of Bangor, *Peritia* 1, 281–95: 284.

Cummian urged acceptance of the Roman date of Easter in a letter to Ségéne of Iona (d. 652) and the hermit Béccán in 632, in which he gives our earliest known reference to *sanctus Patricius papa noster*.[7] There are good reasons for supporting the attribution to Cummian by another Irish exegete of the first commentary on Mark's Gospel.[8] He is identified as author of hymns and texts about the twelve apostles.[9]

---

6   Clancy, Thomas 1991 Saint and Fool: The Image and Function of Cummine Fota and Comgán Mac Da Cherda in early Irish literature, PhD thesis, University of Edinburgh.
7   Walsh, Maura and Ó Cróinín, Dáibhí 1988 *Cummian's Letter De controversia Paschali and the De Ratione Conputandi*, Toronto: Pontifical Institute of Mediaeval Studies 56–97 (84 on Patrick) with discussion of other texts attributed to Cummian on 221-27. See also the informative review of this edition by Charles-Edwards, T. M. 1994, *Peritia* 8, 216–20.
8   Pseudo-Jerome, *Expositio Euangelii secundum Marcum*, edited by Cahill, Michael 1997 Corpus Christianorum Series Latina [CCSL] 82, Turnhout: Brepols; Cahill 1994 voiced caution about Irish authorship: Is the First Commentary on Mark an Irish Work? Some New Considerations, *Peritia* 8, 35–46 and in the introduction to his edition. Yet a *Comianus* is identified as the new author of a commentary on Mark in *Quaestiones vel glose in evangelio nomine. Questiones Evangelii* 43, edited by McNally, Robert E. 1973 *Scriptores Hiberniae Minores* Pars I, CCSL 108B, 142. Cahill's argument that its references to Jews are to living Jews, and was thus written on the Continent is extremely doubtful, like his suggestion that its reference (Cahill, 27) to a boat made from skins derives from continental awareness of Irish practice. *Comianus* is a uniquely Irish name and there is no other commentary to which the reference in the *Quaestiones* could apply. See Wooding, Jonathan M. 2005 The Munster Element in the *Navigatio Sancti Brendani*, *Journal of the Cork Historical Society* 110, 53–67, especially 57–58.
9   See the Latin hymn *Celebra Iuda* attributed to Cummianus Longus in the prologue to *The Irish Liber Hymnorum*, edited by John H. Bernard and Robert Atkinson 1897 Henry Bradshaw Society 13–14, 2 vols, London 1.13.16–21 and 2.108–112. For the *De figuris apostolorum*, see Bischoff, Bernhard 1967 [1932] Regensburger Beiträge zur mittelalterlichen Dramatik und Ikonographie, *Mittelalterliche Studien: ausgewählte Aufsätze zur Schriftkunde und Literaturgeschichte*, 3 vols, Stuttgart: Hiersemann 2.156–68, and Ó Cróinín, Dáibhí 1989 Cummianus Longus and the Iconography of Christ and the Apostles in Early Irish Literature, *Sages, Saints and Storytellers: Celtic Studies in Honour of Professor James Carney*, edited by Donnchadh Ó Corráin, Liam Breatnach and Kim McCone,

The Twelve Abuses was part of this remarkable flowering of learning in seventh-century Ireland.

Breen argued that the Twelve Abuses shares vocabulary and phrasing with the pseudo- Augustine, *De mirabilibus sacre scripture*, addressed by its author to 'the Carthaginians' (presumably the church of Carthach/Mochuda at Lis Mór) soon after the death in 655 of Mancianus, mentioned in its text. *De mirabilibus* is remarkable for its focus on natural science and the historical dimension of the Old Testament.[10] Breen notes parallels in their accounts of how Saul listened to evil spirits, and of how Jeroboam, following the idolatry of his master, Solomon, created division in the kingdom, between Judah and Israel.[11] This led Breen to postulate that the Twelve Abuses was written between 630 and 650.[12]

The internal structure of the Twelve Abuses is remarkably original. It identifies twelve different abusive expressions in which an individual role within society (like king or bishop) is deflected from its proper meaning. It has not been realised that they can be classified into seven stages if we identify five conscious couplets:

(1) The wise man without good works
(2) The old man without religion (3) The adolescent without obedience

---

    Maynooth: An Sagart 268–79. This list occurs in different forms in both Latin and Irish, but is explicitly attributed to Cuimine Fota (*Comianus longus hoc dicit*) in an insertion within the text of the *Sententie Parisienses* (a record of the theological teaching of Abelard) in Paris, BNF lat. 18108, f. 70v, edited by Landgraf, Artur 1934 *Écrits théologiques de l'école d'Abélard*, Louvain: Université catholique 11.

10 *De mirabilibus sacrae scripturae*, PL 35.2149–2200. See MacGinty, Gerard 1987 The Irish Augustine: *De mirabilibus sacrae Scripturae, Irland und die Christenheit* 70–83.

11 *DDA* 6, Breen 202 and 231–33 (875AB); cf. *De mirabilibus* 2.11, 14, 23 (PL 35.2179).

12 Breen 1988 *De xii abusivis* 57–60 and Breen 2002 *De xii abusiuis* 80; Kenney, James F. 1929 *The Sources for the Early History of Ireland: Ecclesiastical*, New York: Columbia University Press 281–82; Breen observes that he follows Kenney against Hellman's dating of the work to 650–70, but for different reasons; Breen, Pseudo-Cyprian and the Bible 232.

(4) The rich man without mercy (5) The woman without shame
(6) The lord without virtue (7) The contentious Christian
(8) The proud pauper (9) The wicked king
(10) The negligent bishop (11) Lay-folk without discipline
(12) People without law

This way of thinking of words as falling from their proper meaning into an abusive expression follows naturally from Isidore of Seville (d. 636), whose writings would enjoy enormous influence in Ireland from around 640.[13] Breen's suggestion that the choice of twelve abuses was structured around the discussion of twelve stages of humility in the Rule of Benedict (or the Rule of the Master) is problematic, given that the Twelve Abuses is not at all concerned with monastic virtue.[14] It could just as well recall the division of Israel into twelve tribes. Breen did not observe that the twelve abuses can themselves be grouped into seven, if five are taken as contrasting pairs, dealing with age, gender, social class, political power and ecclesiastical role. The preface to the Twelve Abuses then comments on how each of these categories suffocates *justitia*—a term that combines justice in society with personal righteousness (as in Romans 10:4).

> By these twelve abuses justice is suffocated. These are the twelve abuses of the age through which the wheel of the age, if any people are in it, is deceived, and, without the help of justice to prevent

---

[13] The oldest known copy of the *Etymologies*, St Gall, Stiftsbibliothek MS 1399a, may be from Ireland, c. 650; see Hillgarth, J. N. 1984 Ireland and Spain in the Seventh-Century, *Peritia* 3, 1–16. Smyth, Marina 2017 Isidorian Texts in Seventh-Century Ireland, *Isidore of Seville and his Reception in the Early Middle Ages*, edited by Andrew Fear and Jamie Wood, Amsterdam University Press 111–30 voices caution about claims to Isidore's presence in Ireland by 650.

[14] *Regula magistri* 10, edited by A. de Vogüé 1964 Sources chrétiennes 105, Paris: Cerf 419–44; *Regula Benedicti* 7, edited by de Vogüé 1972 Sources chrétiennes 181, Paris: Cerf 473–90; Breen 1988, *De XII Abusivis* 96–97. Breen's suggestion of the influence of the Rule of the Master is repeated by Meens, Rob 2014 *Penance in Medieval Europe 600–1200*, Cambridge University Press 61 n. 108.

this, it is propelled into the darkness of hell by the just judgement of God.[15]

This emphasis on *iustitia* as the foundation of all virtue, and as needing to be demonstrated by righteous actions is very different from Augustine's focus on grace. The image of *iustitia* being suffocated in twelve different ways has few parallels, although it may echo an image of virtue being suffocated in the second-century *Pastor Hermas*, strong on moral reform, that is used in the *Collectio Turonensis*, a canonical connection that may have emerged in the mid-seventh century.[16]

The opening chapter, about a *sapiens* without good works, offers foundational advice that a teacher and a preacher (*sapiens et praedicator*) must deliver in action what he says. Although Breen suggested the influence of Augustine's *De fide et operibus*, its core emphasis is moral rather than doctrinal, as it is not concerned to reconcile the teaching of St Paul about faith and of St James about good works.[17] Grace is never mentioned in the Twelve Abuses. Also distinct from an Augustinian perspective is the comment here about Solomon as a *sapiens* whose transgression ultimately led to the division of the kingdom.[18] Neither Jerome nor Augustine discussed at any length the

---

15 *DDA*, Breen 332 (index missing from PL 4.869B): 'I sapiens sine operibus, II senex sine religione, III adolescens sine oboedientia, IIII diues sine helymosina, V femina sine pudicitia, VI dominus sine ueritate, VII christianus contentiosus, VIII pauper superbus, VIIII rex iniquus, X episcopus negligens, XI plebs indisciplinata, XII populus sine lege. His duodecim abusivis suffocatur iustitia. Haec sunt duodecim abusiva saeculi per quae saeculi rota, si in illo fuerint, decipitur et ad tartari tenebras nullo impediente iustitiae suffragio per iustum Dei iudicium rotatur.' I do not follow Breen's argument (278–80) that the prologue contains repetitious statements, and that the sentences from 'Haec sunt' are a later addition.

16 *Pastor Hermae* (uersio uulgata) 5.1.3, 5.1.44, edited by A. Hilgenfeld 1873 Leipzig: Teubner, 44, 87; see for example Cassian, *Collationes* 8.17, edited by M. Petschenig 1886 Corpus Scriptorum Ecclesiasticorum Latinorum [CSEL] 13, Vienna: Tempsky 223. It also occurs in the so-called *Collectio Turonensis*, preserved alongside the first 'Patrick' Synod, in Cambridge Corpus Christi College 279, no. 17 (Heremias dixit ad pastorem angelum), edited by Michael D. Elliot 2014 Canon Law Collections in England ca 600–1066: The Manuscript Evidence, University of Toronto PhD 164 https://bit.ly/2qy33Hd

17 Breen 1988 *De xii abusivis* 104–7.

passage of III Regum (I Kings) 11:1-11, about how Solomon, after building the Temple, strayed into idolatry, provoking God to raise various enemies against the king, including his own servant, Jeroboam, thus leading to scattering of the people (*plebs*) of Israel. Augustine mentions Solomon's wrong behaviour only in passing and not in relation to its political consequences.[19] By contrast, this theme of the bad king leading to division of a kingdom is a central concern of Gildas, who focuses on Solomon's transgression as leading to division of the kingdom.[20] He comments:

> For the Lord, because of Solomon's great sin, divided the kingdom of the House of Israel out of the hands of his children, and because of king David's righteousness, he left the lamp of his generation forever burning in Jerusalem.[21]

Some of the most arresting passages in the Twelve Abuses are about an old man without religion (in the second chapter). They are drawn

---

18 *DDA* 1, Breen, 337 (869C): 'Nam et Solomon dum multae sapientiae transgressionem incurrit, totius Ishraheliticae plebis regni dispersionem solius sui merito praestitit.'
19 Augustine *De ciuitate Dei* 17.9, edited by W. Mountain 1955 CCSL 47, Turnhout: Brepols 573: 'propter peccatum quidem Salomonis regnante filio eis Roboam scimus Israel in duo fuisse diuisum atque ita perseuerasse, habentibus singulis partibus reges suos, donec illa gens tota a chaldaeis esset ingenti uastatione subuersa atque translata.'
20 Gildas, *De excidio Britanniae* 39, edited by M. Winterbottom 1978 *The Ruin of Britain and Other Works*, London: Phillimore 106 (also edited by Hugh Williams 1899/1901 London: Cymroddorion 102): 'Fecit', inquiens, 'Salomon quod non placuerat coram domino, et non adimplevit ut sequeretur dominum, sicut pater eius.' 'Dixit dominus ad eum: quia habuisti hoc apud te et non custodisti pactum meum et praecepta mea quae mandavi tibi, disrumpens scindam regnum tuum et dabo illud servo tuo.'
21 *DDA* 9, Breen 406 (878C): 'Propter piaculum enim Salomonis, regnum domus Israel Dominus de manibus filiorum ejus dispersit. Et propter justitiam David regis, lucernam de semine ejus semper in Hierusalem reliquit (III Reg. XI, 31-35).' Thomas O'Loughlin 2012 examines the use Gildas makes of Scripture, but comments that Gildas passes over the sins of Solomon in *Gildas and the Christian Scriptures: Observing the World through a Biblical Lens*, Turnhout: Brepols 185.

from Cyprian's *De mortalitate* (written in response to the plague of 251/ 2), as well as from Jerome's commentary on Ecclesiastes and Ambrose's writing about Abraham.[22] Its focus, however, is not moral doctrine so much as human frailty:

> For what could be more foolish than that the mind should not strive to attain perfection, when the garb of the physical body, worn out by old age, hasten to its end? When the eyes grow dim and the ears hard of hearing, the head goes bald, the countenance shrunken and pale, the teeth, which start to fall out, become fewer, the skin wrinkled, the breath reeks, the chest becomes stuffed with phlegm and encumbered with a hacking cough, the knees begin to shake, the ankles and feet become swollen with fluid. Even the inward man who does not age is weighed down by these infirmities and all these aforesaid signs betoken the imminent destruction and decay of the physical body.[23]

This reference to the transience of a flowering world (*florida aetas*) echoes that of *Altus Prosator*, a seventh-century Hiberno-Latin text, possibly from Iona, sometimes attributed to Colum Cille, although this has been disputed.[24] It is difficult to affirm if our author knew this text.

Perhaps the most intriguing feature of the Twelve Abuses lies in the way it identifies moral weaknesses at each category in society. Virtues that Cassian had presented as to be pursued by a monk are here presented as relevant to a range of non-monastic groups in society. Just as old people must watch their tongue, so the young should respect

---

22 Breen 1988 *De xii abusivis* 110-114.
23 DDA 2, Breen 340-43 (870BC): 'Quid enim stolidius fieri potest; si mens ad perfectionem festinare non contendat, quando totius corporis habitus senectute confectus ad interitum properat? Dum oculi caligant, aures graviter audiunt, capilli fluunt, facies in pallorem mutatur, dentes lapsi numero minuuntur, cutis arescit, flatus non suaviter olet, pectus suffocatur, tussis cachinnat, genua trepidant, talos et pedes tumor inflat; etiam homo interior qui non senescit, his omnibus aggravatur. Et haec omnia ruituram jamjamque domum corporis cito praenuntiant.'
24 Breen 1988 *De XII Abusivis* 50-56; on *Altus prosator* see *The Irish Liber Hymnorum* 1.62-83; Stevenson, Jane 1999 *Altus Prosator, Celtica* 23, 326-68.

their elders. Its observation that the rich person must give alms, because anyone who just loves gold, silver, land, food, metalwork, wild animals, cannot be loved by these things in return.[25] This matches the fifth abuse, the woman without modesty, who disregards chastity, covets the goods of others, or looks at others with a haughty regard. 'Modesty is the adornment of the noble, the raising up of the lowly, the nobility of the ignoble, the beauty of the weak, the prosperity of the able-bodied, the consolation of the bereaved, the enhancement of all beauty, the adornment of religion, defence against false accusations, the multiplicity of merits, and above all friendship with God, creator of all.'[26] The emphasis here is on virtue that is not gender specific, but is relevant to women. Its final image of friendship with God (*amicitia Dei*), unusual in patristic literature, could derive from a comment of Jerome.[27]

Chapter six, on a lord (*dominus*) without virtue, is concerned with the dangers of abusing power. 'For often the power and capacity to rule are lost through negligence and imprudence of mind, which can be seen to have happened in the case of Eli the priest.'[28] It argues that exercising power requires three elements: 'terror, governance and love (*terrorem, ordinationem et amorem*), a triad not found in any previous writer. Picking up the history of the Hebrews, the chapter invokes the example of the transgressions not just of Saul, but of Solomon, who—despite his evident wisdom—turned to idolatry.

---

25 *DDA* 4, Breen 356 (872C).
26 *DDA* 5, Breen 370–72 (874B): 'Pudicitia ornamentum nobilium est, exaltatio humilium, nobilitas ignobilium, pulchritudo debilium, prosperitas laborantium, solamen moerentium, augmentum omnis pulchritudinis, decus religionis, defensio criminum, multiplicatio meritorum, creatoris omnium Dei amicitia.'
27 Jerome, *Commentarii in Isaiam* 12.41.8, 15.54.9, edited by M. Adriaen 1969, CCSL 73A, Turnhout: Brepols 471, 606.
28 *DDA* 6, Breen 373 (874C): 'Saepe enim dominandi per animi negligentiam perditur fortitudo, sicut in Heli sacerdote factum fuisse comprobatur ... Tria ergo necessaria hos qui dominantur habere oportet: terrorem scilicet, et ordinationem, et amorem.'

It is apparent from these examples that some men are grown more perfect when in high station, and some again become worse, and fall through pride and the arrogance of power. By both of which it is to be understood that they who rise to better things do so through a virtuous disposition and with the help of God and they who turn to meaner pursuits do so through weakness of mind and through negligence.'[29]

The matching figure to the lord without virtue is the contentious Christian, for whom the abuse lies not in the exercise of power, but in pursuit of possessions that do not last.[30] This author offers Christ as the exemplar to follow: 'Behold Christ does not struggle, nor does he shout out: and if you desire to keep likeness to the behaviour of Christ, do not struggle, less you become an abusive Christian in the Church.'[31] The eighth chapter, on the proud pauper, cautions that even one without wealth is not exempt from vice, as merit lies in humility, in being poor in spirit.[32]

The Twelve Abuses is most well known for its ninth chapter on a bad king. Here the word *rex* is explained as one who rules others but also defends strangers, orphans and widows, defends churches, nourishes the poor, and sets good men in positions of responsibility.[33] In appealing to Jeremiah 22:3, 'do not exploit the stranger, the orphan, the widow', it draws on a passage quoted once by Jerome, but otherwise largely ignored by the Church Fathers.[34] Failure to observe justice has disastrous consequences:

---

[29] *DDA* 6, Breen 376-78 (875B): 'Per quae exempla evidenter ostenditur, quosdam in sublimiori statu ad majorem perfectionem crescere, quosdam vero per supercilium dominationis ad deteriora defluere. Per quod utrumque intelligitur eos qui ad meliora transcendunt, per virtutem animi et Dei auxilium posse id facere, et eos qui ad deteriora devertuntur, per mentis imbecillitatem pariter et negligentiam errare.'

[30] *DDA* 7, Breen 390-92 (876BC).

[31] *DDA* 7, Breen 390 (976C): 'Ecce Christus non contendit, neque clamavit: et tu si morum Christi similitudinem tenere cupis, ne contendas, ne abusivus in Ecclesia Christianus existas.'

[32] *DDA* 8, Breen 392-94 (878AB).

[33] Breen 1988 *De XII Abusivis* 31-34, comparing *DDA* 9, Breen 339-65, and *CCH* 25.3-4, Wasserschleben 91-92.

the fruits of the earth are also diminished and the subjection of the peoples is obstructed, many different misfortunes beset the kingdom and hinder its prosperity. Hostile invasions lay waste the provinces on all sides and cause the slaughter of the beasts of burden and the herds of animals, the tempests of the air and the disturbance of the upper atmosphere prevent the fertility of the land and the constancy of the tidal motion of the sea, and frequently blasts of lightning wither the corn on the ground and the blossoms and young shoots on the trees.[35]

The use of the phrase young shoots (*pampinus*) is relatively unusual in early Christian literature but it often comes up in the *Pastor Hermas*, a work with a similar message of moral reform.[36] An unjust ruler loses the right to pass on government to his immediate sons and nephews. The core historical precedent to which he appeals for this is exactly that identified by Gildas in the *De excidio*, that Israel fell into division because of the sinfulness of Solomon.[37] The one author who used Solomon's idolatry to explain how a kingdom could be lost to his natural heirs was Gildas, while this would also be a theme picked up in the *De mirabilibus sacrae scripturae*, written in Ireland c. 655.[38]

But let the king know this, that just as among men he is set highest in his throne, so likewise if he does not administer justice, he shall be set in the foremost place of punishment.[39]

---

34 *DDA* 9, Breen 402 (878B): 'advenis et pupillis et viduis defensorem esse'; cf. Jerome, *In Hieremiam prophetam libri ui* 4.25, edited by S. Reiter 1960 CCSL 74, Turnhout: Brepols 201.
35 *DDA* 9, Breen 400–407, esp. 406-7 (878C): 'hostium incursus provincias undique vastant, bestiae armentorum et pecorum greges dilacerant: tempestates aeris et hyemis terrarum foecunditatem et maris ministeria prohibent, et aliquando fulminum ictus segetes et arborum flores et pampinos exurunt.'
36 *Pastor Hermas* 8.1-5, Hilgenfeld 99-105.
37 *DDA* 9, Breen 406 (878C); see n. 21 above.
38 See above n. 10.
39 *DDA* 9, Breen 408 (878D): 'Attamen sciat rex quod, sicut in throno hominum primus constitutus est, sic et in poenis, si justitiam non fecerit, primatum habiturus est.'

A distinctive feature of the Twelve Abuses lies in the way it combines a prophetic voice with respect for ecclesiastical authority. Chapter ten, on the negligent bishop, begins by reflecting on *episcopus* as a Greek word meaning watchman (*speculator*), the core message of the prophet Ezekiel, about setting a watchman over Israel (33:6–9) and a sword threatening to cut down the watchman who does not do his duty.[40] In his *Sententiae*, Isidore had rebuked uneducated bishops as blind watchmen, not able to bark, namely not nourishing the layfolk (*plebes*) entrusted to them through any word of teaching.[41] This goes back to Jerome's comments on Ezekiel 33:6–9, which he explains could apply equally to the king, bishop or priest.[42] These are also prophetic texts that Gildas invokes to reflect on the failure of Christian *sacerdotes*.[43]

---

40 Isidore, *Etymologiae* 7.12.10, edited by W. M. Lindsay 1912 Clarendon Press: 'Episcopi autem Graece, Latine speculatores interpretantur. Nam speculator est praepositus in Ecclesia; dictus eo quod speculatur, atque praespiciat populorum infra se positorum mores et uitam.'

41 Isidore, *Sententiae* 3.35.2, edited by P. Cazier 1998 CCSL 111, 276: 'Sacerdotes indoctos per Esaiam prophetam Dominus inprobat: Ipsi, inquit, pastores ignorauerunt intellegentiam, et iterum: Speculatores caeci omnes, id est inperiti episcopi, nescierunt, inquit, uniuersi canes muti, non ualentes latrare, hoc est plebes commissas non ualentes resistendo malis per uerbum doctrinae defendere.'

42 Jerome, *Commentarii in Ezechielem* 10 (33), edited by F. Glorie CCSL 75, Turnhout: Brepols 468–69: 'uel iuxta spiritalem intellegentiam ecclesia quae saepe de nouissimis populi sui speculatorem eligit—illum uidelicet quem et apostolus scribens ad Corinthios assumit iudicem—uel certe anima credentis quae mentem atque rationem praeponit populo ac turbae cogitationum suarum—ut non omnia cogitationum incentiua suscipiat, sed iudicet atque discernat quae sectanda sibi quae ue fugienda sint—speculator terrae Iudaeae, uel rex potest intellegi, uel propheta; speculator autem ecclesiae, uel episcopus, uel presbyter, qui a populo electus est et, scripturarum lectione, cognoscens et praeuidens quae futura sint, annuntiet populo et corrigat delinquentem.'

43 Gildas, *De excidio Britanniae* 91.3, Winterbottom 132 (Williams 212–14): 'Et speculator si viderit gladium venientem et non significaverit tuba et populus non observaverit, et veniens gladius acceperit ex eis animam, et ipsa propter iniquitatem suam capta est et sanguinem de manu speculatoris requiram. Et tu, fili hominis, *speculatorem te dedi domui Israel et audies ex ore meo* verbum, cum dicam peccatori: more morieris, et non loqueris, ut avertat a se a via sua impius et *ipse iniquus in iniquitate sua morietur, sanguinem autem eius de*

The Twelve Abuses similarly turns this prophetic tirade against false bishops:

> And if the watchman sees a sword coming and the trumpet does not have meaning and the people do not observe it, the coming sword will take the soul from them and she (Israel) is captured, and I shall exact blood from the hand of the watchman.[44]

While its version of the Ezekiel text is closer to the Vulgate than that of Gildas, the combination of sentences quoted is so close that it seems quite possible that the Twelve Abuses is here relying on Gildas to comment on how a bishop might be deprived of his office if he did not do his duty.[45] Ezekiel 33:6–9 is not a text quoted by Augustine in relation to bishops.

The Twelve Abuses advises the bishop 'to attend diligently to the sins of all over whom he is set in eminence to guard them, and after he has examined those sins, to cause them to be amended, if he can, by word and deed.'[46] In such cases, it explains that:

> he who is subject to the authority of a teacher or bishop, should be expelled from the Church, and he who has been thus expelled ought not to be harboured or received by any other teacher or bishop.[47]

---

manu tua requiram. Tu vero si praedixeris impio viam eius, ut avertat se ab ea, et non se averterit a via sua, hic sua impietate *morietur et tu animam tuam eripuisti.*'

44 DDA 10, Breen 410–13 (878B): 'Quare vero speculator ponitur, et quid a speculatore requiritur, Dominus ipse denudat, cum sub Ezechielis prophetae persona, episcopo officii sui rationem denuntiat, ita inquiens: *Speculatorem dedi te domui Israel. Audiens ergo ex ore meo sermonem, nuntiabis eis ex me.* ... *Si autem* tu annuntiaveris, et ille *non fuerit reversus, ipse* quidem *in iniquitate sua morietur,* sed *tu animam tuam liberasti.*'

45 On the pre-Vulgate and Vulgate elements in the text of the Bible of Gildas, see O'Loughlin 2012, 50.

46 DDA 10, Breen 412–13 (879B): 'Decet ergo episcopus omnium, qui in specula positus est, peccata diligenter attendere, et postquam attenderit, sermone, si potuerit et actu corrigere; si non potuerit, juxta Evangelii regulam, scelerum operarios declinare.'

It then delivers the injunctions of Paul (I Tim 3:2–7) about the requirements for a bishop, that he be sober, prudent, chaste, learned, modest and hospitable, having children in subjection with all chastity, and (among other things) 'having no more than one wife before becoming bishop.'[48] While Jerome would allegorise this Pauline injunction about a bishop having just one wife as about one church rather than one sexual partner, the Twelve Abuses takes St Paul at his word.[49] Its author nonetheless imposes stern standards on bishops as much as kings.

The eleventh abuse, on layfolk (*plebs*) without discipline, provides a balance to the section on the negligent bishop, providing scriptural authority for the imposition of penitential discipline on the Church. This author employs an image developed by Cyprian to maintain the unity of the Church, namely that just as Christ's tunic was not torn, so the discipline of the Church should not be torn.[50] The attention given to Cyprian's image in this penultimate chapter must raise the possibility that its author deliberately attributed the work to Cyprian because he wanted to re-assert this warning against division within the Church. The earliest surviving manuscript of the Twelve Abuses (St Gall, Stiftsbibl. 89, pp. 107–37) unusually includes the Twelve Abuses within a manuscript of Cyprian's works.[51]

---

47   DDA, Breen 414–415 (879C): 'Et qui tali ordine expulsus fuerit, ab alio aliquo doctore vel episcopo non debet recipi.'

48   DDA, Breen 416–17 (879CD): 'ut ad gradum episcopi veniens sit *sobrius, prudens, castus*, sapiens, modestus, *hospitalis, filios habens subditos cum omni castitate*, testimonium habens bonum ab his qui foris sunt, proferens doctrinae fidelem sermonem; antequam episcopus sit, non plures habens uxores quam unam' (cf. I Tim. 3:2).

49   Cf. Jerome, Ep. 69.8, edited by Hilberg, I. 1910 CSEL 58, Vienna: Tempsky 680–98.

50   DDA 11, Breen 422 (880C): 'Sicut enim tunica totum corpus praeter caput tegitur, ita disciplina, omnis Ecclesia, praeter Christum, qui caput est Ecclesiae et sub disciplina non est, protegitur et ornatur.' Cf. Cyprian, *De ecclesiae catholicae unitate* 7, edited by M. Bévenot 1972 CCSL 3, Turnhout: Brepols 254.

51   Scherrer, G. 1875 *Verzeichniss der Handschriften der Stiftsbibliothek von St. Gallen*, Halle 34–35. The text comes after three works of Cyprian (*De dominica oratione, De bono patientiae* and *De opere et eleemosynis*), but is

The final abuse, that of a people without law, is also a simple, but unusual phrase, without clear precedent in patristic tradition. In this final chapter, the author consciously relates his theme to St Paul's insistence that the message of Christ is for all people, Jew and Greek, male and female, slave and free. Rather than use 'the law' in a negative anti-Jewish sense, this author transforms a Pauline statement (Romans 10:4) that the end of the law is Christ, in a way that promotes rather than diminishes respect for law: 'Since therefore Christ is the end of the Law, those who are without law are without Christ.'[52] The only previous author to come up with such an identification is Caesarius of Arles (d. 542).[53] Our author then goes a step further in claiming that 'a people without law is a people without Christ'.[54] Having presented *iustitia* at the outset of the Twelve Abuses as the foundation of the virtues, this author returns to this theme in conclusion, but picks up on how *justitia* is the foundation of both law and Christ. In a profound sense, this author offers a Christological foundation for the canon law of the Church, manifest in the sixth and seventh centuries in penitentials and collections of canon law, most famously in the *Collectio canonum Hibernensis* in around 700.

There is a profound parallel, I suggest, between the emphasis of the Twelve Abuses on law as the foundation of ethical behaviour and the emphasis on canon law in Cummian's letter on Easter, written in 632, following the return of monks from a three-year visit to Rome. They had been sent there after an important meeting of the Irish church at Mag Léne in 629/30, called to consider the request of Pope Honorius (625–38) to adopt the Roman Easter—following papal concern about the potential for liturgical disunity among foundations established by Columbanus (543–641) on the Continent. Cummian reported that a

---

followed by Gregory Nazianzenus, *Oratio VIII* and two further works of Cyprian (*De mortalitate, De ecclesiae catholicae unitate*), and then Ecclus 3:6–17 (*De honore parentum*).

52 *DDA* 12, Breen 428 (881B): 'Dum ergo Christus finis legis est, qui sine lege sunt, sine Christo fiunt.'

53 Caesarius, *Sermo* 106.4, edited by G. Morin 1953 CCSL 104, Turnhout: Brepols 442.

54 *DDA* 12, Breen 428 (882A): 'Igitur populus sine lege, populus sine Christo est.'

certain 'whited wall' (*paries dealbatus*; Acts 23:3) resisted this move, leading to both Armagh and Iona failing to adopt the Roman practice.[55] In this letter, Cummian is particularly concerned with the need not to create division within the universal Church. Contrasting Irish localism with the universalism of the wider Church, he invokes the canons of the 'four-fold apostolic see' (namely of Rome, Jerusalem, Antioch and Alexandria).[56] Above all he singles out Cyprian as 'the most weighty of all about the unity of the Church', before paraphrasing his argument in the *De unitate ecclesiae*, that we must all have one mother, namely the Church, 'just as we have one heavenly father'.[57] Cummian took inspiration from the example of Cyprian, who had to steer a path between rigorists (like Novatian), who refused to accept those who had lapsed at a time of persecution, and laxists for whom this did not matter. Cummian's interest in Cyprian, whose writings are much used by the author of the Twelve Abuses, must raise the question whether he may have been involved in its composition.[58]

The Twelve Abuses also deserves to be compared to the Penitential of Cummian, which introduces specific responses to the eight vices identified by Cassian (gluttony, fornication, avarice, anger, dejection, languor, vainglory and pride) with a prologue about the twelve stages of forgiveness.[59] Cummian's originality is evident from comparison of his discussion of ethical principles to the bare lists of penances offered in

---

55 *De controversia*, Walsh and Ó Cróinín 92–94; Bede reports the initial letter of Honorius II in *Ecclesiastical History* ii.19, edited by Bertram Colgrave and R. A. B. Mynors 1969 Oxford: Clarendon Press 198.
56 *De controversia*, Walsh and Ó Cróinín 58: 'Hoc timui et inquisiui diligenter quid Aebrei, quid Greci, quid Latini, quid Aegiptii de hoc tempore seruarent et sentirent'; 70: 'qui contra statua canonica quaternae sedis apostoicae, Romanae uidelicet Iersolimitanae, Antiochenae, Alexandrinae uenuint, concordantibus his in unitate paschae.' See notes of the editors (69–70) on the Patrick/John distinction, as underpinning the Easter debate.
57 *Ibid*. 78: 'His perscrutatis, uenio ad Cyprianum totum, ut aiunt, sumendum, et inuenio illum pene omnium de unitate aeclesiae grauissimum qui ait: Ab uno patre et ab una matre in hunc mundum uenimus et sic in futurum ueniemus.' Cf. Cyprian, *De ecclesiae catholicae unitate* 6, edited by M. Bévenot 1972 CCSL 3, 253: 'Habere iam non potest deum patrem qui ecclesiam non habet matrem.'
58 Breen, Pseudo-Cyprian and the Bible 234–35.

the earliest penitentials, from which he draws, namely the brief 'Preface of Gildas' and surviving excerpts from the Book of David.[60] Cummian also draws extensively on the so-called Ambrosian Penitential, a text that alludes to a sixth-century British synod 'of the Grove of Victory' and could be the source of the extracts attributed to the Book of David, a figure whose dates are notoriously uncertain.[61] The Preface of Gildas is addressed to both priests and monks, while the *Ambrosianum* and David-related extracts avoid speaking of monks, echoing the influence of Basil, who avoids speaking about monks in his Rule.[62] Cummian's Penitential, although inspired by monastic texts, in particular the

---

59 *Paenitentiale Cummeani*, edited by Ludwig Bieler 1963 *The Irish Penitentials*, Scriptores Latini Hiberniae 5, Dublin Institute for Advanced Studies 108–35, including its preface 109–110.

60 *Praefatio Gildae de Poenitentia*, edited by Bieler 60–65; *Penitentialis Vinniani*, edited by Bieler 74–95. The authenticity of the Preface of Gildas was questioned by Herren, Michael W. 1990 Gildas and Early British Monasticism, *Britain and Ireland: Language and History*, edited by Alfred Bammesberger and Alfred Wollmann, Heidelberg: Carl Winter 65–78, on the grounds that it offers a different perspective on monasticism from that offered in the surviving fragments from the letter of Gildas to Finnian. These texts are different in genre, however. The Preface of Gildas reflects a much less regimented monasticism than Finnian.

61 *Penitentiale Ambrosianum*, edited by Ludger Körntgen 1993 *Studien zu den Quellen der Frühmittaltrlichen Bussbücher*, Quellen und Forschungen zum Recht im Mittelalter 7, Sigmaringen: Thorbecke 258–71, with comment on 1–71, in particular 15–16 and 23–27. It refers to the *Decreta sinodi Loci Victoriae sanctorum sacerdotum* (II.11, edited by Körntgen 260; cf. Bieler 68. In the apparatus to his edition, Körntgen does not mention the parallels to version B of the preface of Columbanus (about spiritual doctors), Bieler 98. Charles-Edwards, T. M. 1997 comments on parallels with the *Ambrosianum* in the Penitential of Columbanus, *Columbanus: Studies on the Latin Writings*, edited by Michael Lapidge, Studies in Celtic History 17, Woodbridge: Boydell 217–39 (at 218 and 228). See the discussion of Meens, Rob 2016 The Irish Contribution to the Penitential Tradition, *The Irish in Early Medieval Europe. Identity, Culture and Religion*, edited by Roy Flechner and Sven Meeder, London: Palgrave 131–46, esp. 133–37. That the *Ambrosianum* is the source of the text introduced as *Excerpta quedam de libro Davidis* is argued by Mews, C. J. and Joyce, S. 2018 The Preface of Gildas, the Book of David, and Penitential Practice in Sixth-Century Britain, *Peritia* 29, 81–100.

62 Silvas, Anna 2013 *The Rule of St Basil in Latin and English: A Revised Critical Edition*, Collegeville MN: Liturgical Press.

Ambrosianum and its version of Cassian's account of eight vices, avoids reference to monks. It goes further than the *Ambrosianum* in its opening analogy of medical remedies for a variety of spiritual wounds by theorizing twelve modes of forgiveness. By comparison, the Penitential of Columbanus is closer to that of Finnian (bishop of Moville, d. 579?) in having separate sections for clerics and monks. Cummian expands Origen's discussion in homilies on Leviticus of seven modes of forgiveness into twelve stages in the penitential process, building on the teaching of Cassian about the fruits of penance.[63] Where Origen had simply listed baptism and martyrdom as the first two modes of forgiveness, Cummian identifies them as the first and last elements framing multiple spiritual stages, each with a pair of ideas:

(1) baptism
(2) the affect of love (*caritas*) (3) the fruit of mercy
(4) profusion of tears (5) confession of sins
(6) affliction of heart and body (7) amendment of ways
(8) intercession of saints (9) the merit of mercy and faith
(10) conversion and salvation of others (11) pardon and remission of ourselves
(12) passion of martyrdom

Just as the Twelve Abuses address society rather than monks, so Cummian's Penitential theorizes forgiveness for any reader, without identifying monks, reflecting the influence of Basil's Rule, as mediated through the *Ambrosianum*. Cummian is thus translating a British model (mediated through the David tradition) while also integrating elements of the Gildas tradition. Finnian's Penitential explicitly reserves to clergy the right to baptise and forbids monks from baptising or collecting alms.[64] In the Twelve Abuses we see a further stage of

---

63 Origen, *In Leuiticum homiliae* 2.4, edited by W. A. Baehrens 1920, Griechischen Christlichen Schriftsteller [GCS] 29, Berlin 292–96, coupled with Cassian, *Collationes* 20.8, Petschenig 561.
64 *Penitentialis Vinniani* 50, Bieler 92: 'Monachi autem non debent baptizare neque accipere elimosinam. Si autem accipiant elimosinam, cur non baptizabunt?'

reflection on ethical principles being transferred to a secular milieu. The placing of the bishop- layfolk doublet after the king-pauper doublet implies that ecclesiastical roles are superior to those in the secular world, as we find in the seventh-century *Críth Gablach* (c. 700), in which the bishop is presented as above the king in matters of religion, although not in secular authority.[65]

An intriguing feature of Cummian's Penitential is that—even if influenced by the *Ambrosianum*—it also goes back to the Preface of Gildas for certain of its rulings, in particular: 'We ought to offer the sacrifice on behalf of good kings, never on behalf of evil kings.' This ruling, not mentioned by Finnian, fits in with the warnings of Gildas in the *De excidio*.[66] The Preface of Gildas opens with rulings about presbyters and deacons who had previously taken a monastic vow. It does not mention episcopal excommunication, but speaks of an abbot as issuing such a punishment.[67] But Cummian clearly thought that some of its rulings still had merit, even if he is much more organised than Gildas on matters of detail. He used Gildas for certain details about penalties of gluttony (*gula*), Cassian's term, which he prefers to *inebriatio*, invoked in the *Ambrosianum*. Fornicating ecclesiastics are similarly judged harshly, with Cummian going further than Gildas in singling out bishops guilty of such vice as incurring an even more severe penance than clerics, monks and layfolk.[68] Cummian also provides much more detail about specific situations of moral abuse than the *Ambrosianum*, making it a much more useful document in a pastoral situation. Nonetheless it concludes by reflecting that human

---

65 *Críth Gablach*, edited by D. A. Binchy 1978 *Corpus iuris Hibernici*, 7 vols, Dublin Institute for Advanced Studies 2.777.6-783.38. I am indebted to Julianna Grigg for pointing out this parallel: how *Críth Gablach* places the bishop's dignity above that of the king due to his religion while at the same time the bishop acknowledges the superior secular authority of the king. See Charles-Edwards, T. M. 1986 *Críth Gablach* and the Law of Status, *Peritia* 5, 53-7.
66 Cummian, *De Penitentia* [*Poenitentiale*] IX.11, edited by Bieler 126, reprising *Praefatio Gildae de Penitentia* 23, edited by Bieler 62: 'Pro bonis regibus sacra debemus offere, pro malis nequaquam.'
67 *Praefatio Gildae de Poenitentia* 1-12, Bieler 60-62.
68 Cummian, *De Penitentia* [*Poenitentiale*] II.1-33, Bieler 112-116; cf. *Praefatio Gildae* 1-5, Bieler 60.

natures are varied, and urges any pastor to reflect on any person's capacity, and to remember their own frailty.[69] In a profound way, Cummian's Penitential offers specific penances for the various abuses outlined in the Twelve Abuses.

Conclusion

The Twelve Abuses offers a remarkable synthesis of ethical reflection in mid-seventh-century Ireland that extends the prophetic voice of Gildas in the *De excidio*, directed so much against bad kings and bishops (*sacerdotes*) into a concise, carefully structured reflection on moral responsibility for different groups in society. Ethical principles that had been formulated by Jerome and Cassian within a monastic milieu were now having to be made relevant to a much more ecclesiastically organised environment. Cummian's letter on the Easter debate from 632 offers a precious window into a society in profound transformation. These developments may have already started in the sixth century. The penitentials of Finnian and Columbanus offer a significant advance on those of Gildas and David in the way they address a perceived need to extend a monastic system of penance to clerical and lay society. By the 630s, however, it was clearly inadequate to rely on fundamentally monastic penitentials that had only limited understanding of what was relevant to a non-monastic milieu. Cummian was committed to asserting the authority of the earliest canons of the Church, not just to establish a common date for Easter, but as a foundation for the legal authority of the Church. In his letter to the abbot of Iona, Cummian drew extensively on patristic authority, above all that of Cyprian, to defend the unity of the Church, while affirming the role of bishops as successors to the apostles. The same theme of true unity as based on justice and law underpins the Twelve Abuses, a work originally circulated as that of Cyprian precisely because it shared Cyprian's concern to maintain the unity of the Church at a time of huge disagreement about how that unity should be enforced.

---

69   Cummian, *De Penitentia* [*Poenitentiale*], Bieler 132–34.

The parallels between the Twelve Abuses and the twelve stages of forgiveness that open Cummian's Penitential suggest that Cummian was either its author or the key intellectual influence on its composition. It demonstrates a profound reading of scripture, comparable to that found in the *De mirabilibus sacrae scripturae*, dated to 655 and addressed to 'the Carthaginians', quite likely the followers of Carthach (d. 636) at Lis Mór. In all probability, the Cummian who wrote to Ségéne of Iona was Cummine Fota of Clonfert Brennain (Co. Galway), in the kingdom of Connacht, and a teacher with strong links to the Eogenacht of Munster, with wide intellectual influence from Connacht to Munster. Cummian promoted the authority not just of Rome, but of a universal Church. From the letter of Pope John IV (640–42), sent to various bishops in the northern part of Ireland (Armagh, Clonard, and Ségéne of Iona), we learn that they were resisting the Roman Easter and were claiming that followers of Pelagius were gaining influence.[70] By the 680s, however, Armagh was proudly asserting its commitment to the traditions of Patrick and thus the liturgical cause promoted by Cummian.

The Twelve Abuses articulates a set of common ethical principles relevant to all society, and thus the foundation of the legal system being formulated by churchmen in seventh-century Ireland. Rather than appealing to the authority of a prophetic individual, it relies on the authority of canon law. As Breen noted, many of its ideas are close to those formulated in the so-called First Synod of Patrick, which claims to be sent by bishops Patrick, Auxilius, and Iserninus to priests, deacons and clergy.[71] It occurs in the same manuscript as the *Collectio Turonensis* (so-called because it was copied in the late ninth century in the region of Tours), which contains many excerpts from Gildas, followed by one about unity attributed to Patrick, and would become a source for the *Collectio canonum Hibernensis*.[72] The 'First Synod' does

---

70 Ó Cróinín, Dáibhí 1985 New Heresy for Old: Pelagianism in Ireland and the Papal Letter of 640, *Speculum* 50, 505–16.
71 *Synodus I S. Patricii*, edited by Bieler 54–59.
72 Breen 1988 *De duodecim abusivis* 8–16 (on *Synodus I Patricii*) and 16–27 (on *Synodus II Patricii*); also published as Breen 1995 The Date, Provenance and Authorship of the Pseudo-Patrician Canonical Materials, *Zeitschrift der Savigny-Stiftung für Rechtsgeschichte, Kanonistische Abteilung* 81, 83–129

not mention monks at all, and insists that no clerics should be vagrant or have a tonsure that was not Roman, but speaks of them having wives.[73] The more widely copied 'Second Synod of Patrick' shares a similar perspective on episcopal authority in providing rules on excommunication procedure, comments on false bishops needing to be degraded, and criticism of false monks who live in solitude. Its concerns are similarly with the authority of bishops and *doctores* as superior to other clergy and layfolk, while monks belonged to a quite separate order.[74] Breen notes that attached to a version of the 'Second Synod of Patrick' are two *Fragmenta Gildae*, urging caution in how excommunication was used.[75] In many ways, this is the emerging world of the Twelve Abuses. Breen's observation that the Twelve Abuses share much in common with the second 'Patrick' or *Romani* synod deserves scrutiny.[76] Cummian was one of a network of scholars who were becoming aware of the universality of the Church, and sought to provide moral and legal authority for its teaching.

Cummian's name is remembered with that of Lathcen (Laithcen) (d. 662/665) at Toureen Peacaun, in County Tipperary.[77] This inscription implies that Cummian was known in Munster, even though his abbey at Clonfert Brenain was in Connacht. It also points to a network of scholars in the region. Lathcen produced an abbreviation of the *Moralia on Job* of Gregory the Great (d. 604) that focuses more on the historical and allegorical than moral sense of the text, and incorporates an excerpt from Isidore's *De ortu et obitu patrum*.[78] This emphasis on the historical reading of scripture is also evident in the

---

(with edition of *Synodus II Patricii* on 112–26 and an excerpt introduced as *De communicatione Gildas* on 121–22). On the First Synod, see Binchy, D. A. 1968–69 St Patrick's 'First Synod', *Studia Hibernica* 8, 49–59.

73 *Synodus I S. Patricii* 3, 6 edited by Bieler, 54: 'Clericus vagus non sit in plebe. … et si non more Romano capilli eius tonsi sint … ab ecclesia separentur.'
74 *Synodus II S. Patricii* 16–20, edited by Bieler 190–92.
75 Breen, Pseudo-Patrician Canonical Materials 121–22.
76 Breen, Pseudo-Patrician Canonical Materials 110–111.
77 Illustrated in Okasha, Elisabeth and Forsyth, Katherine 2001 *Early Christian Inscriptions of Munster. A Corpus of the Inscribed Stones*, Cork University Press 253–56 (Toureen Peacaun 16).
78 *Egloga quam scripsit Lathcen fiius Baith de Moralibus Iob quas Gregorius Fecit*, edited by M. Adriaen 1960 CCSL 145, Turnhout: Brepols 3, quoting Isidore's

De mirabilibus sacrae scripturae from 655. Lathcen also composed the *Lorica Gildae*, claiming it to be a text composed by Gildas to ward off temptation. The poem is presented as placed on the altar of Patrick.[79] The Twelve Abuses may well emanate from the milieu of Cummian and Lathcen, who were committed to combining the prophetic ethos of Gildas with respect for the episcopal authority of Patrick.

The Twelve Abuses combines respect for prophetic authority as formulated by Gildas with insistence that law is the foundation of *justitia*, understood as both righteousness (as embodied in Christ), and as the transcendent moral code from which all law derives. The Twelve Abuses was particularly adept in formulating a profoundly moral message for all members of society, based on the foundational value of *iustitia*. By the early eighth century, respect for prophetic criticism of secular and clerical behaviour was being transmuted into a body of thought structured around respect for law. The particular genius of the Twelve Abuses of the Age was to provide a mirror articulating complaints about justice in society of enduring relevance throughout the medieval period, even if the original identity of its author would be lost to history.

De ortu et obitu patrum (PL 83.136BD) as *Dicta Isidori in libro de vita et exitu prophetarum* near the opening of its first book.

79 The *Lorica* is edited by Herren, M. W. 1987 *Hisperica Famina* II, Toronto: Pontifical Institute of Mediaeval Studies 76–89; see Herren, M. W. 1973 The Authorship, Date of Composition and Provenance of the so-called *Lorica Gildae*, *Ériu* 24, 35–51.

7
Memories of Gildas: Gildas and the *Collectio canonum Hibernensis*

Stephen Joyce

Gildas (*fl.* fifth or sixth century) is arguably the most significant voice describing the British Isles in late antiquity. Active sometime between the late fifth and mid sixth centuries, he is one of only two major Insular voices that survive this period. The other voice is that of the Apostle to Ireland, Patrick (*fl.* fifth century). In a letter to Pope Gregory the Great written around the year 600, the Irish *peregrinus* Columbanus (c. 543–615) called on the authority of Gildas to clarify the correct disciplinary approach to simoniac bishops in Gaul, and of both Gildas and Finnian (died c. 549 or 579) to offer an Insular disciplinary approach to monks who broke their communal vows in order to seek a more religious life.[1] In doing so, Columbanus became our earliest

I would like to thank Professor Constant Mews for reading and commenting on an early draft of this paper, as well as the anonymous reviewer(s) whose notes were most helpful. All errors are, or course, my own.

---

1   Walker, G. S. M. editor 1957 *Sancti Columbani Opera*, Scriptores Hiberniae Latini 2, Dublin Institute for Advanced Studies, ep. I.6.8: 'Ceterum de episcopis illis ... qui contra canones ordinatur, id est quaestu; simoniacos et Gildas auctor pestes scripsit eos'; ep. I.7.8: 'quid faciendum est de monachis illis, qui pro Dei intuitu et vitae perfectioris desiderio accensi, contra vota venientes primae conversionis loca relinquunt, et invitis abbatibus, fervore monachorum cogente, aut laxantur aut ad deserta fugiunt. Vennianus auctor

witness to Gildas as the author of the *De excidio Britanniae* (dated variously from 479–550) and a letter to Finnian (generally dated after the *De excidio*), elements of which survive as the *Fragmenta Gildae* in a range of seventh- or eighth-century canonical texts.[2]

In the *Collectio canonum Hibernensis*, a significant collection of Irish canon law collated in Ireland c. 700, Gildas is cited solely from this letter to Finnian. Curiously, Gildas is not cited from his more noted work, the *De excidio*, a work concerned with the behaviour of kings and bishops written within the prophetic traditions of the Old Testament.[3] The fundamental role of the *Hibernensis*, as Thomas Charles-Edwards notes, was to 'attempt to create a Christian law for a Christian society', as seen in its regulation of secular roles including kingship, and its unusual merging of rules relating to the clergy and laity.[4] Preferring Gildas' *Fragmenta* to his *De excidio* in the context of secular and church leadership is a notable choice by the compilers.

Gildam de his interrogavit, et elegantissime ille rescripsit.' On Gildas' *Epistola ad Vinniauum* (Finnian, variously identified as of Clonard, d. c. 549, or of Moville, d. c. 579), surviving as the *Fragmenta Gildae*, see Sharpe, Richard 1997 *A Handlist of the Latin Writers of Great Britain and Ireland before 1540*, Turnhout: Brepols 149. For further reading on the *Fragmenta Gildae*, see Sharpe, Richard 1984 Gildas as a Father of the Church, *Gildas: New Approaches*, edited by Michael Lapidge and David Dumville, Woodbridge: Boydell 191–206. Sharpe argues that fragments of writings attributed to Gildas in the *Collectio canonum Hibernensis* come from this letter to Finnian. For an overview on the enigmatic figure(s) of Finnian, see Dumville, David N. 2004 The Colophon of 'The Penitential of Uinniau', *Corona Monastica—Moines bretons de Landévennec: histoire et mémoire celtiques—Mélanges offerts au père Marc Simon*, Presses Universitaires de Rennes 167–178.

2   For the *De excidio* and the *Fragmenta Gildae*, see Winterbottom, Michael, editor 1978 *Gildas: The Ruin of Britain and Other Works*, London: Phillimore. This edition will be used for this article. Christopher Snyder has noted various scholastic positions on the dating of the *De excidio* in a useful table: see Snyder, Christopher 2003 *The Britons*, Oxford: Blackwell 123.

3   For Gildas' use of the prophetic traditions of the Old Testament in his *De excidio*, see Joyce, Stephen 2013 Gildas and His Prophecy for Britain, *Journal of the Australian Early Medieval Association* 9, 39–59.

4   Charles-Edwards, T. M. 2005 Early Irish Law, *A New History of Ireland, Volume 1: Prehistoric and Early Ireland*, edited by Dáibhí Ó Cróinín, Oxford University Press 331–370: 353.

In examining how the compilers of the *Hibernensis* remembered the authority of Gildas, this paper will argue that between the mission of Columbanus to the Continent c. 600 and the compilation of the *Hibernensis* c. 700, the memory of Gildas in Ireland was transmuted from that of a prophet shaping the authority of kings and bishops to that of a respected contributor to canon law, one supportive of the church hierarchy and the right of bishops to shape the authority of kings, as represented on a local level by Patrick.

The Collectio canonum Hibernensis and the Fragmenta Gildae

Sometime between the second half of the seventh century and the first half of the eighth century, a collection of canon law—the *Collectio canonum Hibernensis*—was collated in Ireland that cited Gildas in the same breath as illustrious Church Fathers such as Augustine of Hippo (c. 354–430), Jerome (c. 347–420), Gregory the Great (c. 540–604) and Isidore of Seville (c. 560–636).[5] This collection was distinct from equivalent canon collections on the Continent. Aside from its citation of Insular authorities such as Patrick, Gildas and Finnian as well as Insular synods, the *Hibernensis* was unusual in its emphasis on citations from the Latin Fathers and the Bible rather than on papal decretals and church canons as on the Continent.[6] It further distinguished itself by eschewing the chronological systemisation of Continental canon collections for one based on a thematic arrangement of regulations as they related to the proper lives of Christians—whether clerical,

---

5 See Flechner, Roy 2004 *The Hibernensis*—A Study, Edition, and Translation, with Notes, Oxford: D.Phil. thesis, which was recently published as Flechner, Roy 2019 *The Hibernensis, Volume 1: A Study and Edition*, Washington D.C.: The Catholic University of America Press. I would like to thank Dr Flechner for allowing me to use his unpublished edition for this paper. Flechner 17 dates the *Hibernensis* conservatively to 669–748, with a historical argument for 716–747.

6 For its distinctiveness see Flechner 1–6; Elliot, Michael 2013 Canon Law Collections in England ca 600–1066: The Manuscript Evidence, Toronto: D.Phil. thesis 139–140. Gildas is cited fifteen times; Patrick is cited thirty-five times; Finnian is cited once.

monastic or lay—within the church.[7] This distinctiveness was both influential and divisive: while in the ninth century, the *Hibernensis* attracted suspicion from a Gallican and Roman perspective, by the eleventh century it would profoundly influence the structure of Continental canon collections.[8]

The origins of the *Hibernensis* are obscure. As a collation of excerpts from Church Fathers, scripture and canon law, it is likely to have had an origin, or drawn on texts with an origin, prior to the first half of the eighth century in Ireland, a context noted by Roy Flechner as the latest date of its composition as preserved in the manuscript sources.[9] The use of Church Fathers, papal decretals and council canons in the *Hibernensis*, whilst suggesting a desire to preserve traditions, is idiosyncratic for a seventh- or eighth-century text from a Continental perspective. The latest Continental church council to be cited is that of the Council of Orleans in 511, with a significant source of canons concerned with ordination and clerical discipline coming from the Gallican *Statuta ecclesiae antiqua*, dated to the last quarter of the fifth century; a second significant source of canons, predominantly from the Eastern Church, was mined from the *Dionysiana*, collated in Rome in the first quarter of the sixth century by Dionysius Exiguus (c. 470–544).[10] Local canons are assigned to Patrick (with elements

---

[7] See Richter, Michael 1999 *Ireland and Her Neighbours in the Seventh Century*, Dublin: Four Courts Press 217.

[8] Reynolds, Roger 1983 Unity and Diversity in Carolingian Canon Law Collections: The Case of the *Collectio Hibernensis* and Its Derivatives, *Carolingian Essays: Andrew W. Mellon Lectures in Early Christian Studies*, edited by Uta-Renate Blumenthal, Washington: The Catholic University Press 99–136: 101–102, describes early ninth-century attacks on the *Hibernensis* from a Gallican and Roman perspective. Richter 217 points out the standardisation of the *Hibernensis* systemisation in continental Europe in the eleventh century.

[9] On the issue of an Irish origin, Flechner 5 is decisive. However, others still argue for a possible Breton origin: see Elliott 138; see also Davies, Luned Mair 2002 The 'mouth of gold': Gregorian texts in the *Collectio canonum Hibernensis*, *Ireland and Europe in the Early Middle Ages: Texts and Transmission*, edited by Próinséas Ní Chatháin and Michael Richter, Dublin: Four Courts Press 249–267: 249.

[10] See Davies, Luned Mair 2000 *Statuta ecclesiae antiqua* and the Gallic councils in the *Hibernensis*, *Peritia* 14, 85–110. Only one Continental manuscript of

preserved elsewhere as the *Synodus I Patricii* or the so-called First Synod of Patrick) or to local synods, the *Synodus Romana* (with elements preserved elsewhere as the *Synodus II Patricii* or the so-called Second Synod of Patrick) and the *Synodus Hibernensis*.[11] The canons attributed to Patrick (as contained in the *Synodus I Patricii*) appear to represent an Irish church prior to c. 600, while canons attributed to the Insular synods appear to represent the seventh-century Roman liturgical reform movement in Ireland (the *Romani*), a movement reflecting similar and highly contested reform in Britain.[12] What we have is a text of which an earlier version or source may have been compiled with a Continental perspective in the first quarter of the sixth century, and a subsequent version or source compiled with an Insular perspective in the seventh or eighth centuries. This is, perhaps, reflected in the choice of patristic authorities: fourth- and fifth-century Church Fathers such as Ambrose (c. 340–397), Jerome and Augustine are largely complemented by late sixth- and early seventh-century figures such as Gregory the Great and Isidore of Seville, with the latest authority cited being that of Theodore of Canterbury (d. 690).[13] Notably, the sixth-century Irish monastic figures Columba (c. 521–597) and Columbanus are not named in the *Hibernensis*.

---

the *Hibernensis*—Ms Cologne, Dombibl. 210 (K)—cites subsequent Gallican councils up to 540. Flechner 36 notes a potential echo of the Council of Marseilles in 533. For a list of the councils cited in the *Hibernensis*, see Flechner 1035–1039.

11 For an analysis of the canons of the First Synod of Patrick and the Second Synod of Patrick in the *Hibernensis*, see Breen, Aidan 1995 The Date, Provenance and Authorship of the Pseudo-Patrician Canonical Materials, *Zeitschrift der Savigny-Stiftung für Rechtsgeschichte. Kanonistische Abteilung* 81, 83–129. An edition and translation of the Second Synod of Patrick is in the same article. For an edition and translation of the First Synod of Patrick, see Bieler, Ludwig 1963 *The Irish Penitentials*, Scriptores Latini Hiberniae 5, Dublin Institute for Advanced Studies 54–59.

12 Richter, Michael 2000 Dating the Irish Synods in the *Collectio canonum Hibernensis*, *Peritia* 14, 70–84:71. See also Charles-Edwards, T. M. 2000 *Early Christian Ireland*, Cambridge University Press 245–250 for a discussion of the dating of the First Synod of Patrick. He prefers a dating no later than the middle of the sixth century. For an overview of the contested Roman liturgical reform in Britain from an Irish perspective, see 429–438.

13 Flechner 15 and 1033–1051.

The *Fragmenta Gildae*, as laid out in Winterbottom's edition, consists of eight fragments assigned directly to Gildas, and a further two fragments attributed to Gildas.[14] As Sharpe observes, fragments one to seven appear to concern themselves with monastic disputes arising from a desire for stricter discipline, though this is arguably an overview of the material.[15] Only fragments three, four and five strictly relate to monastic discipline. To this can be added the allusion of Columbanus to Gildas' position on monks breaking their communal vows in order to seek a solitary life, a position missing from the *Fragmenta*.[16] The other fragments are more general: fragments one and seven cover excommunication in a clerical and monastic context; fragment two comments on fasting in a clerical, monastic and secular context; fragments six and nine cover judgement in a clerical, monastic and secular context; and fragments eight and ten are Gildasian sayings. The fragments are notable for a tolerant and communal ascetic Christianity cautious of extremism and sober in its warning of the consequences of pride and judgementalism.[17]

What is notable is that the *Hibernensis* did not slavishly copy the *Fragmenta*. Rather the compilers edited the *Fragmenta* in ways that fitted in with the purpose of the *Hibernensis*. Gildas was used to emphasise specific themes: the bishop; the [good] Christian; fasting; honesty; leadership; the monk; excommunication; the tonsure (a theme accorded to Gildas by the compilers but not taken from the *Fragmenta*); and, in a section on a variety of issues, recognising the unjust in a monastic or ascetic context.[18] The majority of these themes lend

---

14 For the *Fragmenta*, see Winterbottom 143–145 (translations 80–82).
15 Sharpe, Gildas as a Father of the Church 197. This article, however, will argue that Gildas' letter to Finnian was advice on the proper exercise of episcopal authority in matters of church discipline.
16 See above, n. 1.
17 See Sharpe, Gildas as a Father of the Church 197.
18 Flechner 1, 4; *Hibernensis*, De episcopo [1] (10, 52), De Christiano [1] (12, 64), De ieiunio [1] (22, 159), De ueritate [1] (36, 287), De principatu [3] (38, 324), De monachis [4] (39, 335), De excommunicatione [1] (51, 454), De tonsura [1] (65, 510), De uariis causis [1]. The amount of times Gildas is cited in the section is noted in square brackets; references to the respective pages of Flechner's edition and translation are in parentheses.

themselves to the ascetic life in general, and Gildas is called upon only once in a specifically clerical context and most often in the section of the *Hibernensis* dedicated to monks, reinforcing the perception of a monastic slant to his authority.[19]

The *Fragmenta Gildae* are preserved in their most complete form in a version of the *Hibernensis* in Cambridge, Corpus Christi College 279, a ninth-century manuscript hailing from Tours, a version edited by Michael Elliot as the *Collectio Turonensis*.[20] This version, systemised by both source and topic, contains the majority of Gildas' *Fragmenta* as published in Winterbottom's edition.[21] All of the fragments, except fragment eight, are to be found under a general heading on Christian sayings, emphasising the general themes of excommunication, fasting, the last days, and monks.[22] This version, quoting the more complete sections of Gildas' letter to Finnian, is not a derivative of the *Hibernensis* as previously held, but rather a major source for the *Hibernensis*.[23] The latest patristic author quoted appears to be from the epilogue to the Penitential of Cummean (d. c. 662), and the relative lack of emphasis on the authority of Gregory the Great and Isidore of Seville combined with a construction prior to the diffusion of Gregory's *Dialogues*, point to a compilation of the *Turonensis* sometime in the second quarter of the seventh century.[24] The single

---

19 For bishops, see *Hibernensis* 1.16, Flechner 17. For monks, see *Hibernensis* 38.5, 38.6, 38.7, 38.9, Flechner 330-332.
20 Elliot 104-105 details Cambridge, Corpus Christi College, MS 279: ninth or tenth century, Tours. The manuscript contains *Collectio canonum Hibernensis* (excerpts), *Synodus I Patricii, Liber ex lege Moysi*, and the *Iudicia Theodori versio discipuli Umbrensis* (excerpts). On the *Turonensis*, see Elliot 161-165. His Latin edition of the *Turonensis* is at 691-728, and will be the edition used in this article.
21 Elliot 163. Gildas occurs at *Turonensis* 42, and *Turonensis* 82-94. See 691-692 for a list of sources for the *Turonensis*. Fragments in Winterbottom's edition not found in the *Turonensis* are sourced from the *Hibernensis*.
22 *Turonensis* 42, Elliot, 704: 'De ueritate praedicanda multi sancti loquuntur'. *Turonensis* 82-94, Elliott 709-713: 'De christianis loquitur quod inuicti sunt'; 'De excommunicatione'; 'De abstinentia ciborum'; 'De nouissimis diebus'; 'De monachis'.
23 Elliot 162. Sharpe, Gildas as a Father of the Church 196.

citation attributed to Patrick in the *Turonensis*, following immediately after the quotes from Gildas, taken together with the presence in the codex of the *Synodus I Patricii*, reveals early efforts to combine the authority of Gildas with that of Patrick.[25]

A potentially earlier source for the *Hibernensis* survives in two Carolingian manuscripts from Germany, manuscripts that, as the late Aidan Breen notes, contain an unattributed version of the *Synodus Romana* or *Synodus II Patricii* along with elements of the *Fragmenta Gildae* and the *Turonensis* under the title *Incipiunt Capitula Canonica* (ICC).[26] The *Fragmenta* used (fragments one and seven on the theme

---

24 Whilst Elliot conservatively dates the *Turonensis* from the middle of the seventh century to the first quarter of the eighth century, this merely duplicates Flechner's dating for the *Hibernensis*. See Elliot 161. On 163 he argues for a date in the second half of the seventh century, perhaps even earlier, based on the use of Cummean. Cummean is quoted at *Turonensis* 123, Elliot 719: 'sed in omni penitentia solenter inquirendum est'. See Bieler 108–135: 132. Cummean's letter on the Paschal controversy, dated c. 632, is the earliest dateable source to mention Patrick in an Insular context. Clarke, Francis 2003 *The 'Gregorian' Dialogues and the Origins of Benedictine Monasticism*, Leiden: Brill 260–274, charts the diffusion of Gregory's *Dialogues*. He argues that the *Dialogues* does not appear in the historical record until the second half of the seventh century. This article sets aside his argument over the authorship of the *Dialogues*.

25 *Turonensis* 95, Elliot 713: 'Patricius de unitate et subditorum: Quis ergo audet scindere unitatem quam nemo hominum soluere uel repraehendere potest'. The source for this quotation attributed to Patrick is unidentified by Elliot. However, Breen has identified Cyprian. See next note.

26 Breen 96–97 details the manuscript tradition underpinning his edition of *Synodus II Patricii*, based on two early ninth-century manuscripts of south German (Carolingian) provenance and containing a number of texts in common: a series of epitomes of conciliar statutes of Gallican and African origin; a section entitled *Incipiunt capitula canonica* containing the canons of *Synodus II Patricii* (without authorial attribution), a number of garbled excerpts from Augustine, Gregory the Great, Jerome, and Gildas, and a number of early Gallican councils, all very similar to the *Collectio canonum Hibernensis* (excerpts) in MS 279 (*Turonensis*). His Latin edition of the ICC is on 121–125; his Latin edition of the *Synodus II Patricii* (with translation) is on 112–121. Patrick's phrase above appears in the ICC and is identified by Breen as being from Cyprian. See Breen 122. Following directly on from Gildas' *Fragmenta*, this expression may be from Gildas' letter to Finnian.

of excommunication) are notably bound in with the authority of Augustine of Hippo. The latest patristic author to be quoted is Gregory the Great, specifically his early works *Homilies on the Gospels* and *Homilies on Ezekiel*, pointing to a composition in the first quarter of the seventh century.[27] What we see is an evolving use of the *Fragmenta* from an early emphasis on excommunication, followed by an emphasis on excommunication, the ascetic life and judgement, and a final emphasis on excommunication, the ascetic life, judgement and leadership. This early and developing focus on excommunication in the context of secular leadership, a power inherent in episcopal authority, alerts us to the possibility that Gildas' letter to Finnian was not concerned with advice on monastic discipline, but rather with advice relating to the proper exercise of episcopal authority.

That the works of Gildas may have been approached selectively by the compilers of the *Hibernensis* can be seen with the attribution of one of Gildas' *Fragmenta*. The fragment at *Hibernensis* 36.31 is attributed to Jeremiah, when it is, in fact, a Gildasian version of 2 Tim 3:1–5, one also found in the *De excidio*:

[*Hibernensis* 36.31 / *Turonensis* 84] Heremias dicit: Nouissimis diebus instabunt tempora pessima. Et erunt homines sui amatores, auarii, adrogantes, superbi, blasfemii, parentibus inobedientes, ingrati, inpurii, sine affectione, sine pace, accusatores, intemperantes, crudeles, odio habentes bonum, proditores magis quam amatores Dei, habentes formam pietatis, uirtutem eius abnegantes.[28]

[*Fragmenta* 3] Gildas in epistolis suis de novissimis diebus: Instabunt tempora pessima et erunt homines sui amatores auari adrogantes superbi blasphemi. parentibus inoboedientes ingrati inpuri sine adfectione, sine pace accusatores intemperantes

---

27 See Breen 121–125.
28 *Hibernensis* 36.31, Flechner 305 (trans. 748); *Turonensis* 84, Elliot 711: 'Jeremiah said: In the last days the worst of times will come. And men will be conceited, avaricious, arrogant, proud, blasphemous, disobedient to parents, ungrateful, unclean, without affection, without peace, accusers, intemperate, cruel, haters of the good, lovers of pleasure rather than God, possessing the form of piety but denying its virtue.'

crudiles odio habentes bonum proditores temerari. inflati uoluntatum amatores magis quam dei habentes formam pietatis et uirtutem eius abnegantes.²⁹

[*De excidio* 104] Hoc enim scitote, quod in novissimis diebus instabunt tempora periculosa. Erunt enim homines semet ipsos amantes, cupidi, elati, superbi, blasphemi, parentibus inoboedientes, ingrati, scelesti, sine affectione, incontinentes, inmites, sine benignitate, proditores, protervi, tumidi, voluptatum amatores magis quam dei, habentes quidem speciem pietatis, virtutem autem eius abnegantes.³⁰

This selective approach to the influence of the *De excidio* and its critical attitude toward bishops and kings alerts us to the fact that the authority of Gildas may have been modified. In order to discern more closely how Gildas' authority was modified, we need to discern whether elements of the *De excidio* survive unattributed in the *Hibernensis*.

The *De excidio* and the *Collectio canonum Hibernensis*

Gildas' criticisms of kings and bishops in his *De excidio* is a tradition, as we have seen, that the Irishman Columbanus brought to the Continent. Curiously, any direct reference to the *De excidio* is missing from the *Hibernensis*, with only the *Fragmenta* being attributed directly to Gildas. A monastic emphasis is seen with the compilers' use of the

---

29 Gildas, *Fragmenta* 3, Winterbottom 143 (trans. 80): 'On the last days Gildas says in his letters: "The worst of times will come: men will be conceited, avaricious, arrogant, proud, blasphemous, disobedient to parents, ungrateful, unclean, without affection, without peace, accusers, intemperate, cruel, haters of the good, traitors, rash, puffed up, lovers of pleasure rather than God: possessing the form of piety but denying its virtue."'
30 Gildas, *De excidio* 104, Winterbottom, 138 (trans. 75): 'Know that in the last days dangerous times will threaten. There will be men who love themselves, greedy, puffed up, proud, blasphemous, disobedient to their parents, ungrateful, wicked, without affection, uncontrolled, cruel, without kindness, traitors, provocative, swollen, lovers of pleasure rather than of God, with a semblance of piety but deniers of its virtue.'

Fragmenta, but also one of leadership (*De principatu*), a sentiment that is surely derived in some form from the *De excidio* and its criticism of secular and clerical leadership. However, on leadership, as with monastic discipline, Gildas appears to be used, once again, as a mediator, one drawing on forgiveness for trifling faults, the importance of stability, and on the need to avoid bad leaders until the appropriate penance has been enacted:

> [*Hibernensis* 36.5 / *Fragmenta* 9] Gildas: En adsentiente Aron in culpando Moise propter uxorem Etiopisam lepra Maria damnatur. Quod nobis timendum, qui bonis principibus detrahimus propter mediocres culpas.[31]
>
> [*Hibernensis* 36.32 / *Fragmenta* 6] Gildas: Vnusquisque in quo uocatus est, in eo permaneat, ut nec primarius nisi uoluntate motetur subiectorum, nec subiectus nisi senioris consilio locum prioris obteneat.[32]
>
> [*Hibernensis* 36.37 / *Fragmenta* 7] Gildas: Quos scimus sine ulla dubitatione esse fornicatores, nisi legitimo ordine peniteant, a pace et missa et mensa cuiuscumque ordinis fuerint, arceamus, ut est illud: Si quis frater nominatur ut est fornicator et reliqua.[33]

As has been noted above, the more strident phrases of Gildas from the *Fragmenta* have been attributed to Jeremiah. To this we can add the rare use of Jer 23.1 in the *Hibernensis* and the *Turonensis*, as referred

---

31 *Hibernensis* 36.5, Flechner 291; Gildas, *Fragmenta* 9, Winterbottom 145 (trans. 82): 'Gildas: Miriam was condemned to leprosy because she and Aaron agreed in blaming Moses because of his Ethiopian wife. We should be afraid of this fate when we disparage good princes for trifling faults.'

32 *Hibernensis* 36.32, Flechner 306; Gildas, *Fragmenta* 6, Winterbottom 145 (trans. 82): 'Gildas: "Let each in God stay where they are called": so that the chief should not be changed except at the choice of his subjects, nor the subject obtain the place of his superior without the advice of an elder'.

33 *Hibernensis* 36.37, Flechner 310; Gildas, *Fragmenta* 7, Winterbottom 145 (trans. 82): 'Gildas: But as for persons we know without doubt to be fornicators, we keep them from communion and our table, unless they do penance in the legitimate manner, according to the order they legitimately belong to. So: "If any man is called a brother and is a fornicator ..." and the rest.'

to by Gildas in his *De excidio*, reinforcing the fact that the earlier *Turonensis* also had an ambivalence in directly assigning authority to the *De excidio*:

> [*Hibernensis* 36.4] Hieremias: Ve uobis pastoribus qui disperdunt et lacerant gregem pascuae meae, dicit Dominus.[34]
>
> [*Turonensis* 74] Hieremias: Uae pastoribus israhel qui disperdunt et delacerant gregem pascuae meae dicit dominus.[35]
>
> [*De excidio* 82.1] Et iterum: 'Vae pastoribus qui disperdunt et dilacerant gregem pascuae meae, dicit dominus'.[36]

Gildas' highly original use of scripture in the *De excidio*—where his criticisms of secular and church leaders are drawn directly from two linear scans through the Bible—contributes to his use of rarely cited scriptural phrases. The reference to shepherds and sheep in Jer 23:1 within *Hibernensis* 36.4, a subsection also quoting Isaiah and Ezekiel on the same theme and one just prior to the use of Gildas' *Fragmenta* at *Hibernensis* 36.5, alerts us to the fact that the tradition embedded in the *De excidio*—that of Isaiah, Ezekiel and John on the role of the good shepherd as the watchman or *speculator*—is also in the *Hibernensis*. This can also be seen in *Hibernensis* 36.22 on Ezekiel's concept of the blood of the sheep being on the hands of the shepherd:

> [*Hibernensis* 36.22] De sanguine subiectorum de manu gubernatorum quesito, si autem corripuerint, licet non audiant, non quesito.
>
> Isaias dicit: Sacerdotes eorum non proderunt eis. Canes muti non possunt latrare. Vos demulgitis lac ouium et comedetis eas. Ego uindicabo sanguinem earum de manibus uestris, dicit Dominus omnipotens.
>
> Dominus ait: Nisi renuntiaueris iniquo iniquitatem suam, sanguinem eius requiram de manu tua.

---

34 *Hibernensis* 36.4, Flechner 290. Jeremiah 23:1: 'Vae pastoribus qui disperdunt et dilacerant gregem pascuae meae! dicit Dominus'.
35 *Turonensis* 74, Elliot 708–709.
36 Gildas, *De excidio* 82.1, Winterbottom 128.

Gregorius: Sanguis morientis de manu speculatoris requiritur, quia peccatum subditi culpe prepositi deputatur, si tacuerit. Vnde quoque hic additur: Si autem tu nuntiaueris et ille non fuerit conuersus ab impiaetate sua et a uia sua impia, ipse quoque in iniquitate sua moritur. Tu autem animam tuam saluasti.

Hironimus: Non solum pro peccatis nostris reddituri rationem sumus, sed etiam pro eorum, quorum abutimur donis et nequaquam de eorum salute solliciti sumus et propter hanc causam mali principes increpanti sunt et considerandi utrum boni an mali.

Vt Paulus ait: Non omnes æpiscopi, æpiscopi habentur. Adtendis Petrum, sed Iudam consideras. Stefanum aspicis, sed Nicolaum aspice.[37]

Hibernensis 36.22 recalls the *De excidio* and its citation of Is 56:10, Ezek 33:1–9, and Jerome's letter to Heliodorus (attributed to Paul in the *Hibernensis*), and also reflects a tradition embedded in the *Fragmenta*:

[*De excidio* 36.4] … ne simus 'canes muti non valentes latrare …'[38]

---

37 *Hibernensis* 36.22, Flechner 300–301 (trans. 743–744): 'That the blood of the subjects is required at the rulers' hands, but if they have rebuked them it is not required, even if they did not obey. Isaiah says: Their priests were of no benefit to them. Dumb dogs are not able to bark. You milk your sheep and eat them. I shall avenge their blood from your hands, says the almighty Lord. The Lord said: Unless you proclaim his wickedness to the wicked man, I will require his blood at your hand. Gregory: The blood of a dying man is required at the hand of the one watching over him, for the sin of a dependant is imputed to the guilt of the superior, if he remained silent. Whence also the following is added: If you have admonished him, and he has not reformed his impiety and his impious way, he dies in his iniquity. You, however, have saved your soul. Jerome: We shall render account not only for our sins, but for the sins of the ones whose gifts we misuse, and whose well-being we were never concerned with, and for this reason wicked princes are to be charged, and they must be examined, whether they are good or evil. As Paul said: Not all bishops are considered true bishops. You think of Peter, but reflect also on Judas. You observe Stephen, but observe also Nicolas.'

38 Gildas, *De excidio* 36.4, Winterbottom 104 (trans. 35): 'to avoid being one of the "dogs that are dumb and cannot bark"'.

[*De excidio* 91.3] Et speculator si viderit gladium venientem et non significaverit tuba et populus non observaverit, et veniens gladius acceperit ex eis animam, et ipsa propter iniquitatem suam capta est et sanguinem de manu speculatoris requiram. Et tu, fili hominis, speculatorem te dedi domui Israel et audies ex ore meo verbum, cum dicam peccatori: morte morieris, et non loqueris, ut avertat se a via sua impius, et ipse iniquus in iniquitate sua morietur, sanguinem autem eius de manu tua requiram. Tu vero si praedixeris impio viam eius, ut avertat se ab ea, et non se averterit a via sua, hic sua impietate morietur et tu animam tuam eripuisti.[39]

[*De excidio* 1.11] beatissimum dicebam Petrum ob Christi integram confessionem, at Iudam infelicissimum propter cupiditatis amorem, Stephanum gloriosum ob martyrii palmam, sed Nicolaum miserum propter immundae haereseos notam.[40]

---

39   Gildas, *De excidio* 91.3, Winterbottom 132–133 (trans. 69): 'But if the watchman sees the sword coming and does not give the signal with the trumpet and the people does not take heed, and the sword comes and takes life from them, that life is taken because of its wickedness. So, son of man, I have set you as a watchman for the house of Israel. You will hear the word from my mouth when you say to the sinner: You will die the death. If you do not speak, so that the wicked man can turn from his way, the wicked man will die for his wickedness: but I shall demand recompense from your hand for his blood. But if you tell the wicked man of his ways in good time, so that he can turn from his way, but he fails to turn, he will die for his wickedness: but you will have got away with your life.'

40   Gildas, *De excidio* 1.11, Winterbottom 88 (trans. 14): 'I used to say it was right that Peter was most blessed because he wholly confessed Christ, Judas most wretched because he loved greed: Stephen glorious because of his martyr's palm, Nicolas unhappy because of the stain of his foul heresy'. See Jerome, ep. 14.9, translated by F. A. Wright 1991 *Select Letters of St Jerome*, Loeb Classical Library 262, Cambridge MA: Harvard University Press, 46–47: 'Attendis Petrum, sed et Iudam considera; Stephanum suscipis, sed Nicolaum respice'. See also Gildas, *De excidio* 67, Winterbottom 119–120: 'Iudam quodammodo in Petri cathedra ... ac Nicolaum in loco Stephani martyris statuunt immundae haereseos adinuentorem'. For more discussion on the use of these opposing images, see O'Loughlin, Thomas 2012 *Gildas and the Scriptures: Observing the World through a Biblical Lens*, Turnhout: Brepols 134–136.

[*Turonensis* 92 / *Fragmenta* 6] 'Quae sunt honesta nostra his honorem habuntiorem circumdamus.' Iudicare ergo satis salubre est subiectos episcopis abbatibusque quorum sanguinem, si eos non bene regnant, de manibus requiret dominus: inoboedientes uero patribus sint sicut gentiles et publicani; et omnibus hominibus tam bonis quam malis praeter suos subiectos illud apostoli: existimantes omnes homines. Rel.[41]

Another scriptural passage in this section on leadership in the *Hibernensis* also reflects the influence of the *De excidio*. The rare use of 1 Tim 3:5 at *Hibernensis* 36.26 reflects *De excidio* 109.1:

[*Hibernensis* 36.26] Item: Quicumque domui sue bene praeesse nescit, quomodo aeclesie Dei potest habere regimina?[42]
[*De excidio* 109.1] Si quis autem domui suae praeesse nescit, quomodo ecclesiae dei diligentiam adhibebit?[43]

The effect is to turn the section in the *Hibernensis* on leadership from three attributed subsections that refer to Gildas' *Fragmenta* (36.5, 36.32, 36.37) to seven subsections (four unattributed) that refer to Gildas' *Fragmenta* and *De excidio* (36.4, 36.5, 36.22, 36.26, 36.31, 36.32, 36.37). Whilst in general the attributions in the *Hibernensis* are poor, as we can see above with the attribution of Jerome's letter to Heliodorus to Paul, there appears to be an awareness when compiling the *Hibernensis*

---

41 *Turonensis* 92, Elliot 712; Gildas, *Fragmenta* 6, Winterbottom 145 (trans. 82): '"Those parts of us that are honourable we surround with more lavish honour." Therefore it is quite proper for bishops and abbots to judge those beneath them, for their blood will be required at their hands by the Lord if they do not rule them well. But those who disobey their fathers shall be as heathen and publicans. And to all men, good and bad, besides their own subjects, in the words of the apostle: "Count all men …" and the rest.'
42 *Hibernensis* 36.26, Flechner 303: 'Likewise: But if a man does not know how to govern his own house, how is he able to steer the church of God?'
43 Gildas, *De excidio* 109.1, Winterbottom 140-141 (trans. 78): 'But if a man does not know how to govern his own house, how can he give due attention to the church of God?'

of placing selected elements of Gildas' *Fragmenta* within sections influenced by Gildas' *De excidio*.[44]

The *De excidio*, with its emphasis on the role of kings and bishops as *speculatores*, as the vocal good shepherds described by Isaiah, Ezekiel and John, clearly influenced the compilation of the *Hibernensis*, but citing Gildas directly on the duties attached to these roles appears not to have been part of the compilers' vision for the *Hibernensis*. In terms of bishops, this is, perhaps, understandable, as Gregory the Great also drew on the good shepherd in his works and, as above in *Hibernensis* 36.22, Gregory is the preferred authority, rightly in the sense of seniority, for commenting on role of the *speculator* in a clerical context. Gildas is directly quoted only once on the role of the bishop, a position drawn from the more moderate *Fragmenta*, one that, at best, alludes to the more strident prophetic criticism in the *De excidio*:

> [*Hibernensis* 1.16] De eo quod nullus debet iudicare episcopos. Gildas ait: Habent quippe sacerdotes et episcopi terribilem iudicem, cui pertinent et non nobis, de illis in utroque seculo iudicare. Item: Conepiscopus et coabbates nec non consubiectos non iudicare melius est.[45]
>
> [*Turonensis* 89 / *Fragmenta* 5] Habent quippe sacerdotes et episcopi terribilem iudicem cui pertinet non nobis de illis in utroque saeculo iudicare.[46]
>
> [*Turonensis* 94 / *Fragmenta* 7] Conepiscopos autem et conabbates et non subiectos non iudicare. Melius est ...[47]

---

[44] For the high level of poorly attributed citations in the *Hibernensis*, see Gorman, Michael 2011 Patristic and Pseudo-Patristic Citations in the *Collectio Hibernensis*, *Revue Bénédictine* 121, 18–93: 20.

[45] *Hibernensis* 1.16, Flechner 17 (trans. 541): 'Gildas said: Indeed, priests and bishops have a terrible judge, to whom it belongs, and not to us, to judge them in both worlds. Likewise: It is better not to judge fellow bishops and fellow abbots and fellow subjects.'

[46] Gildas, *Fragmenta* 5, Winterbottom 145 (trans. 83): 'For priests and bishops have a terrible judge; it is his task, not ours, to judge them in both worlds.'

[47] Gildas, *Fragmenta* 7, Winterbottom 145 (trans. 82): 'It is better for fellow bishops and abbots, and also fellow subjects, not to judge each other.'

This is backed up, perhaps, with the compilers' use of 1 Tim 3:1 at *Hibernensis* 1.1 and *Hibernensis* 1.7, again reflecting Gildas' use of 1 Tim 3 in the *De excidio*.[48]

It is, however, on the role of kings in *Hibernensis* 24 that the absence of Gildas is at its most profound. Whilst Gildas' criticisms of clerics could be replaced by the more senior authority of Gregory the Great, his criticisms of kings in the prophetic tradition in his *De excidio* remained relatively unique in an Insular, perhaps even a Continental, context.[49] Thus, when the compilers put together the section on kings, *De regno*, they led with a quote from Wis 6:2-7, taken directly from the *De excidio*, on the severity of divine punishment on sinful kings:[50]

> [*Hibernensis* 24.1] De increpatione regum. Liber Salamonis sapientiae: Audite ergo reges et intelligite, discite iudices finium terre, prebete aurem uos qui continetis multitudinem et placetis uobis in turbis nationum. Quoniam a Deo data est potestas et uirtus ab altissimo, qui interrogabit opera uestra et cogitationes uestras scrutabitur. Quoniam cum essetis ministri regni eius, non recte iudicastis neque custodistis legem iustiti neque secundum uoluntatem eius ambulastis. Horrende et celeriter apparebit uobis, quoniam iudicium durissimum in his qui presunt fiat. Exiguo

---

48   *Hibernensis* 1.1, Flechner 5: 'Paulus: Qui desiderat episcopatum, bonum opus desiderat'. *Hibernensis* 1.7, Flechner 8: 'Paulus: Si quis episcopatum cupit, bonum opus desiderat'. Gildas, *De excidio* 108.3, Winterbottom 140: 'Si quis episcopatum cupit, bonum opus desiderat'.

49   This can be seen with the influence of the *De excidio* on the Irish text, *De xii abusivis*, a critique of the secular and clerical orders also drawing on a prophetic tradition and possibly dating to 630-650. Like Gildas, it draws on Ezekiel in its criticisms of poor bishops in Caput X, and its criticism of bad kings in Caput IX echoes the sins assigned to the five kings by Gildas in *De excidio* 27, Winterbottom 99 ('peiuriantes, parricidis, adulteris, impius, iniusta'). For the dating and prophetic stance of the *De xii abusivis*, see Breen, Aidan 1987 The Evidence of Antique Irish Exegesis in Pseudo-Cyprian, 'De duodecim abusivis saeculi', *Proceedings of the Royal Irish Academy* 87C, 71-106: 76.

50   Wisdom 6:2-7 is not cited by any patristic author prior to Gildas except for Augustine's *Speculum*.

enim {eis} concedetur missericordia. Salamon: Potentes enim potenter tormenta sustinebunt.[51]

[*De excidio* 63] Sed transeamus ad cetera: 'audite', inquit, 'omnes reges et intellegite, discite, iudices finium terrae: praebete aures vos, qui continetis multitudines et placetis vobis in turbis nationum. Quoniam data est a deo potestas vobis et virtus ab altissimo, qui interrogabit opera vestra et cogitationes scrutabitur: quoniam cum essetis ministri regni illius, non recte iudicastis neque custodistis legem iustitiae neque secundum voluntatem eius ambulastis: horrende et celeriter apparebit vobis, quoniam iudicium durissimum his qui praesunt fiet. Exiguis enim conceditur misericordia, potentes autem potenter tormenta patientur.'[52]

The prophetic voice critical of kings was taken from Gildas and given back to the Bible, in this case Solomon. This tactic by the compilers is further reinforced by another original use of scripture in Gildas' criticism of kings, that of 2 Kgs 24:12–15, this time used in section 26 of the *Hibernensis* dedicated to sin and punishment ('De sceleribus et uindictis eorum'):[53]

---

51 *Hibernensis* 24.1, Flechner 165 (trans. 643): 'The book of Solomon's Wisdom: Hear therefore, o kings, and understand; learn, o judges of the ends of the earth; give ear, you who rule the multitude and who please yourselves in masses of nations. For power is given you by God, and strength by the most high, who will examine your works and inspect your thoughts. For when you were ministers of his kingdom, you have not judged rightly, nor kept the law of justice, nor went by his will. Horribly and speedily will he appear to you, for a most severe judgement shall be for them who bear rule. For to him who is little, mercy is granted. Solomon: The mighty shall be mightily tormented.'

52 Gildas, *De excidio* 63, Winterbottom 117 (trans. 51): 'But let us go on to what remains: "Hear, all you kings, and understand, learn, you judges of the ends of the earth; give ear you who control multitudes, and have your way among the thronging nations. God gave you your power; your virtue is from the most high. He will enquire into what you do, and scrutinise your thoughts. You were servants of his kingdom, yet you did not judge aright, or keep the law of justice, or walk according to his will; swiftly and dreadfully shall he come upon you, for those who rule shall receive the harshest judgement. Pity is granted to the small; but the powerful shall suffer powerful torments."'

53 No patristic author appears to cite Kings 24:12–15 prior to Gildas.

[*Hibernensis* 26.18] De uindictis in unum peccatum mutuatis per electionem peccantis. In Regum libro ad Dauid dicitur: Trium tibi optio datur, elige unum: utrum III-bus annis ueniet tibi famis aut tribus mensibus fugies aduersarios tuos aut certe III diebus erit pestilentia in terminis tuis. Dauid dicit: Melius est, ut incidam in manus Domini, quam hominum. Et moriuntur de populo a Dan usque Bersabe LXX milia uirorum eo quod numerauit Dauid populum suum.[54]

[*De excidio* 39.2–3] Quid David numerando populum evenit? dicente ad eum propheta Gaad: 'Haec dicit dominus: trium tibi optio datur: elige unum quod volueris ex his ut faciam tibi. Aut septem annis veniet tibi fames, aut tribus mensibus fugies adversarios tuos et illi te persequentur, aut certe tribus diebus erit pestilentia in terra tua.' Nam artatus tali condicione et volens magis incidere in manus misericordis dei quam hominum, LXX milium populi sui ...[55]

Once again, the authority of Gildas—as the originator of the biblical citation in the context of a prophetic criticism of kingship—is referred back to the authority of the Bible alone.

---

54 *Hibernensis* 26.18, Flechner 202 (trans. 668): 'That punishments for a sin are changed according to the sinner's choice. In the book of Kings David is told: A choice of three things is given you; choose one: either three years of famine shall come to you, or you shall flee three months before your adversaries, or for three days there shall be a pestilence in your land. David says: It is better that I should fall into the hands of the Lord, than of men. And there died of the people from Dan to Bersabee seventy thousand men, because David counted the people.'

55 Gildas, *De excidio* 39.2–3, Winterbottom 106 (trans. 37): 'What happened to David when he numbered his people? The prophet Gad said to him: "The Lord says this: You have a choice between three things. Choose which you want me to do to you. Either famine will come upon you for seven years, or you will flee from your enemies for three months and thy will pursue you, or there will be pestilence in your land for three days." Under the constraint of these choices, and wishing to fall into the hands of a merciful God rather than men, David was laid low by the death of seventy thousand of his people ...'

The intentions of the compilers in collating this section on kings in the *Hibernensis* can be adduced when we move a little further to sections 24.3 and 24.4 on recognising good and bad kingship from their works ('De eo quod malorum regum opera distruant'; 'De eo quod bonorum regum opera aedificentur'). Both sections—alluding to the *De excidio*'s prophetic emphasis on judgment according to deeds but taken from the apocryphal seventh-century Irish text critical of authority, *De xii abusivis*—are attributed to Patrick.[56] Significantly, this text places the role of bishop at the apex of secular and clerical orders, equal to or above that of kingship.[57] The authority of Gildas, reflecting his letter to Finnian, is now one of a contributer to canon law;

---

56 The *Hibernensis* accords the authorship of the *De xii abusivis* to Patrick. Usually authorship is assigned to Pseudo-Augustine or Pseudo-Cyprian. *Hibernensis* 24.3, Flechner 167–168: 'Patricius: Nonus abusionis gradus est, rex iniquus. Etenim regem non iniquum, sed correctorem iniquorum esse oportet. Inde in semet ipso nominis sui dignitatem custodire debet: nomen enim regis intellectualiter hoc retinet, ut subjectis omnibus rectoris officium procuret. Sed qualiter alios corrigere poterit, qui proprios mores, ne iniqui sint, non corrigit? quoniam in justitia regis exaltatur solium, et in veritate regis solidantur gubernacula populorum.' *Hibernensis* 24.4, Flechner 168–169: 'Patricius: Justitia vero regis est neminem injuste per potentiam opprimere, sine personarum acceptione inter virum et proximum suum juste judicare, advenis et pupillis et viduis defensorem esse, furta cohibere, adulteria punire, iniquos non exaltare, impudicos et histriones non nutrire, impios de terra perdere, parricidas et perjurantes vivere non sinere, ecclesias defendere, pauperes eleemosynis alere, justos super regni negotia constituere, senes et sapientes et sobrios consiliarios habere, magorum, ariolorum pythonissarumque superstitionibus non intendere, iracundiam differre, patriam fortiter et juste contra adversarios defendere, per omnia in Deo confidere, prosperitatibus animum non elevare, cuncta adversa patienter tolerare, fidem catholicam in Deum habere, filios suos non sinere impie agere, certis horis orationibus insistere, ante horas congruas cibum non gustare.' Breen notes that these are not garbled versions of the *De xii abusivis* but a deliberate synopsis and recasting of the original, perhaps taken from an intermediate source such as a synod. See Breen, The Date, Provenance and Authorship 107–108. For more on the *De xii abusivis*, see Professor Constant Mews' article in this volume.
57 For the potential of a bishop to be placed higher in status to that of a king in an Irish context, see Grigg, Julianna 2010 The Just King and *De duodecim abusiuis saeculi*, *Parergon* 27.1, 27–51: 46–48.

Gildas' role as a critic to kings has been given to Patrick. The effect intended by the compilers was to place the prophetic role of the edification of kingship within the apostolic succession.

Conclusion

The compilers of the *Hibernensis* harked back to Patrick and Gildas to affirm the authority of bishops to confirm and edify the kings of Ireland. The readjustment of the memory of Gildas, from an edifier of kings and bishops in the prophetic tradition to an ascetic voice emphasising respect for the church hierarchy and tolerance and moderation in the judgement of leaders, allowed the compilers to emphasise the memory of Patrick and, thus, the apostolic succession as the watchman or *speculator*. Within this readjustment, the compilers drew on a tradition that had recast elements of Gildas' *De excidio* as a Patrician construct. The memory of Gildas as a respected father of the Irish Church was adjusted to address a fundamental change in the nature of authority in Ireland, one that took the edification of secular and church leaders from monastic figures such as Columbanus and placed it in the hands of bishops, as exemplified by Patrick. The result, in an Irish context, was an emerging emphasis on Gildas as Gildas *Sapiens*, as the author of the *Fragmenta* and a contributor to canon law. Significantly, in a contemporary English context, a different image of Gildas was evolving, one that emphasised the *De excidio* and providential history: that of Gildas *Historicus*.[58]

---

58 Bede, *Ecclesiastical History* I. 22, edited by Bertram Colgrave and R. A. B. Mynors 1969 Oxford: Clarendon Press, 68: Qui inter alia inenarrabilium scelerum facta, quae historicus eorum Gildus flebili sermone describit.

8
Armes Prydein as a Legacy of Gildas
Lynette Olson

Roughly four centuries separate Gildas' *De excidio Britanniae* ('On the Downfall of Britain') and *Armes Prydein* ('The Prophecy of Britain').[1] This is not to say that tenth-century people couldn't understand what Gildas was about. No one does it better than Wulfstan, when he writes in *Sermo lupi ad Anglos* ('Sermon of the Wolf to the English'):

> There was a prophet of the people in the time of the Britons called Gildas. He wrote about their misdeeds, how they so angered God that in the end he caused the army of the English to conquer their land and utterly destroy the strength of the Britons. And that was the result of the irregularity of the clergy and the lawlessness of the laity.[2]

---

1 Editions of Gildas with translation: Winterbottom, Michael 1978 *Gildas: The Ruin of Britain and Other Works*, London: Phillimore; Williams, Hugh 1899/1901 *Gildas*, London: David Nutt, 2 vols. Editions of *Armes Prydein* with translation: Williams, Ifor & Bromwich, Rachel 1972 *Armes Prydein, The Prophecy of Britain, from the Book of Taliesin*, Dublin: Dublin Institute for Advanced Studies; Isaac, Graham 2007 *Armes Prydain Fawr* and St David, *St David of Wales: Cult, Church and Nation,* edited by J. Wyn Evans and Jonathan M. Wooding, Woodbridge: Boydell and Brewer 217–32.
2 As translated at the beginning of Winterbottom's Preface, *Gildas* 5 (actually the *Sermo* is early-eleventh-century, but Wulfstan's career began in the late tenth).

'Now, fellow English folk,' says Wulfstan in effect, 'God is going to get *us* for *our* sins: we're about to be taken over by the Danes.' And so they were, though with less catastrophic results than the Britons had suffered. Wulfstan could have known of Gildas via Bede, who in the early eighth century basically rewrote the historical section of Gildas' *De excidio Britanniae* in the early part of his *Historia Ecclesiastica*, or more directly.[3]

The use of Gildas' *De excidio Britanniae* by the compiler of the *Historia Brittonum* ('History of the Britons') in the early ninth century seems to be more often assumed than stated by modern scholars, although Heinrich Zimmer had no doubts when he wrote in *Nennius Vindicatus*:

> Nennius had as the basis for his work a kind of history of Britain, which consisted of two parts very different in nature: the cursory survey of the history of the British up to the time at which Gildas was writing with which in 540 he preceded his Jeremiad addressed to the nobility and clerics of the British ... The main activity of Nennius consisted in seeking to replace the Jeremiad of Gildas with a genuine secular history with facts and dates.[4]

The compiler's dates are ultimately owed to Bede. David Dumville considers that 'it seems likely that the author of *Historia Brittonum* did

---

3   Esp. I.12–16, 22; edited and translated by Colgrave, B. and Mynors, R. A. B. 1969 *Bede's Ecclesiastical History of the English People*, Oxford University Press 40–55, 66–9. Cf. Miller, Molly 1975 Bede's Use of Gildas, *English Historical Review* 90, 241–261.

4   'Als Grundlage für sein Werk hatte Nennius eine Art von Geschichte Brittanniens, die aus zwei sehr verschiedenartigen Theilen bestand: der von Gildas a. 540 seiner Strafpredigt an den Adel und Klerus der Britten vorausgeschickte flüchtige Überblick über die Geschichte der Britten bis zu der Zeit wo Gildas schrieb ... Die Hauptthätigkeit des Nennius bestand darin, dass er an Stelle der Jeremiade des Gildas ... eine wirkliche Profangeschichte mit Fakten und Daten zu setzen suchte', Zimmer, Heinrich 1893 *Nennius Vindicatus. Über Entstehung, Geschichte und Quellen der Historia Brittonum*, Berlin: Weidmannsche Buchhandlung 207–8: On the authorship of the *Historia* see Dumville, D. N. 1975/6 'Nennius' and the *Historia Brittonum*, *Studia Celtica*, 10/11, 78–95.

know Bede's History', and 'extremely likely that he had had access (and probably prolonged exposure) to Gildas's work'.[5] I would go further. Proof of his use of *De excidio Britanniae*, if any be needed, lies in one Old English loanword into Latin. Gildas writes that the first bunch of federate Saxons came in 'tribus, ut lingua eius exprimitur, cyulis, nostra longis navibus' ('three keels, as is expressed by their language, long ships in ours'). The *Historia Brittonum* has *tres ciulae*, using Gildas' English term, while Bede quotes Gildas' Latin gloss on it, *tribus longis navibus*; hence we can be confident both are directly citing Gildas.[6] Another borrowing by the author of the *Historia Brittonum* from Gildas is pointed out by Patrick Sims-Williams:

> The outcome of the war between the Bernicians and the Britons hung in the balance: 'yet at that time sometimes the enemies, sometimes the citizens were vanquished' (*in illo autem tempore aliquando hostes, nunc cives vincebantur*)—this is a deliberate echo of Gildas on the build-up, in the time of Ambrosius Aurelianus, to the earlier British victory at Badon: 'from that time on sometimes the citizens, sometimes the enemy, were victorious' (*ex eo tempore nunc cives, nunc hostes, vincebant*).

Sims-Williams sees the story of the death of Urien in the *Historia Brittonum* as 'an object lesson' in the context of 'the intermittent attempts to unite the Cymry against the Anglo-Saxons as a common foe so as to repeat the success of Badon—*Armes Prydein* being a well-known example from the tenth century.' And he goes on to say,

---

5 Dumville, David N. 1994 *Historia Brittonum*: An Insular History from the Carolingian Age, *Historiographie im frühen Mittelalter*, edited by Anton Scharer and Georg Scheibelreiter, Vienna: R. Oldenbourg Verlag 406–34: 434, 433.

6 *De Excidio Britanniae* 23.3, Winterbottom 97, translation mine; *Historia Brittonum* 31, edited & translated by Morris, John 1980 *Nennius: British History and The Welsh Annals*, London: Phillimore 67, 26 (as is pointed out by editor David N. Dumville 1985 *The* Historia Brittonum, *3. The 'Vatican' Recension*, Cambridge: D. S. Brewer 5, the tenth-century English author of the 'Vatican' recension [20, 82] has modernised the word to 'ceolae'); for the passage from Bede see n. 8 below.

'Following Gildas, the author attributes the initial Saxon settlement to Vortigern's rash gift of land in the east', pointing out that this is Thanet in the *Historia Brittonum* and *Armes Prydein*.[7] That is true in the broadest sense, although Gildas says that the Saxons were given supplies, not land. Bede actually does pretty well at rendering Gildas here, saying that the Britons gave the Saxons a place to stay, a place of habitation among them, stipends; *stipendia* rendering Gildas' *annonas*, *epimenia* and the other two, *locum manendi*, *locum habitationis inter eos*, not incompatible with the framework of *hospitalitas* which underlies his account, in which the Britons are the Saxons' *hospitibus*.[8] The deep thematic continuity from Gildas' *De excidio Britanniae* to *Armes Prydein* and beyond is the main subject of my paper, but first I want to say more about these two sources.

Gildas wrote prose, but, as Neil Wright observes, it is very poetic prose.[9] This is evident from his opening sally against the ruler of Dumnonia, 'Cuius tam nefandi piaculi non ignarus est inmundae leaenae Damnoniae tyrannicus catulus Constantinus'.[10] It is worth pointing out that the written word was commonly sounded at that time, even if persons were reading to themselves. In his study of 'Gildas and

---

7 Sims-Williams, P. 1996 The Death of Urien, *Cambrian Medieval Celtic Studies* 32, 25–56: quotations at 34–5.
8 'Tunc Anglorum siue Saxonum gens, inuitata a rege praefato, Brittaniam tribus longis nauibus aduehitur et in orientali parte insulae iubente eodem rege locum manendi, quasi pro patria pugnatura, re autem uera hanc expugnatura, suscipit. Inito ergo certamine cum hostibus, qui ab aquilone ad aciem uenerant, uictoriam sumsere Saxones. Quod ubi domi nuntiatum est, simul et insulae fertilitas ac segnitia Brettonum, mittitur confestim illo classis prolixior, armatorum ferens manum fortiorem, quae praemissae adiuncta cohorti inuincibilem fecit exercitum. Susceperunt ergo qui aduenerant, donantibus Brittanis, locum habitationis inter eos, ea condicione ut hi pro patriae pace et salute contra aduersarios militarent, illi militantibus debita stipendia conferrent', *Historia Ecclesiastica* I.15, Colgrave and Mynors 50.
9 Wright, N. 1985 Did Gildas read Orosius? *Cambridge Medieval Celtic Studies* 9, 31–42: 31, 33.
10 *De Excidio Britanniae* 28.1, Winterbottom 99. Neil Wright kindly pointed out to me that in the account of how this Constantine killed two royal youths 'under the cloak of a holy abbot' in a place of worship it is the youths rather than Constantine who were *sub amphibalo*, trying to shelter there from the murderous king.

Vernacular Poetry', which overall tends to stress the proximity of the Latin and vernacular traditions, Sims-Williams suggests that imagery from the latter may have influenced Gildas' expression in the former.[11] Yet Gildas does not share in the ethos of Brittonic panegyric, and one can just imagine what he would have done with Cynan and Cadwaladr, the heroes of *Armes Prydein*. To the last but not least of his rulers, Maglocunus, he complains:

> When the attention of your ears has been caught, it is not God's praises in the tuneful voice of Christ's soldiers sweetly singing which are heard, and the strain of the Church's melody, but your own praises, which are nothing, in the mouth of rascally bards filled with lies and liable to bedew bystanders with foaming phlegm, grating away like *Bacchantes*.[12]

It is the reference to music in the passage just quoted that convinces one that more than just the speech of court flatterers is involved. Clerics that Gildas was berating apparently shared in this fault:

> They yawn stupidly at the precepts of holy men—if they ever do hear them: though they should constantly; while they show alert interest in sports and the foolish stories of worldly men, as though they were the means to life and not death.[13]

---

11 Sims-Williams, P. 1984 Gildas and Vernacular Poetry, *Gildas: New Approaches*, edited by M. Lapidge and D. N. Dumville, Woodbridge: Boydell 169–92, esp. from 184 on.
12 I have been happy to insert 'bards' for *praecones* in Sims-Williams' translation, as he recommends, and accept that the parasites mentioned elsewhere are bards (*ibid.* 174ff.). *De Excidio Britanniae* 34.6, Winterbottom 103: 'Arrecto aurium auscultantur captu non dei laudes canora Christi tironum voce suaviter modulante neumaque ecclesiasticae melodiae, sed propriae, quae nihil sunt, furciferorum referto mendaciis simulque spumanti flegmate proximos quosque roscidaturo, praeconum ore ritu baccantium concrepante ...'
13 *De Excidio Britanniae* 66.4, Winterbottom 119, 52–3: 'ad praecepta sanctorum, si aliquando dumtaxat audierint, quae ab illis saepissime audienda erant, oscitantes ac stupidos, et ad ludicra et ineptas saecularium hominum fabulas, ac si iter vitae, quae mortis pandunt, strenuos et intentos ...'

As I have written elsewhere, the stories (and the music) were too good to abandon.[14]

What Gildas' *De excidio Britanniae* and *Armes Prydein* most obviously have in common is prophecy. Here we have to be careful to know what we are talking about. Let us return for a moment to Wulfstan's perceptive statement, which begins in Old English: 'Án þeódwita wæs on Britta tídum, Gildas hátte'. The word *þeódwita* literally means 'wise man or counselor of the people'.[15] Did the translator whom I quoted above stretch it too far to mean 'prophet'? Isn't this what the biblical prophets were? Gildas wrote in their tradition. He does mention non-biblical prophecy, interestingly from an English source:

> The winds were favourable; favourable too the omens and auguries, which prophesied, according to a sure portent among them, that they would live for three hundred years in the land towards which their prows were directed, and that for half the time, a hundred and fifty years, they would repeatedly lay it waste.[16]

Most interestingly, the verb *vaticinabatur* is the same as that quoted by Gildas from Jeremiah: 'falso prophetae vaticinantur in nomine meo'.[17] In the Old Testament tradition in which Gildas writes, true prophets don't practice divination or need omens, auguries or portents, they get their wisdom straight from God.[18] There is also, however, poetic inspiration: the *awen* with which *Armes Prydein* begins, which according to Rachel Bromwich

---

14 Olson, Lynette 2007 *The Early Middle Ages: The Birth of Europe*, Houndmills: Palgrave Macmillan 10.
15 Bosworth, Joseph and Toller, T. Northcote 1898 *An Anglo-Saxon Dictionary*, Oxford University Press, svv *þeód*, *wita* and *þeódwita* (where the Old English quotation is given, clearly to illustrate the meaning 'historian').
16 *De Excidio Britanniae* 23.3, Winterbottom 97, 26: 'secundis velis omine auguriisque, quibus vaticinabatur, certo apud eum praesagio, quod ter centum annis patriam, cui proras librabat, insideret, centum vero quinquaginta, hoc est dimidio temporis, saepius vastaret'.
17 *De Excidio Britanniae* 81.4, Winterbottom 127. Note however 'sancti vates' at 37.3, Winterbottom 105.
18 Cf. Griffiths, Margaret Enid 1937 *Early Vaticination in Welsh*, Cardiff: University of Wales Press, 10–11, 30.

originates in the common Celtic inheritance of technical terms associated with poetry, which are attested in Welsh and in Irish alike ... In both languages, the poet's 'inspiration' implied occult knowledge, and hence the ability to foretell the future.[19]

The rapid transformation of paganism into literary references, as seen in the fifth-century Latin panegyrics of Sidonius Apollinaris and eventually Milton invoking the Muse at the beginning of *Paradise Lost*, may well have had counterparts in vernacular poetry of the world of Gildas, for whom paganism belongs in the past; however, I don't think he would have cared much for them. Yet that is not the point. This paper is about *Armes Prydein* as a legacy of Gildas.

We have one explicit statement from the intervening centuries of how *De excidio Britanniae* was regarded among the Britons. In the Life of St Paul Aurelian, written by Wrmonoc, a priest and monk at Landévennec in western Brittany, in 884, one of Paul's fellow-monks at the Welsh monastery of Illtud is

> the holy Gildas, whose wisdom of nature, industry in reading and expertise in the sacred books of canons that book, well ordered by artful arranging, which they call *Ormesta Britanniae*, declares.[20]

A native name for *De excidio Britanniae* is intriguing. *Ormesta* is a Brittonic loan-word into Latin; but of which word? Is it *armes* 'prophecy' or *gormes* 'oppression'? Were it to be the former, then Gildas' work is another 'Prophecy of Britain' to set beside *Armes Prydein*. Discussion of the matter in Ifor Williams' edition is inconclusive and in the entry for 'Gildas' in the *Dictionary of Welsh Biography* he seems to be trying to have it both ways: 'the word "ormesta" being a Latin form of the Welsh word *armes* or *gormes* or a mixture of both words'.[21]

---

19 *Armes Prydein* line 1, I. Williams and Bromwich 2–3 with note on 17.
20 *Vita Sancti Pauli Aureliani* 3, edited by Cuissard, C. 1881–3 Vie de Saint Paul de Léon en Bretagne d'après un manuscrit de Fleury-sur-Loire conservé à la bibliothèque publique d'Orléans, *Revue celtique* 5, 421: 'Necnon et sanctum Gyldan cujus sagacitatem ingenii industriamque legendi atque in sacris canonum libris peritiam liber ille artificiosa compositus instructione quem Ormestam Britanniae vocant declarat ...' The translation above is mine.

Oliver Padel however has pointed out to me that its form with *O-* is more suggestive of *gormes* than *armes*.[22] This suits its application to Orosius' *History against the Pagans*, titled *Ormesta Mundi* in an apparently Breton context, which, written in the early fifth century to show that there were worse disasters in pagan than in Christian times, is full of oppression, tribulation and misery but not prophecy.[23] It also suits Wrmonoc's statement that Gildas wrote 'de ipsius insulae situ atque miseriis' and Gildas' reference to the latter in the first sentence of his work.[24] Yet Gildas is full of prophecy, and the context of his place and time is there throughout, just as it was for his models, the Old Testament prophets. In reading through *De excidio Britanniae* in Hugh Williams' copiously annotated edition and translation, I was struck by how consistently apposite the chosen biblical passages were to the secular circumstances outlined in the earlier sections of the *De excidio*. Kings are threatened with the loss of their kingdoms, and 'Weep ye priests that serve the Lord, saying, Spare, Lord, thy people; give not thine inheritance to reproach, and let not the Gentiles rule over them, lest the Gentiles say, Where is their God?' would have had powerful resonance among a people threatened by precisely that.[25] So there was a British, yes Celtic, tradition of poetic prophecy, but if anything it

---

21   Viewed at http://yba.llgc.org.uk/en/s-GILD-AS0-0495.html.
22   In private communication; I thank him for kindly answering my enquiry about this matter as well as reading this paper and suggesting a few emendations.
23   Cuissard 458–60, including a useful confirmation by H[enri] G[aidoz] on 459–60. Not everyone was convinced: A. Anscombe identified it as a misreading of *historia mundi* (1903 Ormesta, *Zeitschrift für celtische Philologie* 4, 463) and F. Lot as one of *de miseria mundi* (1927 rpt 1974 De la valeur historique du *De Excidio et Conquestu Britanniae* de Gildas, *Medieval Studies in Memory of Gertrude Schoepperle Loomis*, Geneva: Slatkine Reprints 230n). Cf. Lemoine, Louis 2006 Breton Early Medieval Manuscripts, *Celtic Culture: a Historical Encyclopedia*, edited by John T. Koch, vol. I, Santa Barbara CA: ABC-CLIO 257.
24   *Vita Sancti Pauli Aureliani* 3, Cuissard 421. For the Gildas reference see n. 46 below.
25   *De Excidio Britanniae* 83, H. Williams, 202–3: "'flete, sacerdotes, qui deservitis Domino, dicentes: parce, Domine, populo tuo et ne des hereditatem tuam in opprobrium et ne dominentur eorum gentes, uti ne dicant gentes: ubi est Deus eorum?'" (Joel 2:17).

would have made people even more receptive to the biblical prophecy of Gildas, and indeed his reference to English prophecy, and its application to their circumstances. An important legacy of Gildas to the culture of his people was a prophetic cast to their history. It would have been all the stronger since what Gildas had warned about had so obviously come to pass.

A greater legacy is the history itself, the story of the Britons. Gildas links his people to their pre-Roman ancestors.[26] It is what is said in the *Historia Brittonum* about Roman Britain that Dumville cites in support of the compiler's direct knowledge of Gildas' *De excidio*.[27] Consideration of *Armes Prydein* as a legacy of Gildas focuses on the Saxon settlement in Britain. In the poem the Saxons are ignoble foreigners whose rule in Britain is not by right of descent but by wrong of treachery. *Armes Prydein* has more immediate concerns, but these are subsumed in the centuries-old underlying grievances against the Saxons:

> how much of the country do they hold by right? / where are their lands, from whence they set forth? / where are their peoples? from what country do they come?[28]

A little further on in the poem are two lines for which modern translations differ, 'The kinsmen of Garmon will be paid back with vigour / the four hundred and four years' (Bromwich) to 'With the help of the kinsmen of Garmon, / the four years and the four hundred will be paid for' (Isaac).[29] I would offer a different explanation for Garmon,

---

26 Kelly, Matthew 1989 Aspects of Expression of Identity by the Britons: Fifth to Tenth Centuries AD, BA Honours thesis, Department of History, University of Sydney. So too Turner, Peter 2009 Identity in Gildas's *De excidio et conquestu Britanniae*, *Cambrian Medieval Celtic Studies* 58, 29–48: 35.
27 Dumville, *Historia Brittonum*: An Insular History from the Carolingian Age 432–3.
28 *Armes Prydein* lines 134–6, I. Williams and Bromwich 10–11: 'pwy meint eu dylyet or wlat a dalyant. / cw mae eu herw pan seilyassant. / cw mae eu kenedloed py vro pan doethant.'
29 *Armes Prydein* lines 145–6, I. Williams and Bromwich 12–13: 'ef talhawr o anawr Garmawn garant. / y pedeir blyned ar petwar cant.' Cf. Isaac 230.

the main cause of the difficulty, than either scholar. Bede says that the British called the Anglo-Saxons *Garmani* in his own day, so the 'kinsmen of Garmon' here are the English, which suits the context in this part of the poem very well.[30]

By the end of the poem, the Saxon settlement of Britain is rewinding: 'The foreigners (will be) starting for exile, / one (ship) after another, returning to their kinsmen, / the Saxons at anchor on the sea each day.'[31] This is just one example of maritime references to Saxons in the poem which seem to me particularly Gildasian.[32] In tracing this history back to Gildas I am not arguing that the poet of *Armes Prydein* necessarily knew *De excidio Britanniae* directly; Vortigern, Hengist, Horsa and Thanet of the *Historia Brittonum* if not vernacular tradition are present in the poem. There is a thematic difference: put simply, Gildas blames the Britons, not just their sins but the folly of the *consiliarii* and the *superbus tyrannus* in inviting in the English; *Armes Prydein* blames the English, with a couple of passing swipes at Vortigern.[33] Still, both the *De excidio* and *Armes Prydein* draw on a common memory of the Saxon settlement in Britain; moreover, it is memory that they helped to shape in a particularly significant way.

Here aid to our understanding comes from a rather unexpected source. Now I am no great fan of applying trendy modern concepts

---

30 *Historia Ecclesiastica* V.9, Colgrave and Mynors 476): 'Quarum in Germania plurimas nouerat esse nationes, a quibus Angli uel Saxones, qui nunc Brittaniam incolunt, genus et originem duxisse noscuntur; unde hactenus a uicina gente Brettonum corrupte Garmani nuncupantur.'

31 *Armes Prydein* lines 189-91, I. Williams and Bromwich 14-15: 'Allmyn ar gychwyn y alltudyd. / ol wrth ol attor ar eu hennyd. / Saesson wrth agor ar vor peunyd.'

32 Cf. Sidonius Apollinaris, *Epistulae* VIII.6.13-15 and 9.5 carmen lines 21-27, edited and translated by Anderson, W. B. 1965 *Sidonius. Poems and Letters*, vol. II, Cambridge MA and London: Harvard University Press 428-32 and 446, respectively, and *Carmina* VII lines 369-71, edited and translated by Anderson, W. B. 1980 *Sidonius. Poems and Letters*, vol. I, Cambridge MA and London: Harvard University Press 150 for seagoing Saxons.

33 Rebecca Thomas draws this distinction between *Armes Prydein* and the *Historia Brittonum*; I have extended it to Gildas. I am very grateful to her for kindly sending me a copy of her conference paper Memory and Identity in *Armes Prydein Vawr*.

to early medieval subjects, but have been struck by the appositeness of the following to ours. Paul Salopek applies it to Armenia: '"Chosen trauma" is how the political psychologist Vamik Volkan describes an ideology—a worldview—by which grief becomes a core of identity. It applies to entire nations as well as individuals. Chosen trauma unifies societies brutalised by mass violence. But it also can stoke an inward-looking nationalism.'[34] Volkan defines it as 'The image of a past event during which a large group suffered loss or experienced helplessness and humiliation in a conflict with a neighboring group.'[35] And elsewhere he writes, 'The chosen trauma becomes a significant marker for the large-group identity.'[36] It is thus a way of analysing how a society remembers its past and as such is applicable to the present study. What is at the heart of '*Armes Prydein* as a Legacy of Gildas' is a mother of all chosen traumas, the English settlement at the loss of the Britons. Gildas helped to shape it from the tradition of his time, giving it influential and enduring literary form. The poet of *Armes Prydein* took it and positively polished it in the interests of his day. That there was a large-group identity cannot be doubted. Rebecca Thomas identifies 'the poet's interest in Britain as a whole unit' and 'this vision of Britain as a single unit before the English settlements.'[37] This too is a legacy of Gildas. Sims-Williams writes of Gildas: 'Certainly, whatever his practical limitations, his aspiration is always to generalize about Britannia as a whole ... *Patria, insula*, and *Britannia* seem to be used synonymously.'[38] I would go even further and add *regio*, for he is not the only British scholar having trouble seeing that Gildas could refer to Britain as a *regio*, and consequently trying to work out what part of Britain Gildas is referring to by this term.[39] Yet compare *De excidio*, chapter 5:

---

34 Salopek, Paul, April 2016 Ghost Lands, *National Geographic* 108–131: 126.
35 Volkan, Vamik, Transgenerational Transmissions and 'Chosen Trauma', https://web.archive.org/web/20191207195729/https://www.vamikvolkan.net/.
36 Volkan, Vamik, Chosen Trauma. The Political Ideology of Entitlement, https://web.archive.org/web/20191207195729/https://www.vamikvolkan.net/.
37 Thomas, Memory and Identity.
38 Sims-Williams, P. 1983 Gildas and the Anglo-Saxons, *Cambridge Medieval Celtic Studies* 6, 1–30: 7 and n. 32.
39 E.g. Thompson, E. A. 1979 Gildas and the History of Britain, *Britannia* 10, 216.

The Roman kings, having won the rule of the world and subjugated all the neighbouring regions and islands towards the east, were able, thanks to their superior prestige, to impose peace for the first time on the Parthians, who border on India: whereupon wars ceased almost everywhere.[40]

Regio for Gildas could describe an area of considerable size. Sims-Williams concludes, 'In consequence the *De excidio*, whatever the geographical limitations of its author's effective knowledge, conveyed to posterity a strong sense of Britain's essential unity; Gildas has a fair claim to be regarded as the father of the concept of *Ynys Prydein* ("the Island of Britain"), which was to be so central to subsequent Welsh ideology.'[41]

As mentioned in passing, the poet of *Armes Prydein* clearly had a contemporary agenda, the details of which are much debated and need not detain us here, with one exception to which I will return.[42] Where scholars concur is on the overriding concern for political unity rather than fragmentation. Sims-Williams has been quoted to this effect above. Rebecca Thomas sees the poet's blaming of the English as concealing the disunity of the British. Dumville is another example, if what is said about Cynan and Cadwaladr in the poem is to be interpreted as meaning that 'after the victory there will be harmony between the victorious British leaders (not—the implication would then be—a quarrel over the spoils) and consequently a continuing British unity'.[43] And Helen Fulton writes,

---

40 *De Excidio Britanniae* 5.1, Winterbottom 90–1, 17–18: 'Etenim reges Romanorum cum orbis imperium obtinuissent subiugatisque finitimis quibusque regionibus vel insulis orientem versus primam Parthorum pacem Indorum confinium, qua peracta in omni paene terra tum cessavere bella, potioris famae viribus firmassent'.
41 Gildas and the Anglo-Saxons 30.
42 See the editions cited in n. 1 above; Dumville, D. N. 1983 Brittany and 'Armes Prydein Vawr', *Études celtiques* 20, 145–58, rpt 1993 in his Variorum collection, *Britons and Anglo-Saxons in the Early Middle Ages*, Aldershot XVI; Fulton, Helen 2001 Tenth-Century Wales and *Armes Prydein*, *Transactions of the Honourable Society of Cymmrodorion*, n. s. 7, 5–18.
43 Dumville, Brittany and 'Armes Prydein Vawr' 156.

The issue which unites the entire prophetic tradition in Welsh ... is that of leadership and succession, the devastation caused by the loss of a strong leader in Wales, the armed power struggle that ensues, and the Welsh hopes for victory under an emergent and often yet-to-be-discovered leader ... the clarion call of *Armes Prydein* suggests a Welsh political unity in opposition to the English.[44]

This concern too is a legacy of Gildas: 'External wars may have stopped, but not civil ones.'[45] According to his opening sentence Gildas published the *De excidio* 'grieving with the difficulties and miseries of the country (*patriae*) and rejoicing with its remedies'.[46] Gildas was a patriot and not without hope, so foresight in the *De Excidio* and *Armes Prydein* has something in common, but how much? The situations were rather different. Gildas' age had known peace from external wars, the last to do so, I would think, for a very long time. Certainly tenth-century Britain could not be described thus. What the Britons had done in defeating the barbarians and ruling themselves was extraordinary in the post-imperial West. To borrow from the modern folk-song, Gildas sang of danger and of a warning and about love between his brothers and sisters. Yet within living memory there had been good rulers both secular and sacred (bishops),[47] and could be again (otherwise Gildas' work loses its point). I think he would have liked to see Britain's cities, and certainly access to the shrines of martyrs he mentions, restored;[48]

---

44 Fulton, 17–18.
45 *De Excidio Britanniae* 26.2, Winterbottom 98, 28: 'cessantibus licet externis bellis, sed non civilibus'.
46 *De Excidio Britanniae* 1.1, Winterbottom 87: 'condolentis patriae incommoditatibus miseriisque eius ac remediis condelectantis'; translation mine.
47 *De Excidio Britanniae* 26.2–3, Winterbottom 99: 'et ob hoc reges, publici, privati, sacerdotes, ecclesiastici, suum quique ordinem servarunt. At illis decedentibus ...' and 31.1, Winterbottom 101: (to Vortipor) 'boni regis nequam fili'.
48 *De Excidio Britanniae* 26.2, Winterbottom 98: 'Sed ne nunc quidem, ut antea, civitates patriae inhabitantur; sed desertae dirutaeque hactenus squalent' and 10.2, Winterbottom 92: 'quorum nunc corporum sepulturae et passionum loca, si non lugubri divortio barbarorum quam plurima ob scelera nostra

more than this one cannot say. The poet of *Armes Prydein* sang (one is tempted to say dreamed) of British success, after centuries of loss, through unity and battle prowess, not moral rearmament. Though Christ and St David are invoked, the ethos of the poem, in much the same way as Jones observed concerning *The Song of Roland*,[49] is not Christian, with the most appalling ethnic cleansing, 'When corpses stand up, supporting each other, as far as the port of Sandwich—may it be blessed!'[50] About the unity I have a final point to make.

Armes Prydein forsees an alliance of the Cymry with the men of Dublin, the Irish of Ireland and the Isle of Man and Scotland, the men of Cornwall and of Strathclyde, and the Bretons; 'they will possess all from Manaw to Brittany, from Dyfed to Thanet, it will be theirs ...'[51] Here Bretons and Brittany have raised eyebrows, because the English king Athelstan, to whose reign *Armes Prydein* has usually been dated, is known to have supported the Breton exiles from the Vikings and ultimately assisted them in recovering Brittany. Dumville offers a number of explanations of how the poet could include Bretons in an anti-English alliance, but he favours 'the poet's powerful use of a pre-existing messianic legend—which foretold a pan-Brittonic alliance to drive out the English—in the immediate political context.' Brynley Roberts argues that

> The poem was composed as a response to a particular political situation in the tenth century ... but it derives its strength not merely from a reading of political possibilities and options, but from an emotional appeal to an accepted myth. There was small hope of ... Bretons joining such a coalition and the poet must have known this, but no appeal to the myth ... could omit them.

---

civibus adimerentur, non minimum intuentium mentibus ardorem divinae caritatis incuterent'.

49 Jones, George Fenwick 1963 *The Ethos of the Song of Roland*, Baltimore MD: Johns Hopkins Press.

50 *Armes Prydein* lines 187-8, I. Williams and Bromwich 14-15: 'pan safhwynt galaned wrth eu hennyd. / hyt yn Aber Santwic swynedic vyd.'

51 *Armes Prydein* lines 9-11, 15, 127-32, 147-54, 172-3, I. Williams and Bromwich 2-3, 10-11, 12-13; the last lines are 'o Vynaw hyt Lydaw yn eu llaw yt vyd. / o Dyuet hyt Danet wy bieiuyd.'

Armes Prydein is an example of the use of the Welsh historical myth in a specific contemporary context.

Dumville also inclines to this view, and concludes: 'The political world to which the myth applied stretched "o Vynaw hyt Lydaw".'[52] This is a legacy of Gildas. A pan-Brittonic alliance yes, but perish the thought that it should be anything more, as Dumville instructs us earlier in his article:

> This is no pan-Celtic coalition, a concept inconceivable at that period, but rather a grouping of all the Brython (of Wales, Strathclyde, Cornwall and Brittany) together with the other Insular peoples threatened by the consolidation of English political and military power.[53]

That was received wisdom when I was a postgraduate, but my resistance to it has grown over the years. The reason always given for why it is just an alliance of everyone who isn't English is that it includes the Vikings of Dublin, as if this one exception could rule out ethnic links among the rest. They are not even given an ethnic denominator, but are *gwyr* 'men' or *gynhon* 'gentiles', that is ' pagans' of the place *Dulyn*, unlike *gynhon Saesson* elsewhere in the poem.[54] Pagans could convert and acculturate. Perception of the results of the common Celtic cultural background such as what is said about poetic inspiration above—and entertainers travelled—is possible. True, perception of commonality with the Picts and Scots is not supported by Gildas, who likens them to 'dark throngs of worms who wriggle out of narrow fissures in the rock when the sun is high and the weather grows warm',[55] or Patrick's reference to those

---

52   Dumville, Brittany and 'Armes Prydein Vawr', 158, quoting Roberts, B. F. 1976 Geoffrey of Monmouth and Welsh Historical Tradition, *Nottingham Mediaeval Studies* 20, 29–40: 36.
53   Dumville, Brittany and 'Armes Prydein Vawr' 147.
54   *Armes Prydein* lines 9, 131, 176, I. Williams and Bromwich, 2–3, 10–11, 14–15, with notes on 21 and 56–7.
55   *De Excidio Britanniae* 19.1, Winterbottom, 94, 23: 'quasi in alto Titane incalescenteque caumate de artissimis foraminum caverniculis fusci vermiculorum cunei'.

who questioned his mission among Irish 'enemies who do not know God'.⁵⁶ Yet these Britons were part of the Christianisation of the Irish which linked these peoples. It is from the Irishman Columbanus that we have the first reference to Gildas: that Vinnian had consulted Gildas on a matter of monastic discipline, 'et elegantissime ille rescripsit' writes Columbanus, showing off a bit of eloquence of his own.⁵⁷ The First Life of St Samson of Dol, whose subject travels between Wales, Ireland, Cornwall and Brittany, is the most notable example of links between these regions, but they permeate Celtic hagiography.⁵⁸ Of course contemporaries would not have referred to a pan-Celtic consciousness as such, but we can.⁵⁹

---

56   *Confessio* 46, edited and translated by Hood, A. B. E. 1978 *St. Patrick: His Writings and Muirchu's Life,* London: Phillimore 32, 51: "'Iste quare se mittit in periculo inter hostes qui Deum non noverunt?'"
57   Epistula I.7, edited by Walker, G. S. M. 1957 *Sancti Columbani Opera,* Dublin: Institute for Advanced Studies 8.
58   See Lewis, Barry 2016 The Saints in Narratives of Conversion from the Brittonic-Speaking Regions, *The Introduction of Christianity into the Early Medieval Insular World: Converting the Isles I,* edited by Roy Flechner and Máire Ní Mhaonaigh, Turnhout: Brepols 431–56, esp. 439. An interesting study could be made of the geography of Celtic saints' lives: it is a curious world which does focus on the Celtic-speaking regions, does link them, does exclude England (presumably because it was pagan at the time the genre originated; the Lives of the Irish St Fursey, who was active in conversion there, are an obvious exception) but not Merovingian France or Rome or, in the Lives of St Petroc, the East.
59   There is one useful modern analogy to the term 'Celtic' which I would like to bring to the attention of a wider audience. It concerns the Dinka people of the Sudan, and is quoted from Finnegan, William, Jan. 25, 1999 The Invisible War, *The New Yorker* 60. 'There was so much to try to imagine in Nyamlell. I had seen one or two Dinka bulls at a distance from the village, their tremendous, lyre-shaped horns gliding above the tall grass. They were a reminder that everything one saw on a visit to a Dinka village was incidental, basically, to the real business, the main event, of Dinka life—the *wut*, or cattle camp, which moves with the seasons. There are Dinka groups who primarily fish or farm, but cattle-herding is the unrivalled center of Dinka social, economic, and religious life. Nyamlell might be the *baai*, the homestead, where grain is grown, but the *wut* is where a clan's wealth lives. "The *wut* is my nation," some Dinkas say, when asked about their political loyalties, and one *wut* may in fact wage war against another. On the other hand, the idea of

Armes Prydein as a Legacy of Gildas

In elucidating the deep thematic continuity from *De Excidio Britanniae* to *Armes Prydein*, this study has pointed out a number of legacies of Gildas to the culture of his people. One was a prophetic cast to their history. Another was the concept of Britain as a unit, which had clearly been extended to Brittany and arguably to an even wider common culture in *Armes Prydein*. Another was concern for British unity rather than civil war. The greatest legacy was the 'Welsh historical myth', their 'chosen trauma' in Volkan's more dynamic concept, of the loss of much of Britain to the English, to which Gildas gave influential and enduring literary form. In the terms of the subject of this book of collected studies, the two works draw upon a common memory, while their foresight has something in common albeit with a significant difference in ethos.

---

a "Dinka" nation is thoroughly misleading. The name derives by most accounts from a European explorer's poor transcription of one local chief's name. When I asked people around Nyamlell about their ethnicity, most said "Malual," which is a large tribal group, encompassing a great many *wut*. Nobody said "Dinka." There is a Dinka language, shared, in many versions, by everyone conventionally described as Dinka, and its speakers have in common many cultural values and practices. But there is not and never has been a Dinka paramount chief. The term remains useful.

9
A Woman's Fate: Deirdre and Gráinne throughout Literature

Roxanne T. Bodsworth

Despite the strong parallels in the medieval tales of the love stories of Deirdre and Naoise, Gráinne and Diarmuid, Deirdre has in subsequent literature been more often portrayed in sympathetic terms while Gráinne has been more often vilified. I suggest that the principal difference in the portrayal of these two female characters is because Deirdre is seen as a *victim* of fate, inspiring a heroic response from the predominantly male critics and writers, while Gráinne is seeking to determine her own destiny in a way that is perceived as unattractive even in contemporary times. Hence Thomas Kinsella's assertion that Gráinne's 'selection of Diarmuid over Finn seems more calculating than starry-eyed, and her appetite for manipulation is striking.'[1]

While these two stories have been compared by many scholars, this has mostly involved either consideration of the medieval versions or analysis of specific adaptations that emerged in the Irish Literary Revival. By examining the different literary representations of these female characters from the medieval to the present day, this paper demonstrates the differing attitudes towards the culpability of Deirdre and Gráinne in the tragic consequences that follow their elopement with a hero-lover. Deirdre, despite all her endeavours, is presented as

---

1   Kinsella, T. E. 2009 *The Pursuit of Diarmuid and Grainne and the Exile of the Sons of Uisliu*, Rochester NY: Old Baldy Press 10.

having no control over her predetermined fate while Gráinne does. Hence, Deirdre can be forgiven for breaching social expectations and is presented in revival and contemporary literature as a victim of fate, while Gráinne is frequently depicted as a self-interested and manipulative woman.

Both stories reinforce the idea that a beautiful and independent woman is a danger to male autonomy and social stability. Irish poet, Eiléan Ní Chuilleanáin, suggests that the socio-historical image of women arises firstly in the folk imagination before it becomes anything else.[2] Whether these images made their way into the medieval texts from a pre-existent oral culture or whether they were constructed by the monks who wrote them down is a matter of scholarly contention. There are strong arguments from both sides, but Kim McCone makes the point that 'for all its diversity, early Irish literature as a whole is rooted in a coherent, far-reaching and flexible construct or *senchus* adapted, synthesised and modified by monastic men of letters from the Bible and other Latin writings in conjunction with vernacular traditions both oral and increasingly, as time went on, written.'[3] What is most significant for this examination of the stories is that they were, in their medieval form, predominantly written by men, read by men, and told by men.

Inescapably, the transmission of the stories from the monastic pens was influenced by both their religious devotion and the sublimation of their masculinity into religious life. This may explain the paradoxical tension which characterises many of the Irish stories, where the desire for the woman is coupled with the anxiety of an emasculating loss of autonomy and social status. Lisa Bitel writes that the woman 'tends to be depicted as the object rather than the subject of the narrative, reflecting the projected desires and fears of the male author and his audience rather than her own.'[4] The stories demonstrated that when

---

2 Ní Chuilleanáin, Eiléan 1985 Introduction, *Irish Women: Image and Achievement*, Dublin: Arlen House 1.
3 McCone, Kim 2000 *Pagan Past and Christian Present in Early Irish Literature*, Maynooth: Department of Old Irish ix.
4 Bitel, Lisa M. 1996 *Land of Women: Tales of Sex and Gender from Early Ireland*, New York: Cornell University Press 4.

enslaved to a woman's beauty and his desires, the man could no longer fulfil his social and heroic functions.

This sexual tension continued to be transmitted when the stories were translated into English and then interpreted by two classes of revivalist author. Firstly there were those antiquarians and Celticists primarily interested in the collection of folklore and traditional stories, such as Thomas Crofton Croker (1798–1854), Kuno Meyer (1858–1919), and Eleanor Hull (1860–1935).[5] Secondly, there were those who wanted to use the stories to cultivate a nationalist cultural identification among the Irish people by educating them about their own mythological collection, by bringing the stories from the halls of academia to the common people, and thereby stimulating a pride in the Irish culture and identity. Included in this second group are writers such as Standish James O'Grady (1846–1928), Lady Gregory (1852–1932), Douglas Hyde (1860–1949) and W. B. Yeats (1865–1939).[6]

While the interpretations of the former are still filtered through the context of their personal experience and understanding, the latter have more marked nationalist agendas that thematically shape the reconstruction of the stories. The representation of women in the various translations and adaptations is particularly reflective of attitudes towards women and their place in the social paradigm, though not necessarily on a conscious level. This has been the case throughout

---

5   For a discussion of the contribution of Thomas Crofton Croker see Markey, Anne 2006 The Discovery of Irish Folklore, *New Hibernia Review / Iris Éireannach Nua* 10.4, 26–29. For a brief biography of Kuno Meyer and a summary of his works see Welch, Robert, editor 1996 *The Oxford Companion to Irish Literature*, Oxford: Clarendon Press 365. For a brief biography of Eleanor Hull and a summary of her works see Holmes, Janice 2002 The Century of Religious Zeal, 1800–74, *The Field Day Anthology of Irish Writing IV: Irish Women's Writing and Traditions,* edited by Angela Bourke *et al.* Cork University Press 537–568: 569.

6   See Hull, Eleanor 1916 Standish Hayes O'Grady: A Personal Reminiscence, *Studies: An Irish Quarterly Review* 5.17, 96–103; Doyle, Maria-Elena 1999 A Spindle for the Battle: Feminism, Myth, and the Woman-Nation in Irish Revival Drama, *Theatre Journal* 51.1, 33–46: 34–41; Dunleavy, Janet Egleson and Dunleavy, Gareth W. 1991 *Douglas Hyde: A Maker of Modern Ireland,* Berkeley: University of California Press; Ellmann, Richard 1948 *Yeats: The Man and the Masks,* New York: W. W. Norton and Co.

Irish literary history, including the pre-Norman period, when Bitel says that while gender issues may not have been consciously considered by ordinary people, nevertheless the ideologies of the elite trickled down in what she termed 'vivid tales', as well as in jurist's handbooks, and the lives of saints:

> If people could not read the stories of the literati, they certainly encountered them as repeated around the fire or told along the road. Everyone knew what women were supposed to be and do, and everyone understood that women did not always obey.[7]

The stories, of course, usually concluded with the dire consequences that arose from the disobedience of the women, and this did not change with the adaptations of the Literary Revival of the late nineteenth to early twentieth centuries. While some of the translators, editors and revivalist storytellers were women, they did not undertake this work in order to challenge the orthodoxy of the storytelling in regards to female representation. For example, Lady Gregory's primary consideration was the cultural recognition of Irishness in the stories. Her alterations were focused more upon further romanticising the stories and highlighting the heroic aspects than revising the representation of women.[8] Nevertheless, from the research and publications of Eleanor Hull (1860–1935) to the nationalist poetry of Lady Wilde (1821–1896) using the pen-name of 'Speranza', to the wide-ranging contributions of Lady Gregory (1852–1932), women had entered the field of Irish literature.[9]

Yet it remained male-dominated and while the stories underwent a great deal of change, especially during the Literary Revival, the basic narrative structure was retained as one that perpetuated the theme of the devastating effects of female beauty. While there are many variant texts for both Deirdre and Gráinne, I will mainly refer here to *Longes*

---

7   Bitel 234.
8   Doyle 35–37.
9   Quinn, Antoinette 2002 Ireland/Herland: Women and Literary Nationalism 1845–1916, *The Field Day Anthology of Irish Writing V: Irish Women's Writing and Traditions*, edited by Angela Bourke *et al.* Cork University Press 895–920: 895–900.

mac nUislenn (The Exile of the Sons of Uisliu) as a version of the Deirdre story that was used as foundation material for creative development in the Revival, and for the same reasons, use *Tóruigheacht Dhiarmada Agus Ghráine* (The Pursuit of Diarmuid and Gráinne) for Gráinne.[10]

In both of these stories, a young maiden is betrothed to an older suitor who is a highly respected societal leader. The maiden elects rather to choose her own lover but the young warrior is loyal to his leader and initially rejects her overtures. She then compels her chosen to elope with her. Gráinne does this by laying a *geas* upon Diarmuid; Deirdre by threatening shame upon Naoise. The couple is then pursued by the rejected suitor, forced to live in the wild by their wits and survival skills, until eventually a peaceful return to civilised society is negotiated. The rejected suitor, however, is traitorous and instead engineers the death of the young usurper and this betrayal, in turn, causes the leader to lose respect and therefore authority, with a consequential social upheaval. The stories do diverge at the end, with Deirdre committing suicide while Gráinne survives, but the greatest difference is found at the beginning where one woman, Deirdre, is declared to be predestined to a life of destruction while the other, Gráinne, makes her own choices.

Longes mac nUislenn (The Exile of the Sons of Uisliu) is the oldest known version of the Deirdre story. While Vernam Hull suggests that the story was likely written in the ninth or even the eighth century based upon the language used, Máire Herbert considers it more likely to have been compiled in the period of transition from Old to Middle Irish, that is the tenth century.[11] In *The Exile*, Deirdre cries out from the womb before her birth in the hearing of the king, Conchobar mac Nessa, and his retinue, who have descended upon the household where

---

10 Hull, Vernam 1949 *Longes Mac n-Uislenn: The Exile of the Sons of Uisliu*, New York: The Modern Language Association of America; Ní Shéaghdha, Nessa 1967 *Tóruigheacht Dhiarmada agus Ghráinne: The Pursuit of Diarmaid and Gráinne*, Dublin: Irish Texts Society.

11 Herbert, Máire 1992 The Universe of Male and Female: A Reading of the Deirdre Story, *Celtic Languages and Celtic Peoples: Proceedings of the Second North American Congress of Celtic Studies*, edited by Cyril J. Byrne, Margaret Harry and Pádraig Ó Siadhail, Halifax NS: St Mary's University 53–64: 53.

she is to be born. Prophecies are then made that she will be a beautiful woman who will cause the destruction of the kingdom of Ulster, and further prophecy specifically details those who will be impacted by this destruction including the Sons of Uisliu, being Naoise and his brothers. Herbert writes that:

> The public and private tragedies are traced back to a single, simple cause. That cause is Deirdre, the 'woman of fate'. She was responsible for the death and exile of great men. She offended against the king who apparently professed love for her. She led to his doom a fine warrior whose praise is extolled at length.[12]

There is no escaping the predetermined tragedy of Deirdre's life but paradoxically, instead of engendering condemnation of Deirdre, it seems to render authors and audiences sympathetic. Even in the medieval narration of *The Exile*, it earns the sympathy of the king who, rather than have her killed as his warriors demand, chooses instead to have her reared under his protection, kept separate to society until she is ready to be his queen.[13]

No such prophecies accompany Gráinne; she is simply a woman exercising her own will. In the seventeenth-century *Tóruigheacht Dhiarmada Agus Ghráine (The Pursuit of Diarmuid and Gráinne)*, she is a woman grown and living at her father's castle when Finn's proposal is presented to her by two of his warriors. The emissaries are told by her father, King Cormac, that she has rejected all other suitors and is likely to do the same this time as well. Quite clearly, the final decision is up to her, but surprisingly she seems to accept the proposal.[14]

However, on seeing Finn, she decides she would rather have Diarmuid. Here the two stories intersect again: at her betrothal feast, Gráinne asks the druid about the man who has 'the curling jetblack hair and the two crimson red cheeks ...'[15] Deirdre also describes a

---

12 Herbert, Máire 1991 Celtic Heroine? The Archaeology of the Deirdre story, *Gender in Irish Writing*, edited by Toni O'Brien Johnson and David Cairns, Bristol: Open University Press 13–22: 21.
13 Hull, Vernam 62.
14 Ní Shéaghdha 5.

dream-lover with 'hair like the raven, and a cheek like blood, and a body like snow', identified for her as Naoise.[16] In his examination of the irresistibility of Diarmuid and Naoise, Damian McManus determined that physical beauty was understood to be 'a guarantee of quality in a hero.'[17] Once seen, no other can be considered a suitable lover.

At her betrothal feast to Finn, Gráinne gives everyone a sleeping draught apart from Diarmuid and his companions. In a roundabout fashion, she then informs Diarmuid that he is her choice and when Diarmuid is unwilling, places him:

> under bonds (lit. tabus) of strife and destruction ... that is, the pain of a woman in childbirth and the vision of a dead man over water ... if you do not take me with you out of this house ...[18]

When he seeks the counsel of his companions, they tell him that he has no choice. Similarly, in *The Exile*, Deirdre takes hold of Naoise by his ears and threatens shame on him for all his life if he will not take her. In this way, the young heroes cannot be held accountable for their betrayal of their leaders and this is repeated throughout the stories to make it quite clear that it is the women who have compelled the ill deed.

Yet in the development of Deirdre's character from the ninth-century *Exile* where she is clearly described as responsible for everyone's deaths, to the fifteenth-century version *Oidheadh Chloinne hUisneach: The Violent Death of the Sons of Uisneach*[19] where she is gifted with prescience and wisdom, through to its treatment by the writers of the Revival, Deirdre's character becomes increasingly passive as she succumbs to her fate. She becomes a victim rather than a compelling force, such that Eleanor Hull as early as 1904 commented that:

---

15   Ní Shéaghdha 9.
16   Hull, Vernam 63.
17   McManus, Damian 2009 Good-Looking and Irresistible: The Hero from Early Irish Saga to Classical Poetry, *Ériu* 59, 57–109: 66.
18   Ní Shéaghdha 11.
19   Mac Giolla Léith, Caoimhín 1993 *Oidheadh Chloinne hUisneach: The Violent Death of the Children of Uisneach*, London: Irish Texts Society.

The Deirdre of the ancient tale, forceful of purpose, fiercely determined at all hazards to gain her ends, and, spite of the steadfastness and strength of her devotion, showing in her conduct the savagery of an untamed nature, becomes softened ... into the tearful, sentimental maiden ... It is curious to find the wild woman of the 12th century Book of Leinster version transformed into the Lydia Languish of a later age.[20]

Deirdre's aggressive threat of shame upon Naoise is progressively forgiven over time, but conversely, the trajectory is reversed for the story of Gráinne with *The Pursuit* being a later expansion of the story demonstrating that Gráinne has been increasingly vilified. According to Nessa Ní Shéaghdha, there are at least forty-one manuscript versions of *The Pursuit* and the imposition of the *geas* is mentioned in only three of them with the others either simply stating that Gráinne proposed to Diarmuid, or just that they eloped.[21] Nevertheless, the *geas* is included in Ní Shéaghdha's translation and also in Standish O'Grady's 1857 translation, among other episodes that serve to demonstrate Gráinne's manipulative and self-serving inclinations.[22] For her translation, Ní Shéaghdha chose the earliest version written by Dáibhídh Ó Duibhgeannáin, a highly regarded scribe, in 1651.[23] O'Grady mentioned two sources for his translation of *The Pursuit* and other Fenian tales but the manuscript he used for *The Pursuit* is no longer extant.[24]

This negative portrayal of Gráinne was not apparent in the earlier texts such as the tenth-century *Finn and Gráinne* which gives an account of the wooing of Gráinne by Finn that demonstrates her reluctance from the outset and her growing hatred of Finn as her husband. When Finn overhears Gráinne telling her father of this, Finn

---

20 Hull, Eleanor 1904 The Story of Deirdre, in Its Bearing on the Social Development of the Folk-Tale, *Folklore* 15, 224–39: 225.
21 Ní Shéaghdha xxvii.
22 O'Grady, Standish Hayes 1855 *The Pursuit of Diarmuid O'Duibhne, and Gráinne the Daughter of Cormac Mac Airt, King of Ireland in the Third Century*, New York: Johnson Reprint Corporation 55.
23 Ní Shéaghdha xiv.
24 Ní Shéaghdha xv.

says that it is time for them to separate.[25] Similarly, the tenth-century *Tochmarc Ailbe* (The Wooing of Ailbe) describes conflict between Cormac and Finn, caused because:

> Gráinne had been given in marriage to Finn although she hated him, and had given her love to Diarmait descendent of Duibne.[26]

These representations present rather a more sympathetic view of Gráinne's situation as a reluctant and unhappy wife, which must have been the case for many women in the highly hierarchical Irish society where marriages were primarily economic and political arrangements.[27] Nevertheless, allowances were made in Irish law for the dissolution of unhappy marriages under certain conditions, and *The Separation of Finn and Gráinne* illustrates this right. Máirín Ní Dhonnchadha comments that *The Separation* concerns what she calls the 'restoration of order after marital breakdown.'[28] The important point is that many of the earlier versions show Gráinne as a woman trying to escape from an unhappy marriage to be with a man she can love, rather than the harridan of later versions.

Gráinne's demonisation was also apparent in folk culture, though it cannot be determined if this negative slant was operating as an influence upon the literary or was determined by it. J. F. Campbell's 1860 collection of oral stories includes one version where Gráinne's pursuit of Diarmuid was so insistent and his resistance such that he placed her under spells so she would not appear before him either by night or day, clothed or unclothed, on foot or on horseback, in company or without company. It was only when Gráinne had overcome the restrictions of the spells that Diarmuid eloped with

---

25 Ó Corráin, Donnchadh 2002 Early Medieval Law, c. 700–1200, *The Field Day Anthology of Irish Writing IV*, Cork University Press 6–43: 36–37.
26 Carey, John, Tochmarc Ailbe: The Wooing of Ailbe, unpublished translation (acquired 2016) 3.
27 Kelly, Fergus 2003 *A Guide to Early Irish Law*, Dublin: Dublin Institute for Advanced Studies 70–73.
28 Ní Dhonnchadha, Máirín 2002 Natural and Unnatural Women, *The Field Day Anthology of Irish Writing IV*, Cork University Press 197–249: 225.

her.²⁹ Even so, there is a dichotomy within the folk tradition which may have reflected a male/female difference in perception. While Gráinne was vilified in *The Pursuit* and oral storytelling as the spoilt beautiful king's daughter who tore her lover away from his rightful place in male society, the distribution of dolmens across the country that are known folklorically as the beds of Diarmuid and Gráinne, as well as associated landmarks, attest not only to a widespread knowledge of the story separate to a literary tradition, but also to its popularity as a sexualised love story.³⁰

Máire Mhac an tSaoi alludes to this appeal in her poem, *Gráinne* (1956), where Mhac an tSaoi grants to Gráinne the wild, free nature ascribed to Deirdre in the works of the literary revival. She describes a vibrant young woman about to embark on a journey of 'Blinding love, ceaseless wandering...' and one that that will, while tragic, still be regarded as an experience of life to be envied by 'all the women of Ireland'.³¹ Gráinne's is the story of a woman who has escaped the restrictions of social expectation, followed her heart, and perhaps, if other women could not be so free, then at least they could visit the dolmens and dream about lovers who were. And from the imagination of poets such as Mhac an tSaoi, the representation of women in the stories undergoes subtle shifts and changes such that, as Ní Chuilleanáin writes, women can 'liberate themselves, through achievement in their work, and through their vision and insight as artists, from servitude to an image that has been imposed from without.'³²

Ní Dhonnchadha notes that in the versions which preceded *The Pursuit*, Gráinne's love for Diarmuid 'is fearless and unconditional.'³³ That the feeling is mutual is illustrated in two quatrains in the eleventh-

---

29   Campbell, John Gregorson 1891 *The Fians: Or, Stories, Poems, and Traditions of Fionn and His Warrior Band*, London: D. Nutt 52.
30   Murphy, Gerard 1933 *Duanaire Finn—The Book of the Lays of Fionn, Part III*, London: Irish Texts Society xxxv.
31   Mhac an tSaoi, Máire 2011 Gráinne, *An Paróiste Míorúilteach / the Miraculous Parish*, Dublin: The O'Brien Press 67–68.
32   Ní Chuilleanáin 1.
33   Ní Dhonnchadha 225.

century commentary in *Amra Choluim Chille* (Lament for Colum Cille). In the first, Gráinne sings:

> There is one on whom I should gladly gaze, for whom I would give the bright world, all of it, all of it, though it be an unequal bargain.[34]

In the second quatrain, Diarmuid tells her:

> Good is thy share, O Gráinne, better for thee than a kingdom the dainty flesh of the woodcocks with a drop of smooth mead.[35]

As well, the twelfth-century *Codail Beagán, Beagán Beag* (The Lullaby of Adventurous Love), where Gráinne singing above the sleeping Diarmuid expresses a clear devotion:

> The parting of us two is like the parting
> of children of one home; it is like the parting
> of body and soul, hero of fair Loch Carman.[36]

This mutual romantic affection is displaced in *The Pursuit* where the dominant theme indicates that Diarmuid is an unwilling lover, victim of a scheming, untrustworthy woman. So unwilling is Diarmuid that Gráinne even has to goad him into sex by challenging him that a drop of water on her thigh has more courage than he has shown. It is only when she issues this challenge to his masculinity that Diarmuid takes her as his wife and stops laying clues for Finn such as fish with no bites taken to indicate that he has stayed chaste and loyal.[37]

While there is a developing vilification of Gráinne, the increasing beatification of Deirdre can seem at odds with the earliest versions of the Deirdre story. Edyta Lehmann establishes that in *The Exile*, Deirdre is repeatedly named as the cause of the death of the sons of Uisliu

---

34   Ní Shéaghdha xi.
35   Ní Shéaghdha xii.
36   Ní Dhonnchadha 224–226.
37   Ní Shéaghdha 33.

and the problems of Ulster, and while 'this overt assertion is repeatedly undermined in the text, giving way to other interpretations of her character, the explicit accusation is clearly prominent.'[38] Yet in *The Pursuit*, Lehmann finds only one occasion that explicitly points to Gráinne as a cause of Diarmuid's death.[39]

Deirdre's culpability is not only undermined throughout *The Exile*, but also in the adaptations of the literary revival where she is presented as both a victim of fate and a free spirit. These adaptations include Standish O'Grady's *Deirdre* (1894), which greatly romanticises and embroiders *The Exile*, having Deirdre immured in a forest rather than simply kept within a separate fort, with a god-like Naoise who is immediately enamoured of Deirdre and very willing to be her lover.[40] In her highly romanticised version (1902), Lady Gregory closely follows O'Grady, similarly having Deirdre growing up as a wild, isolated child.

> Deirdre grew straight and clean like a rush on the bog, and she was comely beyond comparison of all the women of the world, and her movements were like the swan on the wave, or the deer on the hill.[41]

Conchobar is treated more kindly in both of these adaptations, where both the king and Naoise are portrayed as driven purely by the forces of love, ultimately towards great tragedy.

Yeats introduces more ambiguity into his 1907 play, *Deirdre*, which begins, as does the sixteenth-century *The Violent Death of the Children of Uisneach*, with the return of Naoise and Deirdre from exile, though he also refers back to her upbringing in wild isolation.[42] Yeats demonstrates how different interpretations can be placed upon the

---

38 Lehmann, Edyta 2010 The Woman Who Wasn't There: Preliminary Observations on the Perplexing Presence and Absence of the Character of Gráinne in the Tóruigheacht Dhiarmada agus Ghráinne, *Proceedings of the Harvard Celtic Colloquium* 30, 116–126: 177.
39 Lehmann 117.
40 O'Grady, Standish James 1894 Deirdre, *The Coming of Cuculain*, New York: Frederick A. Stokes Co. 71–91.
41 Gregory, I. A. 1902 Fate of the Children of Usnach, *Lady Gregory's Complete Irish Mythology*, New York: Chancellor Press 398–420: 399.

moral culpability of the heroine, for example, whether it was Deirdre who lured Naoise away or Naoise who wooed Deirdre. She can appear, in the play, to be deceitful and manipulative, even inconstant, but all the while the audience is made fully aware that it is always to save Naoise from death. Cleverly, Yeats even has Deirdre give her bracelet to one of the singers to prove that this is, indeed, the correct version: 'because you are wearing this / To show that you have Deirdre's story right.'[43] Perhaps Yeats was also implying that his understanding of the story may have had greater insight than that told otherwise. While it is a highly lyricised and stylistic adaptation, particularly with the incorporation of singers who relate the unfolding legend in traditional bardic style, it also offers a new complexity to the depiction of Deirdre.

However, she is returned to the innocent victim in James Stephens' novel, *Deirdre* (1923), another even more highly romanticised adaptation where, rather than being a wild and wilful woman, Deirdre is gentle and peaceful in keeping with her natural and innocent upbringing.[44] While Stephens'depiction was precisely the sort of representation of Deirdre that Eleanor Hull had earlier railed against, such a woman, it seems, is far easier to love from a male perspective, far less threatening to the masculine ideal. In need of rescue from an ominous marriage to the king, she presents an opportunity for the hero to demonstrate his masculine chivalry rather than depriving him of his honour and standing.

Interestingly, Stephens shows great sympathy for women forced into sexual arrangements against their will, putting Deirdre's impending marriage to Conchobar in context of the king's previous disastrous marriage to the unwilling Medb of Connaught.[45] Stephens could even have been describing the feminist process of consciousness-raising when Deirdre's marriage to the king is impending and she attempts to take control of her own life:

---

42 Yeats, W. B. 1934 Deirdre, *The Collected Plays of W. B. Yeats*, London and Basingstoke: Macmillan 169-204: 171-179; Mac Giolla Léith 89-113.
43 Yeats, Deirdre 193-4.
44 Stephens, James 1923 *Deirdre*, London: Macmillan 17-18.
45 Stephens 15-16.

The sense that all the morrows were provided for, and that all the minutes of all the morrows were calculated and ordained, dropped from her for ever, for she had become at last an identity instead of a puppet to be pulled here and ordered there, and to do only what was willed by other people; for first the imagination awakes, and then the sense, and lastly the will, when the urge of life is focussed.[46]

Distressed, Deirdre seeks the aid of Naoise and his brothers. Though they will not support her initially, when she quite clearly states what the king will do to her sexually, and implies that she and Naoise have already had sexual engagements in the forest, Naoise is shamed into eloping with her. The brothers must accompany them to escape the king's vengeance.[47]

Synge's 1910 play, in comparison, strips away the romance, presenting Deirdre as a commonplace woman afraid of losing Naoise's love as she grows old and less beautiful.[48] Yet the very title of the play—'Deirdre of the Sorrows'—emphasises the tragedy of her life rather than any transgression on her part, and the emphasis on the prophecy (that almost becomes self-fulfilling) makes her a *victim* of destiny. The title also creates an association in the highly Catholic nation with 'Our Lady of the Sorrows', one of the titles given to Mary, mother of Jesus. While Deirdre is no saint in Synge's presentation, this nominative aligns her with the process of beatification.

While it has changed somewhat today, with many small theatre groups and musicians inspired by both stories, there were many more adaptations of the Deirdre story than there were of Gráinne's during the literary revival and that in itself demonstrates Deirdre's sympathetic appeal.

Adaptations of the Deirdre Story

1872 J. F. Campbell's collection of ballads

---

46 Stephens 90.
47 Stephens 144.
48 Synge, John Millington (1910) Deirdre of the Sorrows, *Collected Plays: John M. Synge*, Harmondsworth: Penguin 211–265.

1876 R. D. Joyce, *Deirdre*
1880s Samuel Ferguson's poems, 'Deirdre', 'Deirdre's Farewell to Alba', 'Deirdre's Lament for the Sons of Usnach'
1894 Standish O'Grady's chapter *Deirdre*
1896 John Todhunter's *Three Irish Bardic Tales: Being Metrical Versions of the Three Tales Known as the Three Sorrows of Story-Telling*
1902 Lady Gregory's *The Fate of the Children of Usnach*
1904 George Steele's *Deirdre: A Tale of Ancient Erin and Other Verse*
1907 W. B. Yeats's play *Deirdre*
1910 J. M. Synge's play *Deirdre of the Sorrows*
1923 James Stephens' *Deirdre*

Adaptations of the Gráinne Story

1901 play by George Moore and W. B. Yeats *Diarmuid and Grania*
1904 Lady Gregory's *Diarmuid and Grania*
1912 Lady Gregory's play *Grania*
1929 Yeats' poem *Lullaby*

Deirdre is a type of Miranda, untouched and uncontaminated by the world but with a royal future awaiting her. It proves impossible to then reconcile a naturally uninhibited nature such that, as Synge wrote, she has 'the birds to school her, and the pools in the river where she goes bathing in the sun ...'[49] with the trappings of queenhood. While Deirdre's transgression against societal expectations and her wilful rebellion against the prophecies may be more overtly stated than Gráinne's, yet Gráinne is a king's daughter well versed in social expectations and behaviour and so her sin is not so easily forgiven. Quite simply, she should have known better.

Considering *The Exile*, Máire Herbert argues that it is the king who has committed the greatest transgression in the story of Deirdre. The king was only empowered to authority through a just rule that brought prosperity to the land and he exceeds the limits of that authority when he attempts to control Deirdre's life. He pursues his own self-gratification above the interests of his province.[50]

---

49   Synge 216

The nature of sin is especially significant considering the Christian sensibilities of the authors of the medieval texts. As Herbert explains, not only has Deirdre defied the king and entered into an unlawful union with Naoise, when she is captive to the king she commits suicide, considered a mortal sin. Herbert asserts that this influenced the way that the religious authors constructed the story, because 'her depiction had to be made to reflect her culpability.'[51] While the authors retained what she calls 'the original narrative framework', they also inserted material 'which manipulated the rhetoric of the characters so that woman as subversive, as denier of rightful male authority, could be brought into focus.'[52] While the overall tone of the story demonstrates the recklessness of female disobedience, the conclusion with Deirdre's suicide takes it into the realm of the unforgiveable. However, even within the church there could be some sympathy shown for suicide in the face of impending or actual rape. Ní Dhonnchadha writes that:

> In the literature, female suicide is characterised by association with the threat or actuality of sexual violation. This suggests an understanding that ... such violation led naturally to personal disintegration and complete loss of self in suicide.[53]

She proposes that this may have been the thinking of some of the Fathers of the Church when they absolved the sin where suicide had been committed in rape cases.[54]

Perversely, the tragic ending works in Deirdre's favour as far as engendering sympathy and forgiveness, along with many other factors. There is the prophecy, that she is ill-fated through no fault of her own; that she is raised free and innocent of the usual machinations of societal relationships; she seems perfectly content in her life with Naoise in exile living in the wild without luxury; and at the end of the story she raises a lament for her lover that still resonates with contemporary

---

50   Herbert, The Universe of Male and Female 55.
51   Herbert, Celtic Heroine 21.
52   Herbert, Celtic Heroine 21.
53   Ní Dhonnchadha 169.
54   Ní Dhonnchadha 169.

musicians today. She is rendered powerless, then dies tragically, either by falling into the grave of Naoise and his brothers in *The Violent Death*, or after spending a year as Conchobar's sex slave when she leaps to her death after he has passed her on to another man in *The Exile*.[55] The adaptations of the Literary Revival maintain the tragedy of these conclusions.

In *The Pursuit*, however, Gráinne brought about her own downfall and that of her hero-lover through her own choices, not from any predetermined destiny. She was raised in society and fully aware of social etiquette if not accepting of its terms; she always seems dissatisfied with her lot, always wanting something more and pushing her lover to further limits. While Deirdre was content to live with Naoise indefinitely in the wild and it was her natural environment, Gráinne was obviously out of her element, tiring easily and needing to be carried for much of the story, even demanding that Diarmuid act dishonourably in acquiring magical berries. And after a peaceful return is negotiated, she still seeks further social integration, thereby bringing the adversaries into close and deadly contact. While bereft at the death of Diarmuid, to the extent that she falls from the wall and miscarries triplets, she remains self-possessed enough to call their living children to arms to avenge their father's death.

In an alternative ending popularly reinforced through Standish O'Grady's translation, Gráinne even marries Finn and makes a peace between him and her children.[56] Ní Shéaghdha asserts that this ending, used by O'Grady, resembles a late addition to the story found in only one of the forty-one manuscripts.[57] Caoimhín Breatnach contends, however, that there are significant discrepancies to be found in Ó Duibhgeannáin's version which are resolved in the longer version.[58] Because of this narrative cohesion, he argues that the longer version

---

55 Mac Giolla Léith 139; Hull, Vernam 69.
56 O'Grady, *The Pursuit* 209–210.
57 Ní Shéaghdha xviii.
58 Breatnach, Caoimhín 2012 The Transmission and Text of *Tóruigheacht Dhiarmada agus Ghráinne*: a Re-Appraisal, *The Gaelic Finn Tradition*, edited by Sharon J. Arbuthnot, and Geraldine Parsons, Dublin: Four Courts Press 139–150: 145.

with its conclusion of marriage between Finn and Gráinne may be closer to a more complete earlier non-extant version of the story.

However, as the principal theme of *The Pursuit* is the evasion of Finn, it seems a remarkably odd resolution to have Gráinne then marry Finn in the end, especially after he has orchestrated Diarmuid's death and she has called their children to arms to take their revenge. Kinsella states that 'her final acts are damning' when Gráinne distributes Diarmuid's arms to their children but keep his wealth for herself.[59] He considers the ending consistent with the theme of the struggle for power.[60] I would argue that the conclusion which sees Gráinne married to Finn is an anomaly, further censuring the idea of a self-determinative woman.

While Ní Shéaghdha has not reconstructed the story as an artistic artefact in the same way as the revivalist authors, her 1967 translation using Ó Duibhgeannáin's version effectively repositions Gráinne as a woman driven by her desire for love and, in the latter part of the story, for re-establishing the place of her family in society. Her translation offers a legitimate alternative to O'Grady's when undertaking an archaeological excavation of the story.

The writers of the Literary Revival and more contemporary writers, of course, were able to take a poetic licence with the stories, freely reconstructing them to highlight what they considered were the pertinent aspects. Synge presented Deirdre as afraid of losing her physical beauty in *Deirdre of the Sorrows*. A contemporary of his, Irish poet Winifred Letts, found beauty in the ageing and the decay, as part of the natural way of things, offering a different image of beauty to the traditional one.

> Deirdre is dead and all her beauty blown
> Like wind-swept petals underneath the thorn.
> If beauty dies, then beauty is new-born.
> And Deirdre met me in the street to-day,
> Her hair like blackbird's breasts, her shadowed eyes
> Like hazel-circled pools beneath grey skies ...[61]

---

59   Kinsella 24.
60   Kinsella 16.

Contemporary Irish authors still cannot escape the inculcation of the story into Irish consciousness. It is an image that emerges as romanticised tragedy even in the lesbian fiction by Emma Donoghue, in *Hood* when 'She opened her grey eyes until she is Deirdre of the Sorrows. She knows I'm a sucker for that look.'[62] The images are ingrained in contemporary thought from the repetition of stories devised and transmitted by a predominantly male authorship from medieval times to the present day. As Ní Chuilleanáin goes on to say:

> The image created by woman herself may supersede the one presented to her by history and society, but she remains a member of society, an interpreter of history, and thus can never ultimately separate herself from a historical image of the feminine.[63]

The stories of Gráinne and Deirdre have been presented from medieval to contemporary times in a way that reinforces the historical image of a beautiful and independent woman as one who is a danger to both male autonomy and social stability, even while paradoxically delivering oppositional representations with one woman whose fate is predetermined and one who makes her own destiny. This allows audiences to feel sorry for the former, Deirdre, and despise the latter, Gráinne, even while both tell a very similar story of a woman seeking to determine her own life in opposition to the expectations of the society in which she lives, otherwise known as the forces of fate.

---

61 Letts, Winifred M. 1926 Deirdre in the Streets, *The Field Day Anthology of Irish Writing* V 920.
62 Donoghue, Emma 1995 *Hood*, London: Penguin 42.
63 Ní Chuilleanáin 1.

10
'No Remission without Satisfaction': Canonical Influences on Secular Lawmaking in High Medieval Scotland

Cynthia J. Neville

Late in the summer of 1202, after hearing at first hand of a vicious assault on the bishop of Caithness in northern Scotland, Pope Innocent III addressed a letter to the occupant of the nearby See of Orkney. Here he set out in vivid detail the penance that the purported culprit, an otherwise unknown man by the name of Lumberd, must undertake to atone for his 'great and grievous' sin; he further ordered the bishop to ensure that each and every stage of the penance be carried out. The process involved a humiliating and arduous journey for Lumberd on foot—from Rome, no less—to the scene of the crime and, once home, the assumption of penitent garb, a fast on bread and water of fifteen days' duration and the public performance of a carefully prescribed regimen of spoken prayer and physical punishment. Only then, the pope's letter stated, might Bishop Bjarne offer Lumberd remission of his sin, and even this act of clemency was contingent on the offender's

I wish to acknowledge with thanks the support of the Social Sciences and Humanities Research Council of Canada, The Scottish Medievalists and the Humanities Research Centre at the Australian National University (ANU) in the research and writing of this chapter. I am especially indebted, for their insightful comments, to my ANU colleagues, Julie Hotchin, Tania Colwell, Janet Hadley Williams and Carole Newlands.

willingness to undertake an ongoing program of weekly fasts and a further three-year period of crusading in the Holy Land.[1]

Lumberd's brief appearance in papal record has intrinsic value in confirming the extensive reach of Pope Innocent III's influence and more than one scholar has duly noted this fact.[2] But the story is more important still because it lies at the nexus of several transformative developments in the medieval West, details of which, given the fragmentary nature of surviving Scottish record sources, are often impossible to reconstruct with certainty. These developments include, in the realm of ecclesiology, the intensification of church government in hundreds of localities under the direction of a reforming papacy; in political and cultural terms the ongoing expansion of the boundaries of Europe 'as a region and an idea'[3]; and in the economic sphere the struggle among several contenders for control of the great waterways of the North and Irish Seas. This article examines still another strand that runs through the Lumberd story, one that connects this otherwise obscure ruffian to a key moment in the ecclesiastical, political and legal history of Scotland. Lumberd's acts of reparation and Bishop Bjarne's role in overseeing them coincided with a period that saw the development of new ideas about kingship in the realm and the genesis of a successful partnership between ecclesiastical and secular authorities in the making of Scottish common law.

Recent scholarship has made it clear that construction of the 'state' in high medieval Scotland was a considerably more complex process than once thought; it was also, Alice Taylor has argued, one that involved close co-operation between the king and his greatest subjects.[4]

---

1 Innocent III, ep. V.79 edited by Migne, J.-P., *Patrologiae cursus completus, Series Latina*, 217 vols, Paris: Petit Montrouge 214.1062–3.
2 See, for example, Crawford, Barbara E. 1993 Norse Earls and Scottish Bishops in Caithness, *The Viking Age in Caithness, Orkney and the North Atlantic*, edited by Colleen E. Batey, Judith Jesch and Christopher D. Morris, Edinburgh University Press 129–47: 135.
3 Bartlett, Robert 1993 *The Making of Europe: Conquest, Colonization and Cultural Change 950–1350*, Princeton University Press 1.
4 This is the argument that runs through Taylor, Alice 2016 *The Shape of the State in Medieval Scotland, 1124–1290*, Oxford University Press; see especially her concluding remarks at 445–55. Earlier views—some of which argue for a

As was the case elsewhere in medieval Europe, a fundamental prerequisite of the growth of centralised political, legal and fiscal power was the rule of a single king, whose claims rested in turn on dynastic legitimacy. In Scotland, the century or so after 1180 witnessed strenuous efforts to put the building blocks of that state into place. Around the time that the boy king Alexander III succeeded to the throne in 1249, the legitimisation program saw royalist chroniclers begin to create for Alexander both a past and an image of kingship that reflected exemplars of princely authority found in neighbouring England and western Europe. Their goals were, first, to recast, reshape and rewrite the collective memory of royal rule in the kingdom by confirming the direct descendants of Malcolm III and the Anglo-Saxon princess Saint Margaret as the licit occupants of the throne; their second to demonstrate that the king of Scots embraced in image, word and deed the *mores* and practices of the 'civilised' Europe of his day.[5]

---

    less seamless process than Taylor suggests—are discussed in Neville, Cynthia J. 2012 Royal Mercy in Medieval Scotland, *Florilegium* 29, 1–30: 7–8.

5   For the concept of 'civilisation' implicit here see Gillingham, John 1994 1066 and the Introduction of Chivalry into England, *Law and Government in Medieval England and Normandy: Essays in Honour of Sir James Holt*, edited by George Garnett and John Hudson, Cambridge University Press 31–55; Gillingham, John 2000 Conquering the Barbarians: War and Chivalry in Twelfth-century Britain, *The English in the Twelfth Century: Imperialism, National Identity, and Political Values*, by John Gillingham, Woodbridge: Boydell 41–58; Davies, Rees 1993 The English State and the Celtic Peoples, 1100–1400, *Journal of Historical Sociology* 6, 1–14; Davies, R. R. 2000 *The First English Empire: Power and Identities in the British Isles 1093–1343*, Oxford University Press 113–41. Developments in Scotland in the thirteenth century are treated at length in Oram, Richard D. 2011 *Domination and Lordship: Scotland 1070–1230*, Edinburgh University Press 38–73; Brown, Michael 2004 *The Wars of Scotland, 1214–1371*, Edinburgh University Press 17–18, 26–8; Green, Judith 1989 Anglo-Scottish Relations, 1066–1174, *England and Her Neighbours, 1066–1453: Essays in Honour of Pierre Chaplais*, edited by Michael C. E. Jones and Malcolm Graham Allan Vale, London: Hambledon 53–72; Stringer, K. J. 2005 Kingship, Conflict and State-Making in the Reign of Alexander II: The War of 1215–17 and its Context, *The Reign of Alexander II, 1214–49*, edited by Richard D. Oram, Leiden: Brill 99–156; Ross, Alasdair 2011 *Kings of Alba c.1000-c.1130*, Edinburgh: John Donald; Broun, Dauvit 2005 Contemporary Perspectives on Alexander II's Succession,

The construction of this more sophisticated Scottish state found expression, too, in the establishment of centralised offices designed to exploit the fiscal, judicial, territorial and natural resources of the realm at the command (and for the benefit) of the king, namely a regular system of financial accounting, formal assemblies responsible for promulgating laws, judicial officers charged with hearing the king's pleas and an administrative apparatus for negotiating governance of the localities in partnership with the king's aristocratic subjects.[6] More onerous was the challenge of forging an image of divinely sanctioned kingship—another epitome of contemporary European rule—without the benefit of unction and coronation. Although Alexander II (d. 1249) and Alexander III (d. 1286) petitioned Rome diligently and tirelessly for permission to use the rites, English opposition prevailed at the papal court and no king of Scots enjoyed anointing until well into the fourteenth century. Despite their inability to secure these essential attributes of kingship—indeed, it might be said, in large measure precisely owing to it—the thirteenth-century Scottish kings proved thoroughly adept at kingdom-building and equally successful in developing 'top tier monarchical bona fides' in the eyes of their European peers.[7] There can be no mistaking the powerful ideological messages about princely majesty and sovereign authority that underscore the royal commands that issued forth in charters, brieves

---

The Reign 79–98; Duncan, A. A. M. 2002 *The Kingship of the Scots, 842–1292: Succession and Independence*, Edinburgh University Press 53–126.

6 Taylor, *The Shape*; also Broun, Dauvit 2015 Statehood and Lordship in 'Scotland' before the Mid-Twelfth Century, *Innes Review* 66, 7–71; Broun, Dauvit 2008 The Property Records in the Book of Deer as a Source for Early Scottish Society, *Studies on the Book of Deer*, edited by Katherine Forsyth, Dublin: Four Courts Press 313–60. The 'pleas of the crown' were those that canon law defined as 'violations of public peace that were so heinous that the king [alone] had the responsibility of punishing them'; Cairns, John W. 2000 Historical Introduction, *A History of Private Law in Scotland*, edited by Kenneth Reid and Reinhard Zimmermann, 2 vols, Oxford University Press 1.14–184: 22.

7 Hammond, Matthew 2013 Domination and Conquest? The Scottish Experience in the Twelfth and Thirteenth Centuries, *The English Isles: Cultural Transmission and Political Conflict in Britain and Ireland, 1100–1500*, edited by Seán Duffy and Susan Foran, Dublin: Four Courts Press 68–83: 78.

and other letters from the king's writing office in this period. More compelling still are the images of kingship and majesty that the two Alexanders imprinted on the great seals of office with which they authenticated their written acts.[8]

Scholars of medieval Britain almost invariably treat the history of state-making as a predominantly secular phenomenon and to look for evidence of new ideas about kingship in the spheres of the fiscal, judicial and legislative. In the Scottish context, most notably, David Carpenter and Alice Taylor have made compelling arguments for a reappraisal of the state in the high medieval kingdom along these very lines, positing the maturation in the thirteenth century of a political ecosystem in which the exercise of aristocratic power and a relatively unsophisticated system of royal administration functioned in ways that were at once mutually co-operative and co-dependent.[9] Dauvit Broun, likewise, sees the first traces of a recognisable 'state' in Scotland above all in the expansion of royal lawmaking in the secular context.[10] Yet, placing too great an emphasis on the secular sphere risks diminishing recognition of other influences that contributed to shaping expressions of royal power and authority in Scotland in this formative period. Chief among these, and indeed perhaps more important than any other, was the role of the church. Some years ago, Hector MacQueen made the simple but trenchant observation that '[k]ings who claimed to reign by the grace of God had to take account of what the Church said and did about law and legal matters'.[11] He and others have since traced the development of a complex and sophisticated network of nuncios, legates and judges-delegate and shown how, under Innocent III and

---

8   Neville, Cynthia J. 2017 Making a Manly Impression: The Image of Kingship on Scottish Royal Seals of the High Middle Ages, *Nine Centuries of Man: Manhood and Masculinity in Scottish History*, edited by Lynn Abrams and Elizabeth L. Ewan, Edinburgh University Press 101–21: 109–13.
9   Carpenter, David 2013 Scottish Royal Government in the Thirteenth Century from an English Perspective, *New Perspectives on Medieval Scotland, 1093–1286*, edited by Matthew J. Hammond, Woodbridge: Boydell 117–59; Taylor, *The Shape* 495.
10 Broun, Statehood 7–11.
11 MacQueen, Hector L. 2002 Expectations of the Law in 12th and 13th Century Scotland, *Tijdschrift voor Rechtsgeschiedenis* 70, 279–90: 279.

his successors, an ambitious papacy consolidated its control over an ever widening range of concerns within Scotland deemed of interest to the *ecclesia Romana*, including not just marriage, legitimacy and questions relating to the status of clerics and unfree persons, but more complex matters concerning rights in church property, revenues and appurtenances. That the church was in turn able to bring 'effective pressure to bear on the secular law and customs' is apparent in the introduction of new principles in several areas of legal procedure. MacQueen's work, for example, has shown that as early as the twelfth century, in response to ecclesiastical influence, the notion of sanctuary (or girth, as it was known in Scotland) had become closely aligned with grants of the king's specific protection and peace; more specifically, he has argued that Alexander II's legislation concerning girth reflected a sophisticated response to papal condemnation of the ordeals of iron and water.[12]

The limitations of extant record sources relating to medieval Scotland has, however, made it very difficult to link developments in theological and philosophical discourse to specific moments in the project of shaping kingship and a state there. Although there are some notable exceptions, few scholars have ventured to find evidence of the high medieval church's teachings about penance, penitence and the remission of sin in the Scottish rulers' earliest efforts to legislate in the matter of felony or in the development of the related concept of princely mercy.[13] Fewer still have sought to link innovations in European canon

---

12 MacQueen, Hector L. 1991 Girth: Society and the Law of Sanctuary in Scotland, *Critical Studies in Ancient Law, Comparative Law and Legal History*, edited by John W. Cairns and Olivia F. Robinson, Oxford: Hart 333–52: 337, 343; MacQueen, Expectations 286–97.

13 An important exception to this statement may now be found in Simpson, A. R. C. 2016 Procedures for Dealing with Robbery in Scotland before 1400, *Continuity, Change and Pragmatism in the Law: Essays in Memory of Professor Angelo Forte*, edited by A. R. C. Simpson, Scott Crichton Styles, Euan West and Adelyn L. M. Wilson, Aberdeen University Press 95–149. This article amply demonstrates the promise of adopting an approach to legal history that gives due weight to the spiritual and worldly implications of wrongdoing that were the stuff of contemporary ecclesiastical discussion and debate. I am grateful to Andrew Simpson for making his article available to me as I was making final revisions to this essay, and regret that I did not have the

law to the earliest secular legislation in Scotland. This article seeks to tease out of extant legal sources a clearer sense of the ways in which developments in high medieval theology and canon law in particular found expression in a realm that, as one commentator has remarked, lay far away from Rome in a 'frontier area of Christendom'.[14]

§§§

One of the many features of the 'civilising' program set into motion by the high medieval kings of Scots was the gradual control that they came to establish over the definition of serious wrongdoing, a process that (in the late Anglo-Saxon context, at least) has been dubbed the 'criminalisation' of violence.[15] Another was a shift in the Scottish kings' attitude towards corporal punishment and afflictive penalties more generally. During the latter half of his reign Alexander II abandoned judicial mutilation and the public display of brutalised body parts (mostly, but not exclusively, heads) as behaviour inappropriate to a Christian prince.[16] These changes ran parallel with the earliest efforts of the kings of Scotland to enact a kingdom-wide program of legislation that positioned them at the apex of a hierarchy of royal courts and gave them (in name at least) a jurisdiction that was national in its scope and application. There is little reliable evidence to link new ideas about law and law-making in Scotland directly to changes in the nature of secular society there, but neither is there good reason to believe that

---

opportunity to consult it earlier. Dr Simpson and I have been working independently on the subject of canonical influences on secular law in Scotland, and it is both pleasant and encouraging to find that our respective conclusions about the interaction of the medieval legal systems are in essential agreement.

14 Somerville, Robert 1972 Two Notes on Scotland and the Medieval Papacy, *Innes Review* 23, 149–51: 150.

15 The expression appears in Lambert, T. B. 2009 Protection, Feud and Royal Power: Violence and Its Regulation in English Law, c.850–c.1250, PhD dissertation, University of Durham 160, 169, 200–20. The Scottish kings' efforts in this endeavour are examined below.

16 These developments are examined in Neville, Cynthia J. 2016 The Beginnings of Royal Pardon in Medieval Scotland, *Journal of Medieval History* 42, 1–29: 11.

Scotland was too remote from Rome or too unimportant a constituent of Christendom to absorb developments in high medieval theological and canonist jurisprudence or the reformed church's teachings about wrongdoing and punishment.

In fact, thirteenth-century Scottish efforts to articulate ideas about the nature of royal justice, the criminalisation of serious offences and the exercise of royal acts of mercy reflect to a remarkable degree the influence—and the terminology—of new currents of thought then sweeping through the western European church. For a century and a half already before 1250, but in particularly pressing fashion after the appearance and rapid dissemination of the second recension of the great compilation of Gratian's canon law known as the *Concordia discordantium canonum* (the *Decretum*) around 1150,[17] continental theologians and canonists had been discussing the relationship between sin and crime, and the confessional, moral and legal implications of punishment, penance and remission. Among them were the Scotsmen Richard Scott, Adam of Dryburgh, John Scott and Master Michael Scott and, most famously, John Duns Scotus.[18] Several

---

17   The complex authorship of the two recensions of the *Decretum* is unravelled in Winroth, Anders 2000 *The Making of Gratian's* Decretum, Cambridge University Press. For the sake of simplicity, however, references in this essay to the author of the work are to Gratian alone.

18   Richard Scott (c.1123–1173) was also known as Richard de St Victor, after the abbey where he spent most of his life. The prolific author Adam of Dryburgh (c.1140–c.1212) may be the same man who served as a witness to business transacted at the abbey in the early 1190s. Amanda Beam *et al.* editors 2012 *The People of Medieval Scotland, 1093-1314* (*PoMS*) http://db.poms.ac.uk/record/person/8869/. Adam's scholarship and particularly his debt to the Victorine school are examined in Worthen, J. F. 1997 Adam of Dryburgh and the Augustinian Tradition, *Revue des études augustiniennes* 43, 339-347; for Richard Scott and Adam of Dryburgh, see also Broadie, Alexander 1995 *The Shadow of Scotus: Philosophy and Faith in Pre-Reformation Scotland*, Edinburgh: T. and T. Clark 2. For John Scott (fl.1152x1202), see Shead, Norman F. 2007 Compassed about with so Great a Cloud: The Witnesses of Scottish Episcopal *Acta* before ca 1250, *Scottish Historical Review* 86, 159-75: 168. A little later, Master Michael Scot (c.1175–1236), famous as a translator of Arabic-language works, held one and possibly two benefices in Scotland. See Watt, D. E. R. 1977 *A Biographical Dictionary of Scottish Graduates to A.D. 1410* Oxford: Clarendon Press 490; *PoMS* no. 7308

theologians, deeply concerned with the fate of a sinner's soul within an eternal salvific economy, debated especially hotly the purpose of earthly punishment by seeking to understand, on the one hand, the relationship between the priest who forgave sin and, on the other, the judges (secular and religious) who passed sentence upon persons guilty of committing wrongdoing. Particularly important here were the works of Anselm of Laon (d. 1117) and Hugh of St Victor (d. 1141) and his students, who by the middle years of the twelfth century had clarified the distinction between sins meriting eternal punishment and those that might be amended by earthly penance.[19] Other schoolmen sought to illuminate the connection between confession, contrition and absolution, still others to clarify the rationale that underlay punishment, earthly and eternal. Drawing on the work of biblical glossators, civilian commentators and, above all, on the work of Gratian, the 'master of penance',[20] men such as Ivo of Chartres (d. 1115) and the Pseudo-Isidorians, Peter Lombard (d. 1160), Peter the Chanter (d. 1197) and others tackled all these conundra to arrive at working definitions of the closely related notions of penance, contrition (or penitence), purgation and remission. They acknowledged that the sincerity with which a sinner repented, then confessed his or her sins before dying had a direct influence on the fate of that person's soul

---

http://db.poms.ac.uk/record/person/7308/. See also Morpurgo, Piero 2004 'Scot, Michael (d. in or after 1235)' *Oxford Dictionary of National Biography* online edn. Considerably later, of course, but no less remarkable in the later thirteenth century, was the influence of Duns Scotus, see Leff, Gordon 2004 'Duns Scotus, John (c.1265-1308)', *Oxford Dictionary of National Biography*, online edn.

19   Eckert, Raphäel 2011 Peine judiciaire, pénitence et salut entre droit canonique et théologie (XIIe s.–début du XIIIe s.), *Revue de l'histoire des religions* 228, 485–86; Bériou, Nicole 1986 La confession dans les écrits théologiques et pastoraux du XIIIe siècle: médication de l'âme ou démarche judiciaire? *Publications de l'École française de Rome* 88, 261–82: 274–78. See also 'Penance', *The Oxford Dictionary of the Christian Church*, edited by F. L. Cross and E. A. Livingstone, 3rd rev. edn, Oxford University Press 2009 DOI: 10.1093/acref/9780192802903.001.0001 [accessed 24 November 2016].

20   Larson, Atria A. 2014 *Master of Penance: Gratian and the Development of Penitential Thought in the Twelfth Century*, Washington DC: Catholic University of America Press.

in the afterlife. Judicial sentence did not perform the same function and had little to do with the fate of a sinner's soul. Its importance lay, rather, in ensuring that the punishment of wrongdoers repaired the social disruptions that were the consequence of violence and that penal sentences served as salutary warnings against acts that violated legal and political norms.[21]

Theologians and lawmen, religious and secular, were engaged in similar intellectual exercises in England in the eleventh and twelfth centuries. Although they espoused different views about the role of clerics (especially bishops) in the context of earthly punishment, for example, the homilist Ælfric of Eynsham (d. 1010) and Archbishop Wulfstan of York (d. 1023) were in essential agreement in recognising the distinction between 'the spiritual cure for sin'—remorse and, ideally, confession—'and the earthly remedy for crime', the judicial sentence of mutilation or death. The former related to the economy of salvation and was the purview of clerical confessors, the latter belonged to the realm of earthly justice and was ultimately the responsibility of the king.[22] By the close of the twelfth century in Europe, more generally, a well-articulated understanding of the sacrament of penance

---

21 Rolker, Christof 2006 Ivo of Chartres' Pastoral Canon Law, *Bulletin of Medieval Canon Law*, n.s. 25, 114–145: 120–23; Eckert 483–508; Peter the Chanter, *Oxford Dictionary of the Christian Church* DOI: 10.1093/acref/9780192802903.001.0001; Helmholz, R. H. 1996 *The Spirit of Classical Canon Law*, Athens GA: University of Georgia Press 301, 346–57; Goering, Joseph 2008, The Scholastic Turn (1100–1500): Penitential Theology and Law in the Schools, *A New History of Penance*, edited by Abigail Firey, Leiden: Brill 219–38: 221–31; Mansfield, Mary 1995 *The Humiliation of Sinners: Public Penance in Thirteenth-Century France*, Ithaca: Cornell University Press 55–58.

22 Marafioti, Nicole 2009 Punishing Bodies and Saving Souls: Capital and Corporal Punishment in Late Anglo-Saxon England, *Haskins Society Journal* 20, 39–57; Marafioti, Nicole 2014 Earthly Justice and Spiritual Consequences: Judging and Punishing in the Old English *Consolation of Philosophy*, *Capital and Corporal Punishment in Anglo-Saxon England*, edited by Jay Paul Gates and Nicole Marafioti, Woodbridge: Boydell and Brewer, 113–30: 123–24; Hough, Carole 2000 Penitential Literature and Secular Law in Anglo-Saxon England, *Anglo-Saxon Studies in Archaeology & History* 11, 133–42: 134–41; Hamilton, Sarah 2005 Remedies for 'Great Transgressions': Penance and Excommunication in Late Anglo-Saxon England, *Pastoral Care in Late Anglo-Saxon England*, edited by Francesca Tinti, Woodbridge: Boydell

made absolution conditional on the penitent's contrition (*contritio in corde*), confession (*confessio in ore*) and performance of a punishment in satisfaction of the offence (*satisfactio in opere*).[23] So pervasive was acceptance of this teaching that eventually a canon of the Fourth Lateran Council (1215) could confidently require that every Christian who had reached the age of discretion confess his or her sins at least once a year.[24]

The theologians' discussions of penitence and the fundamental notions of redress and reparation that underpinned them had wide appeal and enduring influence in Scotland because they had an immediacy in a society in which compensation for injury was already deeply ingrained in social relations.[25] The revival of canon law studies in the schools and, later, universities of the twelfth and thirteenth centuries reflected the aspirations of a newly reformed papacy anxious to give expression to its claims to supreme jurisdiction over the secular rulers of western Europe, but the theological distinctions between sin and crime acquired new juridical significance when canonists turned their attention to the ways in which they might give worldly application to new ideas about spiritual wrongdoing and punishment.[26] Among

---

83–105; Thompson, Victoria 2004 *Dying and Death in Later Anglo-Saxon England*, Woodbridge: Boydell 174-88.

23 Of particular importance in elucidating the concept of satisfaction was the figure of St Anselm of Laon. See Eckert 486 and Berman, Harold J. 1983 *Law and Revolution: The Formation of the Western Legal Tradition*, Cambridge MA: Harvard University Press 181-98.

24 Canons of the Fourth Lateran Council, edited by Rothwell, Harry 1975 *English Historical Documents, 1189-1327*, London: Eyre and Spottiswoode 654-55.

25 See here, for example, the obligation of compensation that underlies the provisions of the so-called Laws of the of the Bretts and Scots, discussed (albeit from competing points of view) in Woolf, Alex 2007 *From Pictland to Alba 789-1070* New Edinburgh History of Scotland, vol. 2, Edinburgh: Edinburgh University Press 246-49, and Taylor, Alice 2009 *Leges Scocie* and the Lawcodes of David I, William the Lion and Alexander II, *Scottish Historical Review* 88, 207-88: 237-40.

26 See, especially, Fraher, Richard P. 1989 Preventing Crime in the High Middle Ages: The Medieval Lawyers' Search for Deterrence, *Popes, Teachers, and Canon Law in the Middle Ages*, edited by James Ross Sweeney and Stanley Chodorow, Ithaca: Cornell University Press 212-33: 214-15.

the hundreds of topics that preoccupied the masters of the newly established schools of Romano-canonical law (*ius commune*) across Europe, a handful had particular resonance among ecclesiastical and secular princes alike, if for different reasons. These included the role of the prince as earthly judge, the relevance of individual liability in assessing wrongdoing, and the function of punishment in the social economy of this world and the spiritual realm of the next.[27] Modern scholarship remains inconclusive about the chronology in, and the means by, which churchmen imbued with the *ius novum* brought it to the attention of secular rulers in western Europe, and very little has been written about the extent to which the Scottish crown drew on ecclesiastical exemplars in its lawmaking efforts.[28] There is none the less suggestive evidence that in the century after 1180 the king and his advisors sought to give substantive expression to the new canonist learning in the areas just mentioned.

One of the many consequences of the theologians' and canonists' discussions of sin, crime and punishment was the clarification of the role that princes ought to play as earthly judges. Burchard of Worms' (d. 1025) extensive exploration of acts of private vengeance provided a strong theoretical justification for the duty of secular rulers to punish subjects who took part in such violence. His ideas were subsequently the focus of a great deal of discussion in Europe about secular involvement in what today we would call criminal law.[29] By the end of the twelfth century, decretists and decretalists and, eventually, even the pope himself acknowledged that while the church could not afford

---

27 Pennington, Kenneth 1993 *The Prince and the Law, 1200-1600: Sovereignty and Rights in the Western Legal Tradition*, Oakland: University of California Press 38–75; see also, more recently and more briefly, Müller, Wolfgang P. 2007 Violence et droit canonique: les enseignements de la pénitencerie apostolique (XIIe-XVIe siècle), *Revue historique* 644, 771–96.
28 But see now Simpson Procedures for a discussion of legislation concerning robbery.
29 Austin, Greta 2006 Vengeance and the Law in Eleventh-Century Worms: Burchard and the Canon Law of Feuds, *Medieval Church Law and the Origins of the Western Legal Tradition: A Tribute to Kenneth Pennington*, edited by Wolfgang P. Müller and Mary E. Sommar, Washington DC: Catholic University of America Press 66–76: 72–74.

to cede jurisdiction entirely over offences committed by lay persons, it must abandon the older view that 'earthly misdeeds should be tolerated in this life and left to divine judgment.'[30] Princes now must assume an active—albeit a carefully circumscribed—role in the punishment of serious misdoers. In post-Conquest England, such views found immediate resonance when customary laws governing and classifying felony were given legislative force in the Assizes of Clarendon of 1166 and of Northampton in 1176. These in turn became the basis of further legislation and, ultimately, a vigorous expansion of the notion of the king's peace. Thereafter, according to Richard Helmholz, 'the direction of English law was towards assertion of the sole jurisdiction in the Crown over serious crimes.'[31] A similar interest in delineating spheres of jurisdiction and partitioning legal responsibility appears in Scotland in the closing years of that same century, a consequence, at least in part, of the proximity of the two realms. The regular movement between Scotland and England of members of the two royal families, of scholars native and foreign, and of aristocrats ecclesiastical and secular ensured that the kings of Scots were kept abreast of the legal reforms of the Angevin rulers and their thirteenth-century successors.[32] Equally important, however, may have been the ready availability of canonist texts that advocated new views on topics like individual criminal liability and the obligations of Christian rulers to assume responsibility

---

30 Fraher, Preventing Crime 18; see also Mäkinen, Virpi and Pihlajamäki, Heikki 2004 The Individualization of Crime in Medieval Canon Law, *Journal of the History of Ideas* 65, 525–42.
31 Helmholz, R. H. 1983 Crime, Compurgation and the Courts of the Medieval Church, *Law and History Review* 1, 1–26:7; see also the discussion in Helmholz, R. H. 2004 *Oxford History of the Laws of England, Vol. 1: The Canon Law and Ecclesiastical Jurisdiction from 597 to the 1640s*, Oxford University Press 599–604; Hudson, John 1996 *The Formation of the English Common Law: Law and Society in England from the Norman Conquest to Magna Carta*, London: Longman 20, 22, 29–30, 126–85.
32 For an interesting study of the flow of specific ideas about the obligations associated with tenure of land in each of the two realms, see Carpenter, David 2010 Melrose Abbey and English Law (*lex anglicana*): Attitudes to England in the Period before the Wars of Independence, in the database *People of Medieval Scotland 1093–1371*, http://paradox.poms.ac.uk/feature/february10.html.

for the punishment of serious offenders. Some Scottish scholars headed to the schools of France and Italy to learn, but many did not, and among those who remained at home to advise the king few can have been ignorant of the renown of nearby Durham as a centre of canon law studies. Recent studies have, in fact, traced the steady movement of intellectual ideas (and, sometimes, careerist clerics) from the palatinate into Scotland.[33]

There are good reasons to argue that the discussions of twelfth- and thirteenth-century European theologians and canonists about the nature of sin, the growing tendency on the part of canonists (from Burchard through Ivo of Chartres and his imitators and thence into the *Decretum*) to link sin and crime,[34] the role of satisfaction or reparation in the economy of sin and their emphasis on the duty of secular princes to punish serious offences all had a more direct impact in Scotland

---

33 For which see Landau, Peter 2011 The Origins of Civil Procedure: Treatises in Durham during the Twelfth Century, *Canon Law, Religion, and Politics: Liber Amicorum Robert Somerville*, edited by Ute-Renate Blumenthal, Anders Winroth and Peter Landau, Washington DC: Catholic University of America Press 139–43 and the extensive survey of relevant Durham manuscripts in Kuttner, Stephan and Rathbone, Eleanor 1951 Anglo-Norman Canonists of the Twelfth Century: An Introductory Study, *Traditio* 7, 279–358: 294, 296, 297, 303, 320–21. See also Piper, A. J. 1978 The Libraries of the Monks of Durham, *Medieval Scribes, Manuscripts and Libraries: Essays presented to N. R. Ker*, edited by M. B. Parkes and Andrew Watson, London: Scolar Press 213–49 and Dalton, Paul 1994 Scottish Influence on Durham 1066–1214, *Anglo-Norman Durham, 1093–1193*, edited by David Rollason, Margaret Harvey and Michael Prestwich, Woodbridge: Boydell 339–52: 344. The twelfth- and thirteenth-century manuscripts housed in Durham are examined in detail in Watson, Andrew G. editor 1987 *Medieval Libraries of Great Britain: A List of Surviving Books*, edited by N.R. Ker, Supplement to the Second Edition, London: Royal Historical Society 16–34. For an example of a Durham cleric who moved north, see Greenaway, Diana E. editor 1971 *Fasti Ecclesiae Anglicanae 1066–1300: Volume 2, Monastic Cathedrals (Northern and Southern Provinces)*, London: Institute of Historical Research, 30, 37, 105 and n. 107. These entries record the life of William Cumin, who became chancellor of King David I. His near-contemporary, Geoffrey prior of Canterbury, became abbot of Dunfermline in 1128. *Ibid.* 8–12.
34 Hyams, Paul 2000 Does It Matter when the English Began to Distinguish Between Crime and Tort?, *Violence in Medieval Society*, edited by Richard W. Kaeuper, Woodbridge: Boydell 107–128: 109.

than most historians have hitherto appreciated. This was especially the case after the kingdom acquired the status of a 'special daughter' of the papacy in the 1190s and the establishment in 1225 of the provincial council of the Scottish church subject directly to the pope.[35] The new relationship between Rome and the bishops of the *ecclesia Scoticana* is apparent in the volume of letters that circulated between the curia and Scotland in the period immediately before 1190s and then regularly afterwards.[36] Likewise, the keen interest of the papal court in reserving to the church's exclusive jurisdiction disputes that threatened to accroach the authority of canon law or to threaten ecclesiastical prerogative is well attested in the activities after 1160 of nuncios, legates and judges delegate in Scotland, some of whom may have been equipped with an up-to-date *ordo iudiciarius* of the jurist Pseudo-Ulpianus that adapted civilian procedure to the requirements of Scottish ecclesiastical courtrooms.[37] At the heart of many of the disputes over which these men presided were the very issues that preoccupied canonists anxious to implement the reform agenda of the papacy, among them the appropriateness of subjecting clerics to the

---

35   Barrell, Andrew D. M. 1995 The Background to *Cum Universi*: Scoto-Papal Relations, 1159–1192, *Innes Review* 46, 116–38; Watt, D. E. R. 2000 *Medieval Church Councils in Scotland*, Edinburgh: T. and T. Clark 43–53; Ferguson, Paul C. 1997 *Medieval Papal Representatives in Scotland: Legates, Nuncios, and Judges Delegate, 1125–1286*, Edinburgh: Stair Society 22–28, 63–64, 202–03.

36   Discussed extensively in Watt, *Church Councils* 25–42 and Barrell, Andrew D. M. 2005 Scotland and the Papacy in the Reign of Alexander II, Oram, *Reign* 157–78.

37   Gouron, André 2010 Un traité écossais du douzième siècle: l'*ordo* "*Ulpianus De edendo*", *Tijdschrift voor Rechtsgeschiedenis* 78, 1–13: 10–12; see also Brasington, Bruce 2016 The Anglo-Norman *Ordo iudiciarius*: Pseudo-Ulpianus, *De edendo, Order in the Court: Medieval Procedural Treatises in Translation*, by Bruce Brasington, Medieval Law and its Practice 21, Leiden: Brill, 112–71: 112, 120–23, 125–30. Both articles discuss not merely the twelfth-century text of *De edendo* found in British Library Harley MS 2355, but the intriguing series of notes appended to it. Innocent III appears to have assumed familiarity with Tancred's *Ordo iudiciarius*, written c. 1215, in Scotland: see Ferguson 281. The work of papal nuncios, legates and judges delegate in Scotland is comprehensively examined in Ferguson; see also Cooper, T. M. 1914 *Select Scottish Cases of the Thirteenth Century*, Edinburgh: W. Hodge & Co.; MacQueen, Canon Law 221–53.

secular custom of judicial combat, the proper procedure to follow when people accused clerics of theft or homicide, the validity of ecclesiastical and lay testimony in courtroom testimony, the implications (spiritual and mundane) of excommunication. In Scotland, as in England, the appearance of the terminology drawn from new *ordines iudiciarii* suggests that before the end of the twelfth century there was a demand for expertise both in the stuff of civil and canon law and in the new procedures that were now being widely implemented.[38]

The pope himself sometimes took the lead in ensuring that the distant kingdom of the Scots complied with new developments in canon law. In the early 1180s, for example, Alexander III wrote to the bishop of St Andrews—and, through him, to King William I (d. 1214)—to remind Scottish jurists that authority in the prosecution and punishment of tonsured clerics (i.e. those who had not yet taken orders) belonged to the church alone;[39] twenty years later Innocent III personally instructed King William I on the canonical rules governing the treatment of felons who took sanctuary in churches, and cited specifically 'the prescriptions of the sacred canons and the teaching of the civil laws'.[40] Innocent was equally quick to reprimand the king (if in a fit of pique) in the matter of a custom then in operation in the Anglo-Scottish region, which compelled clerics to participate in judicial combat. This, Innocent declared, was 'destructive' and 'offensive to God and the sacred canons'.[41] Annoying though these papal

---

38   Brasington 123.
39   Somerville, Robert, editor 1982 *Scotia Pontificia: Papal Letters to Scotland before the Pontificate of Innocent III*, Oxford: Clarendon Press no. 102.
40   Edited by Robertson, Joseph 1866 *Concilia Scotiae: ecclesiae Scoticanae statuta tam provincialia quam synodalia quae supersunt, MCCXXV–MDLIX*, 2 vols, Edinburgh: Bannatyne Club 2.236, translated in Patrick, David, editor 1907 *Statutes of the Scottish Church, 1225–1559*, Edinburgh: Scottish History Society 205. The letter was dated 1200.
41   Innes, Cosmo, editor 1843 *Registrum episcopatus Glasguensis*, 2 vols, Edinburgh: Bannatyne Club 1, no. 110; for the background of the bull, see Patrick 288–93. Innocent's sharp rebuke may have reflected his frustration that the Scottish custom so clearly violated the very specific condemnation issued in the decree *Sentenciam sanguinis*. This had comprised chapter 38 of the extensive Lateran IV legislation issued only months earlier, copies of which Innocent knew had been taken back to Scotland.

intrusions into royal concerns may have been, eventually they had tangible results. While disputes concerning teinds (*Anglice*, tithes) remained frequent in Scotland well into the thirteenth century, a notable feature of William's later charters is his readiness to acknowledge in more than merely nominal fashion the force of canon law in a wide range of circumstances and to defend, sometimes vigorously, episcopal claims to such revenues. In one deed of this period the king deferred openly to 'the requirements of the *Lex Christiana*' that governed the assessment of teinds; in another he acknowledged the 'laws and rights of Holy Mother church' in similar matters.[42] Words such as these may well have been designed to remind the papacy that lack of unction in no way diminished the piety of the king of Scots, but William's support of the clerical law on teinds offers important evidence of his awareness that royal justice and royal authority themselves derived considerable strength from the king's championing of the church.

Thirteenth-century synodal and episcopal legislation in Scotland, perhaps not surprisingly, demonstrates a thorough familiarity with contemporary Romano-canonical treatments of sin, penance, remission and punishment as laid out not only in the widely circulated *Concordia discordantium canonum* of Gratian, but in the very recently updated Decretals issued under the name of Pope Gregory IX.[43] There is clear evidence, moreover, that already in the twelfth century, recent debates about substantive issues in Romano-canonical law (for example, the claim of *praescriptio*) were already the stuff of litigation in Scottish courts.[44]

---

42 Edited by Barrow, G. W. S. 1971 *Regesta Regum Scottorum, Vol. II: The Acts of William I, King of Scots, 1165–1214*, Edinburgh University Press nos. 179, 281. For relations between the crown and the papacy in the late twelfth and early thirteenth centuries generally, see Oram, *Domination* 332–34, 341–46.
43 For numerous examples, see Watt, *Church Councils* 55–102.
44 On prescription generally, see Brasington 120–23; for Scottish examples, see Shead, Norman F. editor 2016 *Scottish Episcopal Acta, Vol. 1: The Twelfth Century*, Edinburgh: Scottish History Society no. 208; Innes, C. editor 1832 *Registrum monasterii de Passelet*, Glasgow: Maitland Club 229–30; Lindsay, W. A., Dowden, J. and Thomson, J. M. editors 1908 *Charters, Bulls and Other*

From the reign of King Alexander II (1214–49), however, there comes more compelling evidence that changes to the substance and procedure of canon law which zealous reformers were effecting in continental European church courts were receiving due notice in Scotland and in contexts beyond that of the religious life. Alexander's legislative program, in fact, demonstrates both in its overall design and in the carefully chosen terminology of some of its provisions that the king was closely in touch with new juridical trends and that he enacted measures designed to give effect to his obligations as an earthly judge as the canonists understood the concept. In 1230, a royal assize made special provision for 'those who cannot fight' by introducing the visnet (or jury) as a method of proof in the trial of some cases of robbery and theft.[45] The assize reserved the use of the jury specifically to categories of persons whom canon lawyers had long identified as especially deserving of protection by secular authorities: clerics, women (and widows in particular), children and the infirm.[46] The scope of this 1230 legislation was then extended in 1244 to include homicide,[47] and eventually had as one of its most important effects the restriction of trial by ordeal across much of the realm. The introduction of testimony by the visnet to the secular legal process system as an alternative to the existing custom of personal accusation spoke in clearer terms still to Alexander's understanding of, and his responsiveness to, other innovations in canonistic jurisprudence. The new laws no doubt served the very useful purpose of making it easier for secular authorities to detect, prosecute and punish crimes both open and occult.[48] But they

---

Documents relating to the Abbey of Inchaffray, Edinburgh: Scottish History Society, 1st Series no. 111.

45   Thomson, T. and Innes, C. editors 1814–24 *Acts of the Parliaments of Scotland*, 11 vols, Edinburgh: Record Commission 1.399, discussed in Taylor, *The Shape* 277–78 and Simpson Procedures 109–11.

46   The antecedents of this canonical tenet are reviewed briefly in Helmholz, *The Spirit* 120–26.

47   Thomson and Innes 1.371. This edition of the assize is unreliable; for the original text, see the discussion in Taylor, *The Shape* 139, 240–43, 293–94.

48   Alexander II's actions also made a strong statement about the independence of the Scottish church from English domination; see here Simpson, Andrew A. C. and Wilson, Adelyn L. M. 2017 *Scottish Legal History Volume One: 1000–1707*, Edinburgh University Press 76.

bore strong witness, too, to Alexander's familiarity with a new emphasis in canon law on concepts of individual responsibility and *mens rea* in sin and crime, and to his awareness of Innocent III's recent preoccupation with public utility in secular lawmaking.[49] Connections such as these have recently been argued for contemporary England,[50] but they are apparent also in Scotland, perhaps most obviously in 1197, when legislation of William I made an explicit distinction between homicide and murder.[51] The thirteenth-century popes, it is true, were never able to eradicate the 'execrable abuses' that remained customary in Alexander II's Scotland (and well thereafter), most notably in the survival of judicial combat in the Anglo-Scottish border region.[52]

---

49 The shift from accusatorial to inquisitorial process in the thirteenth century and the connection of this shift to the broader notion that 'public utility' required the active intervention of the king in secular lawmaking are examined at length in Fraher, Richard M. 1984 The Theoretical Justification for the New Criminal Law of the High Middle Ages: '*Rei publicae interest, ne crimina remaneant impunita*', *Illinois Law Review* 577–95: 581–82; Fraher discusses the implications of the new papal focus on criminal detection and punishment in the secular realms of the thirteenth century in Fraher, Richard M. 1992 IV Lateran's Revolution in Criminal Procedure: The Birth of *inquisitio*, the End of Ordeals, and Innocent III's Vision of Ecclesiastical Politics, *Studia in honorem eminentissimi cardialis Alphonsi M. Stickler*, edited by Rosalio Iosepho, Studia et Textus Historiæ Iuris Canonici 7, Rome: Libreria Ateneo Salesiano 97–111: 99. Fraher's arguments have deeply influenced recent discussions of high medieval changes in the procedure of church courts in criminal matters; it is now generally accepted, moreover, that canonist influence on secular law making in the area of criminal law was comprehensive. See, for example, Pihlajamäki, Heikki and Korpiola, Mia 2014 Medieval Canon Law: The Origins of Modern Criminal Law, *Oxford Handbook of Criminal Law*, edited by Markus Dubbler and Tatjana Hörnle, Oxford: Clarendon Press 210–24: 217–19.
50 Kamali, Elizabeth Papp 2015 *Felonia Felonice Facta*: Felony and Intentionality in Medieval England, *Criminal Law and Philosophy* 9, 397–41: 399–401, 413–18.
51 Taylor, *Leges* 272. The latter are here designated *interfectores in murthedric*.
52 For the later medieval period, see Neville, Cynthia J. 1998 *Violence, Custom and Law: The Anglo-Scottish Border Lands in the Later Middle Ages*, Edinburgh University Press 4, 6, 40, 76–77, 79, 134, 190 and Forte, A. D. M. 2010 'A Strange Archaic Provision of Mercy': The Procedural Rules for the *Duellum* under the Law of *Clann Duib*, *Edinburgh Law Review* 14, 425–29.

Nevertheless, by the middle decades of the thirteenth century the influence of canonist legal thought had real, rather than merely nominal, application within Scotland in a variety of legislative contexts.[53]

The dialogue between secular and ecclesiastical legal thinking in Scotland proved as fruitful as it did in large part because it accorded so well with the Scottish kings' own designs to give vigorous new expression to their dynastic legitimacy and to their princely ambitions as lawmakers. From as far back as the reign of Alexander I (d. 1124) the papal curia had had occasion to instruct the rulers of distant Scotland in the qualities of a Christian prince and the most appropriate ways in which to conduct the business of governing. More than once, too, the pope carefully explained to the king of Scots the canonical arguments that linked the prince's governance in this world with the fate of his soul in the next.[54] But papal missives to Scotland were never only admonitory; they were also vehicles through which the church lent its support to the essential project of creating for the descendants of Malcolm III and Margaret an image of Christian kingship across the length and breadth of a realm that was still in the high Middle Ages territorially and linguistically fragmented. In a letter of 1110x1113 addressed generally to the 'clergy and laity' of Scotland, for example, Pope Paschal II accentuated the role of King Alexander I as a 'protector of the catholic faith'.[55] Likewise, in 1139/40 and again in 1186 Innocent II and Urban III contributed to dynastic image-making in Scotland when they memorialised King David I as a 'catholic prince and an expander of the Christian faith'.[56]

Cordial relations between pope and king created a propitious atmosphere for the exchange of ideas about legal reform between Roman core and Scottish periphery. An equally influential factor was the maturation of the king's council in the late twelfth and the

---

53 MacQueen, Expectations 283–84, 288; MacQueen, Hector L. 1993 *Common Law and Feudal Society in Medieval Scotland*, Edinburgh University Press 110–11, 250–51; Taylor, *The Shape* 337, 340, 347–48.
54 See, for example, Somerville, *Scotia Pontificia* nos 1, 2, 21, 22, 141, 166.
55 Bethell, Denis 1970 Two Letters of Pope Paschal II to Scotland, *Scottish Historical Review* 49, 33–45: 44; Somerville, *Scotia Pontificia* no. 2.
56 Somerville, *Scotia Pontificia* nos. 21, 137.

thirteenth centuries and the steady entrenchment of its members as advisors to the crown in the day to day business of governing the realm. While lay noblemen jealously monopolised the offices that afforded them prestige in the secular hierarchy (notably those of the steward, the constable and the butler), the growth of more sophisticated administrative and legal systems for implementing the royal will was largely the achievement of the king's clerical counsellors, and above all of his chancellors (all but one of whom between c. 1171 and 1292 were churchmen). The prominent roles that senior Scottish clerics played at the heart of the royal court in turn gave the contemporary church unusually weighty influence in shaping new secular law in the thirteenth-century kingdom. The men who occupied episcopal office in the kingdom were sometimes themselves university graduates;[57] in their dual capacities as representatives of the church and royal counsellors they played unique and important roles as conduits through which the king and his secular advisors received instruction in the stuff of debate and dispute that animated the schools and earliest universities. Some high-ranking clerics, moreover, had first-hand knowledge of new developments in canon law, personally bringing back to court eye-witness accounts of the proceedings and copies of the legislative decrees of the ecumenical councils that convened at the Lateran palace and elsewhere in the twelfth and thirteenth centuries. The Scottish episcopate was well represented at most of the major councils held between 1139 and 1274 and, while not all bishops had formal university training, their extant acts demonstrate that, as was the case in England, they had access to wide ranging expertise in canon law and theology among the many men who staffed their households.[58]

---

57 Shead, Compassed 167–68 should be read alongside his comprehensive edition and study of extant bishops' records in Shead, *Scottish Episcopal Acta*; see also Watt, *Church Councils* 25, 36–37, 87–88.
58 Brasington 117. For comments about a 'similar process of exchange which kept the ecclesiastical lawyers in Scotland in touch with the mainstream of European canonical studies', and which 'had an important effect ... on making the canon law available to Scottish jurists', see Ollivant, Simon 1982 *The Court of the Official in Pre-Reformation Scotland*, Edinburgh: Stair Society 130.

The closing years of the twelfth century are notable for the appearance in Scotland of the terminology of the canonists and theologians, deployed now in new ways and more specifically in the secular context of the king's courts, the king's justice, the king's peace and the king's mercy. That language, moreover, demonstrates familiarity with the range and the ambiguity of theological and canonist texts. Alice Taylor, for example, has dated to the reign of Alexander II the earliest Scottish use of the term *crimen* and *felonia* in the modern sense of secular crime;[59] nevertheless, the former had long denoted sin in canonical and confessional texts.[60] Royal assizes of William I and Alexander II that refer to serious offenders both as *calumpniati* or *defamati* speak to deliberate word choice and familiarity with the distinctive terms used in canonical sources to distinguish prosecutorial methods.[61] The use of canonist language in other legislation of the twelfth and the thirteenth centuries intended specifically for secular application—for example, the terms *iniuria, contumelia, malum, vindicia, maleficia*—suggests more than merely an effort to deploy ornamental language; it reveals an impressive grasp of the canonists' views about degrees of culpability and personal responsibility for transgressing societal norms.[62] Even before Pope Innocent III considered it appropriate to instruct William I in the laws governing sanctuary, the king demonstrated his full understanding of the legal immunities associated with girth when he directed a brieve to the keepers of the sanctuary at Wedale, ordering them to preserve the jurisdiction of the abbot of Kelso despite the church's special status.[63] Other legislation of William I, notably an assize of 1177 that concerned

---

59   Taylor, *The Shape* 138–39.
60   It is used in its dual sense in the letter of Pope Alexander III of 1180/1 cited above at n. 39. See also the use of the term and its cognates in some of the ecclesiastical legislation collected in Robertson, for example at 18–20, 26–28.
61   Taylor, *Leges* 250–56, 265–68, 274–76 (*calumpn-*); 256 (*defamatus*).
62   For a discussion of these terms in the specific context of brieves of protection, see Taylor, *The Shape* 165–67. Taylor does not discuss the evidence for the widespread use of any of these terms in Scotland earlier than the reign of William I. The terms appear, however, in other legislation, royal and episcopal.
63   Barrow, *William I* no. 68, dated 1165/1171.

the movement of people, goods and animals, represents an effort to give expression in the sphere of secular law to the medieval canonists' extensive discussions of the Mosaic principle that the killing of a thief taken by surprise in the home is a crime (*crimen*) if committed by day, but if done at night the killer remains *sine culpa*.[64] Familiarity with, and perhaps an intention to emulate, canonistic views concerning the appropriate delegation of jurisdiction appears also in new royal legislation on fire-raising. The Gaelic, Anglo-Saxon and Anglo-Norman legal traditions all had long histories of treating the offence with severity,[65] but it is probably no accident that in 1180 the offence of arson, which members of the Second Lateran Council had specifically excoriated as 'wicked, devastating, horrible and malicious' and 'surpassing all other depredations' was first identified clearly as one of the pleas reserved to the crown for adjudication.[66] The assize of

---

64 The distinction between killings committed at night and during daylight was the subject of extensive discussion by St Augustine (in his commentary of the Book of Exodus) and later included in Justinian's *Digest* (D 9.2.4.1). It passed eventually into the *Panormia*, traditionally (if no longer exclusively) attributed to Ivo of Chartres (*Panormia*, V.74). The arguments against Ivo's authorship are succinctly reviewed in Rolker, Christof 2008 Ivo of Chartres and the *Panormia*: The Question of Authorship Revisited, *Bulletin of Medieval Canon Law*, n.s. 28, 39–70.

65 Owen, Morfydd E. 2006 *Tàn*: The Welsh Law of Arson and Negligent Burning, *Tair Colofn Cyfraith: The Three Columns of Law in Medieval Wales: Homicide, Theft and Fire*, edited by T. M. Charles-Edwards and Paul Russell, Bangor: Welsh Legal History Society 131–45; Summerson, Henry 2012 Burning Issues: The Law and Crime of Arson in England, 1200–1350, *Laws, Lawyers, and Texts: Studies in Medieval Legal History in Honour of Paul Brand*, edited by Susanne Jenks, Jonathan Rose and Christopher Whittick, Leiden: Brill 101–28: 101–03. The influence of twelfth- and early thirteenth-century canonists on the contents and redaction of Welsh law is discussed in Watkin, Thomas Glyn 2007 *The Legal History of Wales*, Cardiff: University of Wales Press 71–74.

66 A text of the canon is available in Schroeder, H. J. editor 1937 *Disciplinary Decrees of the General Councils: Text, Translation, and Commentary*, New York: B. Herder 207; for the assize reserving the plea to the king, dated 1180, see Taylor, *Leges* 261, c. 7. However, like Simpson (Procedures 97n), I prefer to translate the *rapina* of this passage as 'robbery', rather than 'plunder'. Interestingly, the near-contemporary Cyfnerth Redaction of Welsh laws also grouped secret killing, arson, rape and robbery, as did the earliest manuscript

1180, moreover, associated arson with other grievous offences against the person (robbery, rape and secret killing), the punishment of which contemporary canonists all agreed should first be the responsibility of the prince and only then of a spiritual confessor.[67] The legislative efforts of the Scottish kings William I and Alexander II, then, suggest a pattern of legal change in tune with recent theological and canonistic discussions in the schools of Paris, Laon and elsewhere, and a sophisticated grasp of the conceptual links between punishment, remission and reparation. A similar understanding of serious offences as both sin and crime runs through the decrees issued by the thirteenth-century Scottish church councils which, in step with royal legislation, formally condemned acts of homicide, theft, robbery and fire-raising.[68] Clearly, there was a great deal of cross-fertilisation between the thinking of learned clerics and secular lawmakers going on in this period.

Among the many clerics who counselled the twelfth- and thirteenth-century kings of Scots a handful were in an ideal position to instruct legislation-minded rulers about new currents in canonist thinking. While lists of the manuscript holdings of most of the religious houses of Scotland have long been lost, there is plenty of evidence to suggest that the writings of European canonists and theologians circulated widely in Scotland. There were extensive libraries in places such as St Andrews, Aberdeen, Glasgow, Melrose, Dunfermline, Jedburgh and Kelso, and small collections elsewhere.[69] The libraries at

---

copies of *Tair Colofn Cyfraith*. Pryce, Huw 1993 *Native Law and the Church in Medieval Wales*, Oxford: Clarendon Press 45.

67 Helmholz, *The Spirit* 116–17; Helmholz, Crime 3–4.
68 Robertson 18–20, 26–27, 29, 38.
69 In the very early twelfth century Pope Pascal II sent copies of Ivo of Chartres's *De exceptiones ecclesiastiarum regularum* and the *Panormia* to the bishop of St Andrews. The latter was still in the priory library in the middle years of that same century, together with works by several church fathers, Bernard of Clairvaux's *Sententiae* and glosses on biblical books. The bishop gifted all these books to the new monastery at Loch Leven. Higgitt, John, editor 2006 *Scottish Libraries*, London: British Academy 24–25. The richness of Scottish libraries in the fourteenth century is apparent in the list of works that Higgitt brings together in Index IV of this book, 420–29. See also Higgitt, John 1998 Manuscripts and Libraries in the Diocese of Glasgow before the Reformation,

Durham, with whose bishops and priors the Scots maintained close personal, professional and intellectual communications, housed dozens of copies of works by such authors as Augustine, Gregory I, Pseudo-Isidore, Ivo of Chartres (and his imitators), Hugh of St Victor, Peter Lombard and Peter Comestor (among others), as well as up-to-date canonical collections (notably by Gratian and early decretalists) and copies of the earliest *summae* by scholars such as Thomas Aquinas.[70] Excerpts from some of these works in turn made their way into Scottish episcopal legislation in the mid-thirteenth century.[71] The identities of individual owners of works of law and of the men who may have acted as transmitters of expertise in canonical procedure are much more difficult to trace, but not atypical, perhaps, was the Berwickshire-born Peter of Paxton who owned, in addition to a glossed Bible, a complete collection of civilian and canon law texts, which he used in 1219 as pledges for a debt.[72] Recent scholarship on twelfth-century manuscripts of Boethius's work, moreover, has demonstrated beyond doubt that, however peripheral may have been the kingdom's geographic location, Scottish monks from houses large and small were deeply integrated into a 'lively network of textual exchange and transmission' with manuscript writers in England and Europe.[73]

Medieval Art and Architecture in the Diocese of Glasgow, edited by Richard Fawcett, Leeds: British Archaeological Association 102–10; and Higgitt, John 2005 Dunfermline Abbey and Its Books, *Royal Dunfermline*, edited by Richard Fawcett, Edinburgh: Society of Antiquaries of Scotland 177–86; Webber, Teresa 2006 Monastic and Cathedral Book Collections in the Late Eleventh and Twelfth Centuries, *The Cambridge History of Libraries in Britain and Ireland: Volume 1, to 1640*, edited by Elisabeth Leedham-Green and Teresa Webber, Cambridge University Press 109–25: 118; and Rouse, Richard H., Rouse, Mary A. and Mynors, R. A. B. editors 1991 *Registrum Angliae de libris doctorum et auctorum veterum*, London: British Library 303–08. Much of the information from the *Registrum* is now readily available at the website *Medieval Libraries of Great Britain*, at http://mlgb3.bodleian.ox.ac.uk/.

70   Watson 16–34.
71   Watt, *Church Councils* 67–68; Somerville, Two Notes 150.
72   Foster, C. W., Mayer, K. *et al.* editors 1931–73 *The Registrum Antiquissimum of the Cathedral Church of Lincoln*, 10 vols, Lincoln: Lincoln Record Society 3, no. 816.
73   Murray, Kylie 2015 Books Without Borders: Fresh Findings on Boethius' Reception in Twelfth-Century Scotland, *Medievalia et Humanistica*, new ser.

The kings of Scots were able to keep in close touch with new currents in scholastic thinking thanks to the clerics prominent within their inner circles. Some years ago, Donald Watt identified some 600 'university men' in Scotland in the period between 1200 and 1340 alone.[74] The tools for social network analysis associated with the database *People of Medieval Scotland* are now making it possible to represent the personal and professional relationships of individuals in graphic form and, more promisingly still, to link some of these men firmly with the legislative changes of the late twelfth and the thirteenth centuries.[75] A few examples here will suffice. Matthew Scott, who eventually served as chancellor of Scotland in the late 1220s, began his intellectual career at the university of Paris. After his studies in theology he stayed in Paris, where he acquired such an impressive reputation as a teacher that the pope endowed a chair for him.[76] Peter Ramsay may have been a student of Scott's at Paris; he achieved the degree of doctor of theology before returning to Scotland, where he eventually became bishop of Aberdeen.[77] Two Williams, Malveisin and de Lindsay, also became masters after studying in Paris, the former earning the

---

41, 7–44: 8; see also Harrison, Julian 2013 Cistercian Chronicling in the British Isles, *The Chronicle of Melrose Abbey: A Stratigraphic Edition, Vol. 1 Introduction and Facsimile Edition*, edited by Dauvit Broun and Julian Harrison, Woodbridge: Boydell and Brewer 13–28.

74 Watt, D. E. R. 1986 Scottish University Men of the Thirteenth and Fourteenth Centuries, *Scotland and Europe 1200–1850*, edited by T. C. Smout, Edinburgh: John Donald 1–18:2; Watt, *Biographical Dictionary passim*.

75 See *PoMS* http://www.poms.ac.uk/social-network-analysis/ for an explanation of what kinds of relationships may be studied on the database; see also Jackson, Cornell and Hammond, Matthew 2014 Use of Social Network Analysis to Explore the People of Medieval Scotland, *Proceedings of the Digital Humanities Congress 2014*, edited by Clare Mills, Michael Pidd and Jessica Williams https://www.hrionline.ac.uk/openbook/chapter/dhc2014-hammond.

76 *PoMS* no. 864 http://db.poms.ac.uk/record/person/864/; Theiner no. 17.

77 *PoMS* no. 2047 http://db.poms.ac.uk/record/person/2047/; Watt, *Biographical Dictionary* 460. The *PoMS* entry for Ramsay makes it possible to display the complex series of relationships that linked Ramsay to several dozen other people with the assistance of Gephi visualisation software. Men who served in episcopal households as *magistri* and *iuris periti* are discussed in Shead, Compassed 167–68.

title *utriusque juris peritus* in recognition of his expertise in civil and canon law.[78] All four of these men served as chancellors of Scotland, in precisely those decades when theologians and canonists in Europe were disseminating to wide audiences their conclusions on the nature of penance and its relationship to judicial punishment.[79] Their views were eventually given full elaboration in the work of Thomas Aquinas, in which discussions of punishment and restitution foregrounded the victims of crime, likening acts of compensation and restitution to the restoration of equilibrium, earthly and divine, and epitomising this argument in the dictum that '[r]estitution belongs to justice, because it re-establishes equality'.[80] Scott, Ramsay, Malveisin and de Lindsay, together with others of their ilk—Richard de Inverkeithing (d. 1272), William Wischard (d. 1279), William Fraser (d. 1297), Thomas Charteris (d. 1292), all *magistri*, successively chancellors of King Alexander III and well schooled in the latest currents in canonist thought—were in a unique position to advise their royal employers in the minutiae of canon law and on the ways in which Christian kings might give legislative expression in the secular sphere to the teachings of the church.

Extant documents occasionally make explicit reference to the involvement of these learned clerics in the task of lawmaking. Studies of the witness lists of royal charters have enabled historians to reconstruct with great accuracy the membership of the royal councils of successive Scottish kings during the period between the reign of David I and that of Alexander III as well as the professional backgrounds of many of the clerics who may have been responsible for advising the king in matters of canon law.[81] Early manuscript witnesses of Scottish legal texts sometimes make reference to the promulgation of assizes before

---

78 Watt, *Biographical Dictionary* 375–76, 354.
79 Bériou 263–64.
80 Aquinas, *Summa Theologica*, II.2, Q. 62, Art. 4, accessible at http://dhspriory.org/thomas/summa/SS/SS062.html#SSQ62A4THEP1. See also Nemeth, Charles P. 2008 *Aquinas on Crime*, South Bend IN: St Augustine's Press 146–47.
81 The published volumes in the *Regesta Regum Scottorum* series cover the reigns of Kings David, Malcolm IV, William I and Alexander III. The witnesses to the acts of all these rulers, together with those of King Alexander

the king's 'bishops and abbots,' or the 'nobles and prelates' of the realm.[82] While such clerical lawmakers are not always identified by name in these sources,[83] their prominence in other written materials (most notably in the witness lists of the royal *acta* just mentioned) makes it clear that while allusions in the law books to ecclesiastical expertise may be frustratingly vague, they represent more than just empty words. William I and his thirteenth-century successors understood that a wise king was one who solicited the counsel of his churchmen in making secular law—and was seen publicly to do so.[84] To the preface of a twelfth-century law concerning thieves taken with stolen goods, accordingly, a later transcriber considered it appropriate to add the words '[i]t was ordained by the king on the advice of his prelates earls and barons'.[85] Likewise, in recording the text of an assize enacted at Stirling in 1180 that made provision for the holding of franchisal courts, a later copyist thoughtfully inscribed alongside its rubric a note to the effect that the councillors who had advised the king on the new law included not merely 'earls and barons', but also 'prelates'.[86] That royal advisors gave more than a passing nod to canonical texts and the fundamental role of the church in the making of law is even more apparent in the efforts of some compilers to graft canonical authority into the stuff of early legislation. This occurs, for example, in the *Liber de judicibus*, an early fourteenth-century treatise, parts of which are datable to the reigns of William I and Alexander II. The compiler of an early recension of the treatise added to its contents several paragraphs on *infamia*, the killing of thieves caught in the act of stealing at night, liability in cases of fire raising, counterfeiting, and

---

II, may be found in the searchable *People of Medieval Scotland* database, at http://www.poms.ac.uk/.

82 See, for example, Thomson and Innes 1.374–75, 376, 377, 382, 383.
83 But for exceptions to this general observation, see Thomson and Innes 1.397, 403–04.
84 The prominence of the office of chancellor at the heart of the government of King Alexander II and, by extension, in the making of new law is examined in Stringer, K. J. 2013 The Scottish 'Political Community' in the Reign of Alexander II (1214–49), Hammond, *New Perspectives* 53–84.
85 Taylor, *Leges* 257, c. 4 and n. 351.
86 Taylor, *Leges* 260, c. 7 and n. 455.

accessory to theft. All these passages originated in the Pseudo-Ivonian treatise *Panormia*; they were repeated in the later version of Gratian's *Concordia discordantium canonum* and are found afresh in the Decretals of Gregory IX.[87] From the Decretals they made their way in turn into the texts of the thirteenth-century decrees of the Scottish church.

§§§

It was above all in their efforts to legislate for the new burghs of the realm that Scottish rulers drew on principles of the *ius commune* and the early texts that expounded them. They found in the works of one of Gratian's most influential predecessors, the compiler of the *Panormia* (written c. 1115),[88] a rich font of information about the law-worthiness of different sorts of people and how to treat pledges. Some of these same passages were regarded as so authoritative in the context of urban dispute settlement that they rapidly acquired the status of local Scottish custom. In this way they were seamlessly woven into early compilations of burgh law in the thirteenth century, then copied and recopied in the fourteenth century and later.[89] From the Ivonian and Pseudo-Ivonian *Decretum* and *Panormia*, for example, comes a list in an early version of the burgh laws of the kinds of people who should be considered *infames*, among them thieves and persons guilty of other 'capital crimes', adulterers, fugitives and so on. The list draws almost verbatim

---

[87] Stein, Roman Law 278–79; see also Smith, David Baird 1936 Canon Law, *An Introductory Survey of the Sources and Literature of Scots Law*, by various authors, Edinburgh: Stair Society 183–92. The earliest extant manuscript version is National Library of Scotland, MS 21246, fos 67v–119r, with a slightly later version in British Library, MS Additional 18111, fos 138v–139r (new numeration).

[88] Rolker, Christof 2010 *Canon Law and the Letters of Ivo of Chartres*, Cambridge University Press 283–85.

[89] Stein, Peter 1988 Roman Law in Medieval Scotland, *The Character and Influence of the Roman Civil Law: Historical Essays*, by Peter Stein, London: Hambledon 269–317: 275; MacQueen, Hector L. and Windram, William J. 1988 Laws and Courts in the Burghs, *The Scottish Medieval Town*, edited by Michael Lynch, Michael Spearman and Geffrey Stell, Edinburgh: John Donald 208–27: 210–12.

from these earlier canonist sources.[90] Similarly, the treatise known as the *Liber de judicibus*, noted above, incorporates material of considerably earlier provenance including, once again, passages from both the *Decretum* and *Panormia*.[91] Still again, Peter Abelard's term 'positive law', which cannot have come to Scotland earlier than the 1160s, was apparently well enough known to one of King William's advisors to be included in the text of an early-thirteenth-century treatise concerning the burgh laws. The source of the information, in the opinion of Peter Stein, was 'probably a canonist *Summa* of recent publication'.[92]

The efforts of William I and Alexander II to expand the notion of the king's peace and to establish their jurisdiction over offences that they considered exclusively their purview spoke not to inchoate ideology or inarticulate political ambition, but rather to carefully calculated efforts to appropriate canonist and theological arguments about fundamental princely obligations to protect the weak and to uphold the law. They sought also to demonstrate by word, deed and act that they were prepared to put into practice the advice that the papal curia was so ready to dispense. That the learning of the schools in respect of these notions was absorbed into Scottish political thinking is apparent in some of the earliest writs issued from the royal writing office. In these, the king granted his special protection to individuals or corporations; here, he commanded his subjects to act in such a way that 'there be no complaint made of default of justice'. Scottish pronouncements about the king's obligation to 'do right' following default of justice in the courts of ecclesiastical and secular aristocrats were based on canon law discussions of the same topic probably

---

90 Thomson and Innes 1.744; Ivo of Chartres, *Decretum*, V.291 and *Panormia*, IV.66, both available at The Virtual Canon Law Library, at https://ivo-of-chartres.github.io/decretum/ivodec_5.pdf and https://ivo-of-chartres.github.io/panormia/pan_4.pdf, both with date/revision stamp 2015-09-02. Although the earliest manuscript of burgh laws dates from c. 1270, most historians agree that the origins of the burgh laws lie in the later twelfth century. See, for example, Oram *Domination* 273–74.
91 For the dating, see Windram, W. J. 1984 What Is the *Liber de judicibus*? *Journal of Legal History* 5, 177–78: 178.
92 Stein, Roman Law 277.

mediated, like so much else in the juridical context, through ecclesiastical counsellors familiar with the writings of university men.[93] More tellingly still, the obligation to 'do right' came to be embedded in the terminology of royal letters of remission, which threatened with royal sanction anyone who dared to contravene the secular and ecclesiastical protection that the king's pardon extended to the remorseful.[94] Scholars have argued that changes in twelfth- and thirteenth-century canon law gave new impetus to the high medieval papacy's designs to control and punish persons who committed the most heinous of ecclesiastical sins, simony and heresy.[95] In a comparable development, legal changes in the secular sphere gave King William and his thirteenth-century successors the theoretical justification and the practical tools that they required to enact secular legislation concerning crime and other serious wrongdoing. The ideology and the vocabulary of canonical writing are apparent in the thoughtful deployment of the terms noted above (*crimen, iniuria, contumelia, maleficia*) and found expression in the development of a more coherent sense of the king's peace.[96]

Of especial interest to the king of Scots and the people he governed must have been the notion that absolution—earthly or spiritual—was valid only if an offender had made satisfaction to the injured party. Canonists, theologians and the thirteenth-century decretalists commented at length about the implications of penance in the *Concordia discordantium canonum*,[97] eventually settling on the broadly

---

93 Barrow, G. W. S. editor 1984 *Regesta Regum Scottorum, Vol. 1: The Acts of Malcolm IV, King of Scots, 1153–1165*, Edinburgh University Press no. 258 and see no. 149; see also Barrow *William I* nos. 197, 507, 513; MacQueen, Expectations 282, 290; MacQueen, *Common Law* 194–95.
94 Neville, The Beginnings 3–4.
95 Fraher, Preventing 214.
96 On the king's peace, see Neville, Royal Mercy 8–18; Harding, Alan 1966 The Medieval Brieves of Protection and the Development of the Common Law, *Juridical Review*, n.s. 11, 115–149 and the correctives introduced by Taylor, *The Shape* 148–52, 164–75.
97 For which, see the website Decretum Gratiani, at http://www.gratian.org. A link to the newly edited First Recension, by Anders Winroth and others, is available via the site. Gratian's treatment of penance is most extensively presented in the treatise *Tractatus de penitentia*, Distinctio 1, part of the

conceived dictum *non valet pœnitentia sine satisfactione*, that is, that there could be no penance, and no remission of fault, in the absence of reparation to God and to the offended party.[98] This concept will have resonated deeply in contemporary Scotland, where, throughout the medieval period (and well into the modern), Gaelic legal custom required persons who committed the serious offences of theft, homicide and other acts of violence involving injury to make reparation, not only to the lords whose peace they had broken (including that of the king), but also to the victim of the injury or the kindred of a homicide.[99] The centrality of the payment of compensation within the context of Scottish criminal law runs through the earliest law codes of Scotland, and assizes of William I and Alexander II sought to limit the circumstances under which the victims of theft, murder or plundering might licitly seek revenge outside the king's own courts.[100] The deeply embedded notion of kindred compensation likewise found its way into the earliest registers, formularies of brieves and legal treatises.[101] In the later 1200s, as Taylor has shown, the crown may not have wielded exclusive power to punish all incidents of serious crime,

---

larger work *Concordia discordantium canonum*. The *Tractatus* is available at the above-named website, pp. 763–845; see also Wei, John C. 2016 *Gratian the Theologian*, Washington DC: Catholic University of America Press 69–185.

98 Helmholz, *The Spirit* 389. The argument was later incorporated into the decretals of Gregory IX.

99 Taylor, *The Shape* 124–30, 139–52; Neville, Royal Mercy 3, 10–11, 15.

100 Thomson and Innes 1.375; Taylor, *Leges* 256–57, 263–65, 274, 278–79 (the last reference here offers a new edition of the so-called *Leges inter Brettos et Scotos*. Relevant here, too, is the *Leges Marchiae* of 1249, edited by Nielson, George 1971 The March Laws, *Miscellany One*, Edinburgh: Stair Society 11–77. The *LBS* laid out a series of graduated penalties liable to the kindred of a slain man in order to avoid the feud, and carefully distinguished from other fines the *cró* and *kelchin* payable to the kindred. The laws of the marches similarly devoted considerable space to the sums payable to injured parties.

101 The enduring nature of the customs requiring compensation is perhaps most forcefully illustrated in parliamentary legislation of 1366, which nullified royal letters of remission (pardon) in cases of serious wrongdoing if satisfaction had not been made to the injured parties within one year. Brown, K. M. *et al.* editors 2007–2016 *The Records of the Parliaments of Scotland to 1707*, http://www.rps.ac.uk/trans/1366/7/12. See also Wormald, Jenny 1980

but with the support of their canonist contemporaries the kings of Scots exercised *de facto* and *de jure* the same authority to make and to defend the law that other European princes enjoyed.

§§§

Over the course of the late twelfth and the early thirteenth centuries, the kings of Scots looked to the law of the church for inspiration and for the means to give substantive expression to their power to establish the legal rules and norms of secular society. In similar fashion they began to articulate, then to execute, a more fully informed understanding of the connection that theologians and canonists made between royal justice and princely mercy. By the mid-twelfth century secular lawyers and canonists alike agreed that clemency and judgment were indelibly linked. In the secular sphere, they wrote, mercy was most palpably demonstrated in the king's obligation to rule justly.[102] Here again, the popes sometimes assumed personal responsibility for instructing the descendants of Malcolm III and Margaret in these matters. Thus, in a letter to David I dated 1130/40 Innocent II reminded the king of this duty when he likened David's

---

Bloodfeud, Kindred and Government in Early Modern Scotland, *Past & Present* 87, 54-97: 80.

102 A good summary of medieval thought on this topic appears in Sullivan, Robert G. 2001 *Justice and the Social Context of Early High Medieval German Literature*, London: Routledge 46–55. For discussions in the British context, see Davies, R. R. 2009 *Lords and Lordship in the British Isles in the late Middle Ages*, edited by Brendan Smith, Oxford University Press 170, 175 and the little known, but cogently argued McCune, Patricia Helen 1989 The Ideology of Mercy in English Literature and Law, 1200–1600, PhD dissertation, University of Michigan 71–110. *Glanvill's* opening statement about a prince's duty to rule justly, which was itself based on a passage from the *Institutes* of Justinian, was well known in Scotland by the later thirteenth century; Hall, G. D. editor 1965 *Treatise on the Laws and Customs of the Realm of England Commonly Called Glanvill,* London: Nelson xxxvi, 1–2. Earlier still, legislation of King Alfred 'saw the system of compensations as an integration of mercy and justice'. Treschow, Michael, 1994 The Prologue to Alfred's Law Code: Instruction in the Spirit of Mercy, *Florilegium* 13, 79–110: 106.

authority to that of the heavenly ruler Himself.[103] The papal directive that in 1218 restored William del Bois to the office of chancellor of Scotland following a lengthy sentence of excommunication was redolent of the language of penitence and clemency. It served a more general didactic purpose in its solemn declarations about the obligation of a lord, even a wronged one—and even the king—to grant clemency.[104] Less subtle was a missive that the pope addressed directly to Alexander II early in 1225; here, Honorius III reminded the king that acts of royal mercy were all the more appropriate in circumstances in which anger had coloured royal judgement.[105] Coronation oaths all over Europe included explicit statements of the princely duty to exercise clemency, and there is every reason to believe that the oaths taken by Alexander II in 1214 and Alexander III in 1249 made statements to this effect as well.[106]

In the thirteenth-century canonical discussions of sin and crime and theological arguments that princes acted as God's representatives when they extended their mercy to the genuinely repentant all found fertile ground in Scotland. The Caithness layman Lumberd, with whose story this essay began, was made to complete a well prescribed series of acts the purposes of which were at once penitential, punitive and prescriptive. Public humiliation, arduous physical exertion, rituals of supplication and abject demonstrations of contrition: as early as the eleventh century, canonists such as Ivo of Chartres and Anselm of Bec wrote at length about the role that each of these aspects of contrition, submission, satisfaction and peacemaking played in earning grace (*misericordia*) and a formal act of absolution.[107] The ramifications of

---

103 Somerville, *Scotia Pontificia* no. 21; see also Barrow, *Malcolm IV* no. 319.
104 Theiner, Augustinus, editor 1864 *Vetera Monumenta Hibernorum et Scotorum*, Rome: Typus Vaticanis no. 16, discussed in Stringer, Kingship 139, 148–49.
105 Bliss, W. H. editor 1893 *Calendar of Entries in the Papal Registers Relating to Great Britain and Ireland. Papal Letters. Vol. 1: 1198–1304*, London: Her Majesty's Stationery Office 1.104.
106 Duncan, A. A. M. 2003 Before Coronation: Making a King at Scone in the 13th Century, *The Stone of Destiny: Artefact and Icon*, edited by Richard Welander, David John Breeze and Thomas Owen Clancy, Edinburgh: Society of Antiquaries of Scotland 139–68.

their discussions were by no means exclusive to the ecclesiastical and confessional spheres; here, as in so much lawmaking more generally, the language and the speech acts that were the stuff of penitential practice exerted a profound influence on the secular world.[108] The rulers of western Europe, even those in faraway Scotland, drew heavily on the literature of penance of the high Middle Ages and in turn adapted its substance to suit their specific aims. In doing so they elided the distinctions between rites of public penance and those ritual ceremonies of political submission that have so intrigued historians influenced by the anthropological turn.[109] The deployment in these 'theatres of penance' of props, *viva voce* appeals for royal grace, acts of contrition done on bended knee, exchanges of the kiss of peace and gestures of *amicitia*, all intended to secure remission of the Scottish king's 'rancour of spirit'—itself an expression borrowed from canon

---

107 Rolker, Ivo of Chartres' Pastoral Care 120–21; Bossy, John 2004 Practices of Satisfaction, 1215–1700, *Retribution, Repentance and Reconciliation*, edited by Kate Cooper and Jeremy Gregory, Studies in Church History 40, Woodbridge: Boydell 106–18: 107–09.

108 For the borrowing of penitential thought and ritual in secular ceremonies in secular Europe generally, see Meens, Rob 2014 *Penance in Medieval Europe, 600–1200*, Cambridge University Press 10–11; Bossy, John 1983 Postscript, *Disputes and Settlements: Law and Human Relations in the West*, edited by John Bossy, Cambridge University Press 289; Althoff, Gerd 2001 Satisfaction: Peculiarities of the Amicable Settlement of Conflicts in the Middle Age, *Ordering Medieval Society: Perspectives on Intellectual and Practical Modes of Shaping Social Relations*, edited by Bernard Jussen, Philadelphia: University of Pennsylvania Press 270–84: 271–22; Vollrath, Hanna 2002 Rebels and Rituals: From Demonstrations of Enmity to Criminal Justice, *Medieval Concepts of the Past: Ritual, Memory, Historiography*, edited by Gerd Althoff, Johannes Fried and Patrick J. Geary, Washington DC: German Historical Institute 89–110: 97–101; Marafioti, Nicole and Gates, Jay Paul 2014 Introduction, Gates and Marafioti, *Capital* 13; Mansfield 77–80.

109 The literature here is now very substantial, but see, for example, Koziol, Geoffrey 1992 *Begging Pardon and Favor: Ritual and Political Order in Early Medieval France*, Ithaca NY: Cornell University Press; Althoff, Gerd 2002 The Variability of Rituals in the Middle Ages, in Althoff, Fried and Geary 71–87; Petkov, Kirik 2003 *The Kiss of Peace: Ritual, Self, and Society in the High and Late Medieval West*, Leiden: Brill 33–135. For Scottish examples, see Neville, The Beginnings 20–21.

law[110]—were merely performances in a secular context of the penitential acts that so preoccupied theologians.[111] Collectively, indeed, these accounts confirm the observations of more than one historian that 'sometimes the line between political peacemaking and religious reconciliation is difficult to draw' and that 'the borrowing of public penance by secular powers was much more common than one might imagine'.[112] But they indicate also that the chroniclers who wrote about these events, closely in touch with the learned schoolmen who were the king's chief counsellors—and, in Scotland, often also papal legates well versed in canon and civilian law[113]—were thoroughly attuned to the penitential significance of the gestures and words that informed the scripts of such ceremonies. Beginning in the very late twelfth century and increasingly in the thirteenth, the kings of Scots put into practice what their clerical (and papal) counsellors had taught them and exercised the princely prerogative of clemency both in public and private settings.[114] Moreover, they did so not only overtly, by means of letters that remitted the king's 'rancour of spirit' against felons and rebels, but more subtly, too, in grants that remitted amercement and debt.[115] Such acts of clemency echoed—if, indeed, they did not openly imitate—the practice of almsgiving that Thomas

---

110 The term *rancor animi* was 'a phrase well-known to students of medieval feud.' Jordan, William Chester 2009 *A Tale of Two Monasteries: Westminster and Saint-Denis in the Thirteenth Century*, Princeton University Press 150. See also Hyams, Paul R. 2003 *Rancor and Reconciliation in Medieval England*, Ithaca NY: Cornell University Press 130, 255, 297. The term was used, for example, in Peter of Poitiers's *Sententiarum libri quinque*, edited by Migne, J.-P., *Patrologiae cursus completus, Series Latina*, 217 vols, Paris: Petit Montrouge 211.1077 (written c. 1179).

111 For discussions of the 'theatre of penance' in a specifically Scottish (if slightly later) context, see McGavin, John J. 2007 *Theatricality and Narrative in Medieval and Early Modern Scotland*, Aldershot: Ashgate 18, 20–25 and Todd, Margo 2002 *The Culture of Protestantism in Early Modern Scotland*, New Haven CT: Yale University Press 127–82.

112 Mansfield 277.

113 Ferguson *passim*.

114 Neville, The Beginnings 11–15.

115 These are recorded both in royal charters and, if only partially, in extant Exchequer records of the period. The author's study of such remissions is ongoing.

McSweeney has uncovered to such good effect among the curia regis rolls of their contemporaries in England, John and Henry III.[116] More definitively, they drew deliberately on both secular and religious notions associated with the term *misericordia*.

The Scottish kings of the twelfth and thirteenth centuries had good reason to appropriate to their own uses the clerical significance of ceremonies of personal subjection. They did so because the church's views gave added weight in the secular sphere to relations between ruler and ruled. The profound transformation that occurred in power relations between the crown and the Scottish aristocracy in this period—what Taylor has dubbed the 'shaping' of the Scottish state—was effected without benefit of the advantages associated with sacral kingship (unction) that were the norm almost everywhere else in Christendom. Public displays of lawmaking implicitly co-opted these attributes and served to emphasise the superior lordship of the king of Scots. By and large, moreover, Scottish chroniclers were prepared to portray their rulers as exemplars of Christian kingship. Taylor's analysis of the high medieval Scottish state argues convincingly that despite the inability to add unction and anointing to their enthronement ceremonies, Alexander II and Alexander III were regarded as 'fully fledged Christian kings' within their own realm and well beyond. Both enjoyed especially strong reputations as lovers of justice and models of merciful rule.[117]

The contents of the royal assizes of William I and Alexander II attest efforts on the part of the king of Scots to give meaningful expression to kingly authority. In some respects, the new secular legislation may have represented 'a response to learned laws, both as a form of competition with them and as a means of marking the validity of customs within the terms of the learned laws themselves'.[118] But

---

116 McSweeney, Thomas J. 2014 The King's Courts and the King's Soul: Pardoning as Almsgiving in Medieval England, *Reading Medieval Studies* 40, 159–75.

117 Taylor, Alice 2010 Historical Writing in Twelfth- and Thirteenth-Century Scotland: The Dunfermline Compilation, *Historical Research* 83, 228–52: 252.

118 Ibbitsen, David 2005 Custom in Medieval Law, *The Nature of Customary Law*, edited by Amanda Perreau-Saussine and James Bernard Murphy, Cambridge University Press 151–75: 154.

the legislation bears witness also to a growing appreciation for the canonists' teachings about the responsibility of a Christian ruler to govern well. Only two generations after the death of William I, the multivalent meanings associated with royal lawmaking had been so thoroughly absorbed at the Scottish court that a royal charter of 1264 could refer casually to both native custom and the *ius commune* in a reference to rights of transit through lands held in secular hands.[119] By the late thirteenth century the canonist dictum *legista sine canonibus parum valet* or 'a civil lawyer without the canons is worth very little' was as relevant in Scotland as it was anywhere else in Europe.[120] When in 1291–92 the two chief claimants to the throne appealed to 'the laws and usages of Scotland' and to the 'laws by which kings reign,' they evoked the juridical authority, ecclesiastical and secular, upon which their predecessors had successfully fashioned an image of secular majesty. Each also sought to demonstrate to the crowd gathered to hear them their conviction that royal justice in Scotland was all the stronger for its canonical underpinnings.[121] The lawyers who acted on behalf of the claimants probably grasped more firmly still the fact that the successful candidate would ultimately owe his throne (and the future of his realm) to the churchmen who had been such crucial partners in the making of the kingdom.

---

119 Neville, Cynthia J. and Simpson, Grant G. editors 2012 *Regesta Regum Scottorum, Vol. IV, Pt 1: The Acts of Alexander III King of Scots, 1249–1286*, Edinburgh University Press no. 49.
120 The background to the expression is reviewed in Merzbacher, Friedrich 1967 Die Parömie 'Legista sine canonibus parum valet, canonista sine legibus nihil', *Studia Gratiana* 13, 273–82. The debt of early fourteenth-century Scottish law to Goffredus of Trano (d. 1245) in particular is discussed in Stein, Peter 1969 The Source of the Romano-Canonical Part of *Regiam Maiestatem*, *Scottish Historical Review* 48, 107–23; see also Godfrey, Mark 2004 Arbitration in the *Ius Commune* and Scots Law, *Roman Legal Tradition* 2, 122–35: 131–33.
121 Stones, E. L. G. and Simpson, Grant G. editors 1978 *Edward I and the Throne of Scotland 1290–1296: An Edition of the Record Sources for the Great Cause*, 2 vols, Oxford University Press, 2.30, 167, 168, 169, 171, 181, 182, 246, 264 (*leis et usages*); 166, 167, 170, 171, 172, 202, 205 (*la ley par quele reys regnent*).

11
Esoteric Tourism in Scotland: Rosslyn Chapel, *The Da Vinci Code*, and the Appeal of the 'New Age'

Carole M. Cusack

The Collegiate Chapel of St Matthew, better known as Rosslyn Chapel, was named 'best attraction' in the 2015–2016 Scottish Thistle Awards, selected ahead of other tourist attractions including the Wallace Monument, Stirling and Born in the Borders, an artisan brewery and visitor centre in Jedburgh.[1] The Chapel also received a 'prestigious Sandford Award for its education work' and was certified Gold by the Green Tourism Business Scheme in 2016.[2] Rosslyn Chapel is a small, elaborately decorated fifteenth-century church in Roslin village, seven miles south of Edinburgh. The foundation stone was laid by William Sinclair, Third Earl of Orkney and First Earl of Caithness, in 1446. The chapel is owned by a trust administered by the Sinclair (St Clair) family, and in 2000 was in urgent need of repairs.[3] The publication of Dan Brown's sensationalist novel about Robert Langdon (a Harvard scholar of religious 'symbology') and Sophie Neveu (a French cryptologist)

---

1 I am grateful to Donald Barrett for his sympathetic interest in my research and his company on many visits to Rosslyn Chapel between 2006 and 2015.
2 King, Diane 2016 Rosslyn Chapel Strikes Green Tourism Gold, *Edinburgh Evening News*, 22 December. At: http://www.edinburghnews.scotsman.com/our-region/edinburgh/rosslyn-chapel-strikes-green-tourism-gold-1-4323790.
3 St Clair-Erskine, Peter (7th Earl of Rosslyn) 1997 *Rosslyn Chapel*, Roslin: The Rosslyn Chapel Trust 7.

investigating Jesus and Mary Magdalene's bloodline and the whereabouts of the Holy Grail, *The Da Vinci Code*, featured Rosslyn prominently.[4] The film, starring Tom Hanks and Audrey Tautou as Langdon and Sophie (2006), had a climactic sequence at the site, and created a touristic audience with interests far removed from the original Catholic function of the Chapel, and from the research of Medieval Studies scholars.[5]

A *mélange* of motifs from the Western esoteric tradition, including the Knights Templar, Freemasonry, Pagan 'Green Men' and ley lines, coalesce in alternative 'histories' of the site, which are decried by scholars, and denied by the Trust (which nevertheless makes skilful use of Brown's novel as a 'pull factor' for its lucrative tourist trade).[6] This 'esoteric' material attracts an audience that, while not self-identified 'New Agers', is nevertheless attuned via popular culture (novels, films, television and so on) to 'alternative' spiritual currents, which are often esoteric and implicitly anti-Christian. This chapter draws on the author's visits to Rosslyn Chapel between 2006 and 2015, and charts the remarkable transformation of a once-dilapidated and scarcely visited site to a global attraction, with a state-of-the-art visitor centre, sophisticated internet presence, and a steady stream of fascinated visitors, who listen to the 'orthodox' historical narrative of the guides, but are attracted by unorthodox interpretations, often discovered through reading Brown's novel.[7] I commence with a brief history of Rosslyn Chapel and then examine the 'alternative' narrative crafted by Michael Baigent, Richard Leigh, and Henry Lincoln in *The Holy Blood and the Holy Grail*.[8] The appeal of this conspiracist, fringe interpretation of the site, popularised by Brown's novel, will be assessed

---

4 Brown, Dan 2003 *The Da Vinci Code*, London: Corgi.
5 Howard, Ron (dir.) *The Da Vinci Code*, Culver City CA: SONY Pictures. See also Martin-Jones, David 2014 Film Tourism As Heritage Tourism: Scotland, Diaspora and *The Da Vinci Code*, *New Review of Film and Television Studies* 12.2, 156–177.
6 Martine, Roddy 2006 *The Secrets of Rosslyn*, Edinburgh: Birlinn 171–175.
7 Rosslyn Chapel 2017 *The Official Rosslyn Chapel Website*. At: http://www.rosslynchapel.com.
8 Baigent, Michael, Leigh, Richard and Lincoln, Henry 2006 [1982] *The Holy Blood and the Holy Grail*, New York: Random House. The book was reissued

Figure 11.1 Rosslyn Chapel, south side. Photo by Donald Barrett.

using the six-point typology of Western esotericism proposed by Antoine Faivre.[9] I then consider tourism to the Chapel in relation to 'New Age' ideas of sacred places, sites of power, and hidden histories.

The History of Rosslyn Chapel and *The Holy Blood and the Holy Grail*

The foundation stone of the Collegiate Chapel of St Matthew was laid on 21 September 1446, the feast day of Saint Matthew. This building was the third church to be erected in Roslin village, replacing an older St Matthew's church and supplementing the chapel within Roslin Castle.[10] It was part of a construction programme that resulted in around fifty

---

in a revised format in 2005, due to the success of Brown's *The Da Vinci Code* (2003) and has sold over two million copies worldwide.
9   Faivre, Antoine 1994 *Access to Western Esotericism*, Albany NY: State University of New York Press 10–15.
10   Campbell, George, Old, Madge, Combe, Andrew and Stevenson, Winnie 2006 *A Short History of the Churches of Roslin* (revised edition), Roslin: Roslin Church Publishing 17–19.

collegiate churches (so called as they were staffed by a college of canons, rather than by monks) existing in Scotland at the time of the Reformation.[11] The Chapel's founder, Sir William Sinclair, whose ancestor William 'the Seemly' St Clair had received the lands of Roslin in a charter dated 1070, intended to build a much larger church, but he died in 1484 and 'was buried in the unfinished Chapel and the larger building he had planned was never realised.'[12] The existing Chapel consists of an aisled choir of five bays twenty-one metres in length, four east chapels in a chevet formation, and a sacristy in the crypt.[13] Rosslyn Chapel was endowed with a staff of nine, consisting of six prebendaries, two choristers and a provost, and in 1523 land was granted for surrounding houses and gardens.

In 1571 the Chapel's endowments were confiscated and the staff expelled as the Reformation took hold. The St Clair family were Catholic and for twenty years resisted despoiling the altars of the Chapel. However, in 1592 Oliver St Clair appeared before the Church of Scotland General Assembly and was 'threatened with execution if the altars remained standing after August 17th 1592.'[14] By 31 August the altars were demolished and the Chapel became ruined, no longer used as a place of worship. During the English Civil War Rosslyn Chapel was used as a stable by the troops of the Roundhead General Monk, and in 1688 just prior to the accession to the throne of William of Orange and Queen Mary, local vandals further damaged the building in an attempt to obliterate all 'popish or idolatrous' features.[15]

The eighteenth century marked a change of fortunes, with the Romantic delight in the picturesque resulting in a new appreciation of the Rosslyn Chapel. In 1700, Father Richard Augustine Hay (1661–c.1736), a Catholic priest and chaplain to the Sinclairs, compiled a history of the family that was published as *A Genealogie of the Sainte Claires of Rosslyn* in 1835. James St Clair repaired the roof, glazed

---

11   [Anon] 2005–2017 Rosslyn Chapel, *Sacred Destinations*. At: http://www.sacred-destinations.com/scotland/rosslyn-chapel.
12   St Clair-Erskine 2.
13   McWilliam, Colin 1978 *Lothian Except Edinburgh*, Harmondsworth: Penguin Books 411–412.
14   St Clair-Erskine 4.
15   Martine 107.

the windows, re-laid the flagstones, and constructed a boundary wall in 1736. In 1803 William and Dorothy Wordsworth visited Rosslyn Chapel, and it featured in Walter Scott's *The Lay of the Last Minstrel* (1805).[16] The Romantic sensibility expressed in Gothic novels like those of Matthew 'Monk' Lewis and Ann Radcliffe delighted in what Victoria Nelson terms 'faux Catholic trappings', which were in abundance in the Chapel.[17] Queen Victoria, a lover of Scotland, came in 1842, and in 1862, James Alexander, Third Earl of Rosslyn, recommenced Sunday services after the chapel was rededicated. In 1880 the church was extended by a small baptistery at the west end, a 'vestry and [an] organ chamber by Andrew Kerr',[18] an Edinburgh architect who published papers on Roslin Castle and Rosslyn Chapel in the *Proceedings of the Society of Antiquaries of Scotland* in 1877.

The official narrative of Rosslyn Chapel as a dazzling example of a private place of worship erected by a devout Catholic in the Middle Ages, which was rediscovered in modernity due to its architectural distinction and beautiful natural setting is sober compared to the 'alternative' histories that have proliferated about the site. Roddy Martine's *The Secrets of Rosslyn* (2006) expounds legends that have accreted over the centuries regarding Rosslyn Chapel and the Sinclairs, while acknowledging that the historical evidence for these tales is slim. The Sinclair family's role in the Knights Templar and the Crusades, the foundation of Freemasonry and purported links to the Priory of Sion and the alleged bloodline of Christ, are canvassed with attendant disclaimers. Yet this narrative has gained traction in the thirty-five years since the publication of *The Holy Blood and the Holy Grail*, and is now a thriving subcultural industry producing newspaper and magazine articles, books, websites and television documentaries. Martine's alternative history of the Sinclairs and the Chapel includes: the possible marriage of Hugh de Payens, founder and first Grand Master of the Templars, to a daughter or sister of the Sir Henry Sinclair

---

16 Martin-Jones 167–168.
17 Nelson, Victoria 2007 Faux Catholic: A Gothic Subgenre from Monk Lewis to Dan Brown, *boundary 2: an international journal of literature and culture* 34.3, 87–107.
18 McWilliam 413.

who fought in the First Crusade; the legend that another Henry Sinclair explored the New World two decades before Christopher Columbus, evidenced by carved friezes at Rosslyn that are said to depict corn and cacti; Augustine Hay's claim that the Sinclairs were 'hereditary Grand Masters ... of the Masons of Scotland'; the possibility that Hay was involved in the secret return of the head shrine of Saint Margaret in the eighteenth century; and the location of Rosslyn Chapel at the conjunction of powerful ley lines.[19] For Martine, Rosslyn Chapel is at the centre of the story; he is dismissive of more outrageous claims, and protective of the reputation of the Sinclair family.

The narrative of Baigent, Leigh and Lincoln in *The Holy Blood and the Holy Grail*, by contrast, is focused on the claim that Jesus and Mary Magdalene married and had children, and that the Holy Grail of the Arthurian legend is in fact the 'bloodline of Christ'.[20] This bloodline is alleged to have survived to the present, having passed through the early medieval Merovingian dynasty in France, and protected by the Templars, 'a proto-secret society',[21] whose role is continued by the Masons and the Priory of Sion, a mysterious fraternity that, while purportedly ancient, was founded by Pierre Plantard (1920–2000) in 1956. Plantard spread tales about Berenger Saunière (1852–1917), a parish priest of Rennes-le-Château, situated in medieval 'Cathar country', who had supposedly discovered a Templar treasure that contained 'documents confirming the old Southern French legends that Jesus Christ, rather than ascending into Heaven, had come to live in France with his wife, Mary Magdalene'.[22] Despite the treasure and the Priory of Sion being modern fabrications, Berenger Saunière most likely having defrauded the church,[23] many conspiracy theorists and alternative subcultural groups accepted the story of an 'underground' true Christianity that was preserved among fringe groups including

---

19 Martine 23, 58, 84, 120 and 129.
20 Baigent, Leigh and Lincoln 339–340, 382, 390, 393, 436–442 and 448–449.
21 Marshall, David W. 2007 Introduction: The Medievalism of Popular Culture, *Mass Market Medieval: Essays on the Middle Ages in Popular Culture*, edited by David W. Marshall, Jefferson NC and London: McFarland 1–12: 2.
22 Introvigne, Massimo 2004 Beyond 'The Da Vinci Code': What is the Priory of Sion? *CESNUR: Center for Studies on New Religions*. At: http://www.cesnur.org/2004/mi_davinci_en.htm.

the ancient Essenes, medieval Cathars, early modern Rosicrucians and Illuminati.[24]

In this secret history of Christianity, the key disciple and interpreter of Jesus is Mary Magdalene, whose burial site had long been linked to southern France. In the eleventh century it was claimed that she died and was buried at Saint Baume, forty miles north of Marseilles. Rival sites included the abbey of La Madeleine, Vézelay and Saint Maximin in Aix-en-Provence. The legend underlying these destinations stated that after the crucifixion Mary arrived in France with a child named Sarah ('princess' in Hebrew). The coastal town of Saintes Maries-de-la-Mer in the Camargue holds a festival from 23 to 25 May in honour of the arrival by boat of Mary Magdalene, Martha, Lazarus, and Sarah. Occult Christianity posits that Sarah is the daughter of Jesus and Mary Magdalene, and that the cult of the 'Black Madonna' found throughout Europe is a disguised form of goddess worship focused on Mary Magdalene, rather than Mary, mother of Jesus.[25] One of the reasons for the sudden popularity of these hitherto obscure tales was the mid-twentieth century discovery of both the Dead Sea Scrolls (1946–1947) and the Nag Hammadi codices (1945), both of which broadened academic and general knowledge of the more varied and less determined context of early Christianity.[26] For example, Gnostic texts that have attracted attention include gospels attributed to Mary Magdalene and Judas.[27]

---

23   Radford, Ray 2017 'Ruined Narratives': Urban Exploration and the *Dérive* in Search of New Meanings, Sydney: University of Sydney, unpublished Honours thesis, 28–30.
24   Guffey, Robert 2006 The Illusion of Control: The Priory of Sion and the Illuminati, *New Dawn* Special Issue No. 2, 45–47.
25   Starbird, Margaret 1993 *The Woman with the Alabaster Jar: Mary Magdalene and the Holy Grail*, Rochester VT: Bear and Co. 60–61. See also Mullen, Peter 1998 *Shrines of Our Lady*, London: Piatkus 155.
26   Vermes, Geza 2011 [1962] *The Complete Dead Sea Scrolls in English*, London: Penguin Books; Robinson, James M. general editor 1981 [1978] *The Nag Hammadi Library*, New York: Harper and Row.
27   Meyer, Marvin 2004 *The Gospels of Mary: The Secret Tradition of Mary Magdalene the Companion of Jesus* (with Esther A. DeBoer), San Francisco CA: Harper San Francisco and Ehrman, Bart D. 2008 *The Lost Gospel of Judas Iscariot*, New York: Oxford University Press.

Figure 11.2 Rosslyn Chapel, west end. Photo by Donald Barrett.

Tales of the Holy Grail, which was traditionally understood as the chalice that Jesus drank from at the Last Supper, which Joseph of Arimathea later used to catch the blood of Jesus as he stood beneath the cross, began circulating in Europe at the end of the twelfth century. Historians argue that this is directly related to the Crusaders' loss of territories in the Holy Land, and of sacred relics such as the fragment of the True Cross 'lost in specular fashion to the Saracens at the disastrous defeat at the Horns of Hattin in 1187'.[28] As pilgrimage routes became perilous, or closed altogether, Christians sought other relics to link them to the life of Jesus. Once the Holy Places were no longer under Christian control, legends connecting Jesus with Europe (like the tradition he came as a child to Glastonbury) spread, creating various 'holy lands' in Europe.[29] Baigent, Leigh and Lincoln (and Brown following their lead) make much of the fact that the term 'San Graal' (Holy Grail) can also be interpreted as 'Sang Real' (royal blood). In the Arthurian cycle this was the blood that Joseph of Arimathea collected when Jesus' side was pierced by the centurion's lance, but in the esoteric 'history' of Mary Magdalene and Jesus it is the blood of their descendants. Brown downplays certain aspects of the alternative history, including the role of the Cathars. The most significant event in Cathar history for esoteric Christianity was the fall of the stronghold of Montsegur in March 1244, after which more than two hundred Cathars were burned.[30] Before the castle fell it was alleged that certain Cathars stole away, taking with them a mysterious 'treasure', speculatively identified with the Holy Grail, and possibly also the treasure of Rennes-le-Château associated with Berenger Saunière.

Rosslyn Chapel features briefly in the revised edition of *The Holy Blood and the Holy Grail* (2006). It is claimed that the Chapel is 'associated with both Freemasonry and the Rose-Croix', and that the Sinclairs are Grand Masters of Scottish Freemasonry.[31] Further,

---

28 Barber, Richard 2004 *The Holy Grail: Imagination and Belief*, Cambridge MA: Harvard University Press 125.
29 Digance, Justine and Cusack, Carole M. 2002 Glastonbury: A Tourist Town for All Seasons, *The Tourist as a Metaphor of the Social World*, edited by Graham Dann, Wallingford: CABI International 263–280.
30 Lambert, Malcolm 1998 *The Cathars*, Oxford: Wiley-Blackwell 167–169.
31 Baigent, Leigh and Lincoln 195.

Baigent, Leigh and Lincoln attempt to demonstrate that the Sinclairs are part of the list of Grand Masters of the Priory of Sion, despite the fact that in 1993 (after the original publication of *The Holy Blood and the Holy Grail* but before the revised edition) Plantard, when questioned by a judge, 'admitted that he had fabricated his story, founded the Priory of Sion (with a few friends), and with an associate forged the documents'.[32] Yet the contemporary conspiracist milieu is not deterred by such confessions of the falseness of its complex of beliefs; as David G. Robertson notes, '"conspiracy theories" are constructed as those which challenge "official accounts" ... [and] appeal to counter-epistemic strategies'.[33] Rosslyn Chapel features in chapter 104 of Brown's novel: he asserts it lies on the Rose Line, a ley line running through Glastonbury, the Arthurian Avalon; that it is also on the location of a Mithraic temple, and features 'a mind-boggling array of symbols from the Jewish, Christian, Egyptian, Masonic and pagan traditions'.[34] All of these claims are false, but are woven into the web of stigmatised and rejected 'knowledge' that has considerable appeal for those in the 'cultic milieu', which sociologist Colin Campbell characterises as an oppositional subculture.[35]

When Langdon and Sophie enter the church, she realises that she has been there before, in the company of her grandfather Jacques Saunière. Her identity as a princess of the bloodline of Christ is confirmed when the young guide at the Chapel turns out to be her brother, long believed dead (a plotline that was omitted from the film), and she is reunited with her grandmother Marie who raised him. The scenes at Rosslyn Chapel are the emotional climax of *The Da Vinci Code*, as Langdon and Sophie also begin a romantic relationship.[36]

---

32 Lacy, Norris J. 2004 *The Da Vinci Code*: Dan Brown and the Grail That Never Was, *Arthuriana* 14.3, 87.
33 Robertson, David G. 2016 *UFOs, Conspiracy Theories and the New Age: Millennial Conspiracism*, London and New York: Bloomsbury 52-53.
34 Brown 564.
35 Campbell, Colin 1972 The Cult, the Cultic Milieu, and Secularization. *A Sociological Yearbook of Religion in Britain* 5, 119-136.
36 Maddux, Kristy 2008 The Da Vinci Code and the Regressive Gender Politics of Celebrating Women, *Critical Studies in Media Communication* 25.3, 237.

The Da Vinci Code and Faivre's Typology of Western Esotericism

Antoine Faivre's typology of Western esotericism was devised to overcome issues in the academic study of esoteric traditions. He argues that esotericism 'conjures up chiefly the idea of something "secret" ... of restricted realms of knowledge.'[37] Esotericism can also refer to the transcendence of methods employed in specific religions in order to achieve higher knowledge that 'is identical to all who achieve it; experience of its attainment is the proof or guarantee of the "transcendent unity of religions".'[38] These ideas, secrecy and the *philosophia perennis*, are seemingly religionist and uncritical; Faivre's typology represents an attempt to identify empirically verifiable elements of esoteric traditions. Wouter J. Hanegraaff applied the Faivre typology to New Age ideas and practices, arguing that they were secularised manifestations of the Western esoteric tradition. No longer secret, elitist, and lofty, New Age was exoteric, public and incorporated elements from popular culture.[39] Critically examining *The Da Vinci Code* through Faivre's model is fascinating, in that the novel fits each of the six descriptors closely. The first aspect, Correspondence, posits that '[s]ymbolic and real correspondences ... are said to exist among all parts of the universe, both seen and unseen. ("As above so below").'[40] Correspondences are identified to be interpreted; the 'universe is a huge theater [sic] of mirrors, an ensemble of hieroglyphs to be decoded'.[41]

---

37 Faivre 5.
38 Faivre 5.
39 Hanegraaff, Wouter J. 1998 [1996] *New Age Religion and Western Culture: Esotericism in the Mirror of Secular Thought*, Albany NY: State University of New York Press 397. The 'New Age' is a contested concept and it is worth noting that scholars have offered other formulations of its core structures. See Sutcliffe, Steven 2003 Category Formation and the History of the New Age, *Culture and Religion: An Interdisciplinary Journal* 4.1, 5–29. Sutcliffe reviews the definitions and models of New Age proposed by Hans Sebald, J. Gordon Melton, Michael York, Wouter Hanegraaff, and Paul Heelas, noting their overlaps and discontinuities.
40 Faivre 10.
41 Faivre 10.

Figure 11.3 Rosslyn Chapel, north side. Photo by John Lord (https://bit.ly/2PHpcwD).

The fundamental belief that the universe is a text to be decoded is in evidence from the outset in *The Da Vinci Code*. Jacques Saunière (who shares a surname with the priest of Rennes-le-Château), the elderly curator and Grand Master of the secretive Priory of Sion, who is murdered in the Louvre at the start of the novel, taught his granddaughter Sophie Neveu puzzles, and left coded messages as he lay dying. When Robert Langdon, the hero, sees the body he recognises that Saunière has arranged himself in the pose of Leonardo da Vinci's *Vitruvian Man*, and has a pentacle drawn in blood on his chest.[42] As Langdon and Sophie decode the messages left by Saunière, themes are articulated and replicated. For example, the interwoven scenes from Langdon's classes at Harvard adumbrate motifs; one example is the far-fetched identification of the 'Mona Lisa' (who is described by a

---

42   Brown 58–65.

student as 'one ugly chick') as a portrait of androgyny, her name being the anagram of the Egyptian gods, Amon and Isis (allegedly 'L'Isa'). This technique of interpretation is also applied to da Vinci's 'The Last Supper.' The conversation, involving Grail expert Sir Leigh Teabing (whose name is an anagram of Baigent and Leigh), to whom Langdon and Sophie have fled not realising his villainy, posits that the disciple usually identified as John 'the beloved' is in fact Mary Magdalene, Jesus' wife. Teabing asserts that there are symbols in the painting giving the letter 'M', and also the chalice and blade symbols ('v' and inverted 'v'), exemplifying divine femaleness and maleness.[43] At the novel's close Langdon realises that the glass pyramid of the Louvre, and its subterranean counterpart, *la Pyramide Inversée*, on the Rose Line running through the church of Saint-Sulpice, are also signs of the fusion of the goddess and the god, in plain sight.[44]

Faivre's second characteristic is Living Nature: 'Nature, seen, known, and experienced as essentially alive in all its parts, often inhabited and traversed by a light or a hidden fire circulating through it'.[45] This is chiefly manifest in *The Da Vinci Code* by the presence of the female divine as an abiding preoccupation. Occult histories claim that the rise of warlike cultures is associated with the male divine (monotheistic God or polytheistic gods) and his aggressive need to dominate, subjugate and rape both nature and women. By contrast, the religions of the divine feminine worship nature as alive and a goddess; have a positive and non-violent view of sexuality; and create egalitarian societies that encourage personal fulfilment, emotional, spiritual and artistic.[46] It is undeniable that monotheism (Jewish, Christian and Islamic) displaced many female deities, and the Bible speaks of the Canaanite worship of Astarte or Ashtoreth, a version of Ishtar. As Christianity advanced in the Greco-Roman world, the Virgin Mary (the mother of Jesus) took the place of the goddess in the

---

43 Eisler, Riane 1987 *The Chalice and the Blade: Our History, Our Future*, San Francisco CA: Harper San Francisco xiii–xxi.
44 Brown 592.
45 Faivre 11.
46 See French, Marilyn 1985 *Beyond Power: Women, Men and Morals*, London: Jonathan Cape 355.

hearts of the people, her churches being built on the sites of goddess temples, such as the Temple of Diana at Ephesus.[47] In the novel much is also made of symbols derived from nature, chiefly the rose, which resembles the female genitals and is thus a goddess symbol, and also through the use of the Latin phrase *sub rosa* (under the rose), which identifies a secret.

Faivre's third characteristic is 'a form of imagination inclined to reveal and use mediations of all kinds, such as rituals, symbolic images, mandalas, intermediary spirits'.[48] The novel begins with Jacques Saunière's body being discovered in the Denon Wing of the Louvre. Robert Langdon, American professor of 'religious symbology', is summoned by Interpol to help decode Saunière's message and the arrangement of his body in the pose of Leonardo da Vinci's *Vitruvian Man*. This is an image that mediates meaning. Langdon explains to Bezu Fache that the pentagram was a symbol of the divine feminine which da Vinci and Saunière shared an interest in. When Langdon is saved from imminent arrest by cryptographer Sophie Neveu, Saunière's granddaughter, she tells him that the suit of pentacles was her Tarot suit when she played with Saunière as a child.[49] The goddess theme continues with the identification of the Mona Lisa as a goddess and the Priory of Sion as a goddess-worshipping cult. Langdon and Sophie are then led to Leonardo's *The Madonna of the Rocks*, which Langdon says is 'notorious among art historians for its plethora of hidden pagan symbolism'.[50] At the Bank of Zurich they use the Priory key to retrieve a cryptex (a stone puzzle cylinder containing a scroll). Da Vinci had made these as a hobby, as did Saunière. Langdon determines that it is the keystone of the Priory of Sion, which will reveal the location of the Holy Grail. The cryptex is finally opened when the word 'Sofia' (wisdom) is spelled, only to reveal an inner cryptex requiring further decoding. This opens to the word 'apple,' the object that ensured Adam's

---

47 Warner, Marina 1976 *Alone of All Her Sex: The Myth and Cult of the Virgin Mary*, London: Picador 33–37.
48 Faivre 12.
49 Brown 129.
50 Brown 191–192.

fall in Genesis, and the consignment of Eve and all subsequent women to the category of sinful temptresses.[51]

The fourth element of the Faivre typology is 'the experience of transmutation ... the passage from one plane to another ... the modification of the subject in its very nature'.[52] A crucial quality of the Western esoteric tradition is that its focus is on personal transformation. Whereas medieval Catholicism taught that Christ's death resulted in salvation for humanity, through the tradition and institution of the Church, esoteric movements posit that being initiated and deepening one's *gnosis* (knowledge) results in a transmutation of the person which is akin to the alchemical notion of changing base metal into gold.[53] Another important distinction is that Christianity taught that salvation was realised in heaven as a spirit after death, and that this life might involve hardship and self-denial, and that certain aspects of human life, such as sexuality, should be repressed. In *The Da Vinci Code* Sophie's estrangement from her grandfather is because she witnessed him participating in a sexual ritual. In chapter 74, Langdon reveals the true meaning of this rite to her:

> although what she saw probably looked like a sex ritual, *Hieros Gamos* had nothing to do with eroticism. It was a spiritual act. Historically, intercourse was the act through which male and female experienced God. The ancients believed that the male was incomplete until he had carnal knowledge of the sacred feminine. Physical union with the female remained the sole means through which man could become spiritually complete and ultimately achieve *gnosis*—knowledge of the divine. Since the days of Isis, sex rites have been considered man's only bridge from earth to heaven. 'By communing with woman,' Langdon said, 'man could

---

51 Crispin, Philip 2008 Scandal, Malice and the Kingdom of the Bazoche, *Medieval Sexuality: A Casebook*, edited by April Harper and Caroline Proctor, London and New York: Routledge 165.
52 Faivre 13.
53 Schwarz-Salant, Nathan 1998 *The Mystery of Human Relationship: Alchemy and the Transformation of the Self*, London and New York: Routledge.

Figure 11.4 Gargoyle, Rosslyn Chapel. Photo by Davie Bicker (https://bit.ly/2WMo9NG).

achieve a climactic instant when his mind went totally blank and he could see God'.[54]

This illustrates the esoteric tendency to interpret things metaphorically or non-literally. Brown's characters are what Carl Jung called *archetypes*; Langdon and Sophie become the male and female divine, and their romantic relationship is assumed from the novel's onset.[55] Sophie is named for Sophia (divine wisdom, *hokmah* in Hebrew) which features in both the Old Testament as an hypostatised quality of God, and in the Gnostic Gospels as a major figure in the myth of salvation. More obscure, but still recognisable, is the identification of the lame Sir Leigh Teabing with the king of the Grail Castle, who has various personal names (for example,

---

54 Brown 410.
55 Jung, Carl G. 1959 *The Archetypes and the Collective Unconscious*, London and New York: Routledge 175–176.

Anfortas) but is generally known as the Fisher King.[56] The Fisher King was wounded in the thigh by the Dolorous Stroke; his realm is blighted and the wound cannot be healed until the Grail Knight (Perceval, Lancelot or Galahad, in various versions of the legend) arrives to experience the Grail. This identification leads the reader to trust Teabing, making his unmasking as a villain more effective.

The fifth element of Faivre's system is the praxis of concordance, which he defines as 'a consistent tendency to try to establish common denominators between two different traditions or even more, among all traditions, in the hope of obtaining illumination, a *gnosis*, of superior quality'.[57] Most readers are interested in what *The Da Vinci Code* alleges about Christianity, although the sources that Brown employs are well known to scholars, who regard the *mélange* of occult motifs he has assembled as a pseudo-history. In chapter 55, this 'occult' version of Christianity is expounded by Sir Leigh Teabing, the Grail expert that Langdon and Sophie have taken refuge with. He takes pains to detail Christianity's links with and legacies from many religions. He mentions: the Gnostic Gospels, rediscovered in 1945 at Nag Hammadi; the adoption of pagan dates in Christianity (for example, 25 December for Jesus' birth, which was the Roman feast of Saturnalia, Germanic Yule, and the birth of the Persian god Mithras); the adoption of pagan customs (the resemblance between the Christian Eucharist and the initiatory agape feasts of the Hellenic mystery cults, not to mention their 'dying and rising god' theology); and the alleged marriage of Mary Magdalene to Jesus.[58]

This last point is vital for the novel, as the Holy Grail is identified with the womb and descendants of Mary Magdalene. It is true that the combining of the three women (Mary Magdalene, Mary of Bethany and the nameless prostitute who washes Jesus' feet with ointment) is an error, and that Magdalene's position as the patron saint of prostitutes is undeserved.[59] It is also true that unmarried men

---

56 Nitze, W. A. 1909 The Fisher King in the Grail Romances, *Publications of the Modern Langugage Association* 24.3, 365–418.
57 Faivre 14.
58 Brown 311–319.
59 Haskins, Susan 1993 *Mary Magdalen: Myth and Metaphor*, New York: HarperCollins 14.

were unusual in Jewish culture. Teabing cites a famous passage from the apocryphal *Gospel of Philip*:

> [a]nd the companion of the Saviour is Mary Magdalene. Christ loved her more than all the disciples and used to kiss her often on her mouth. The rest of the disciples were offended by it and expressed disapproval. They said to him, 'Why do you love her more than all of us?'[60]

Mary Magdalene and Jesus are purportedly of the bloodline of David, and their daughter Sarah is too. Jesus is claimed to have been a feminist and left his church in Mary's hands. Peter is therefore not 'the Rock', but a mere pretender to authority. Mary Magdalene went to France after Jesus' death, and the bloodline of Jesus and endures to this day. When she hears Teabing expound this version of events, Sophie Neveu understands why her grandfather always called her 'Princess Sophie.'

The sixth point in Faivre's typology is an '[e]mphasis on transmission [which] implies that an esoteric teaching can or must be transmitted from master to disciple following a pre-established channel, respecting a previously marked path'.[61] The posited existence of the Priory of Sion, allegedly founded in 1099 by Godfrey de Bouillon, the conquering commander of the First Crusade who became King of Jerusalem, is an example of this. Langdon expounds the occult history of the Knights Templar to Sophie in chapter 37; it asserts that Pope Innocent II gave the Templars so much power because they were in possession of a secret that could topple the Christian Church, and that the secret they guarded was the 'Holy Grail'.[62] In 1307 the Templars were dissolved by the Pope and the French King Philip IV, and the last Grand Master Jacques de Molay was burned in Paris with his two deputies in 1314. The reason for this was desire on the part of the church and the state to seize their property, but the occult history argues they were a threat, and were

---

60   Brown 331.
61   Faivre 15.
62   Brown 216–222.

accused of heresy and trumped-up charges, so that the Catholic Church could protect itself.[63]

The alleged bloodline of Christ is another example of such initiatory and secret transmission of sacred knowledge. This analysis of Brown's novel using the Faivre typology reveals that in the twenty-first century much that was formerly esoteric has become part of mainstream culture, and *The Da Vinci Code* is but one fiction that exploits this fact. Needless to say, Christian commentators have been less positive, arguing that 'Brown has created a pseudo-history which appeals to ... readers of an age in spiritual crisis',[64] or engaging in rebuttal to draw attention to 'the real Jesus code ... something worth believing'.[65]

Visiting Rosslyn Chapel: Mediatised and New Age Tourism

My first visit to Rosslyn Chapel was in 2006, and was motivated by the entry on the Chapel in the Lonely Planet city guidebook, which termed it 'Scotland's most beautiful and enigmatic church', with symbolism that 'has led some researchers to conclude that Rosslyn is some kind of secret Templar repository, and it has been claimed that hidden vaults beneath the Chapel could conceal anything from the Holy Grail or the head of John the Baptist to the body of Christ himself'.[66] The filming of *The Da Vinci Code* was mentioned in the entry, and the film was released a week after we visited with friends from St Andrews. At that time, a makeshift information centre operated from an old building (now integrated into the new Visitor Centre), and the Chapel was scaffolded and covered by a canopy (which had been set up in 1997 by James Simpson, the architect superintending its restoration by Nicholas

---

63 Barber 306–313.
64 Morgan, Gwendolyn A. 2006 *The Invention of False Medieval Authorities as a Literary Device in Popular Fiction: From Tolkien to the Da Vinci Code*, Lewiston NY: Edwin Mellen Press 76.
65 Bock, Darrell L. 2004 *Breaking the Da Vinci Code*, Nashville TN: Nelson Books 167.
66 Wilson, Neil 2006 *Edinburgh City Guide*, London: Lonely Planet Publications 184.

Boyce Stone Conservation) so that work on the roof could be done. The restoration was complete in 2013, and cost approximately ten million pounds, raised by 'the Rosslyn Chapel Trust and supporters, including the National Lottery [and] Historic Scotland'.[67] Roddy Martine, reflecting on the impact of *The Da Vinci Code* tourism, noted that in 2005 approximately 120,000 visitors were recorded, there were around 32,000 websites referring to Rosslyn Chapel, and 'the Chapel's official website ... gets an average of 30,000 hits per week'.[68]

My second visit was in 2010, by which time a coach park had been built, the exhibits curated for visitors were more elaborate, and there were guided tours of the Chapel. Emphasis was placed on explaining Rosslyn Chapel in a conventional Christian framework, and no mention was made of Dan Brown or *The Da Vinci Code* (though the flood of tourists that contributed funds to the restoration undoubtedly visited because of the novel and film). My third visit to Rosslyn in 2015 saw a remarkable transformation of a once-dilapidated and scarcely visited site into a global attraction, with a new visitor centre, sophisticated internet presence, and a steady stream of enthusiastic tourists, who listen to the 'orthodox' historical narrative of the guides, but are attracted by the fictional explanation of Brown.[69] In the eleven years since Martine's book was published, visit numbers remain at around 150,000 per year, with 176,000 in 2006 as the recorded high, stimulated by the release of the film starring Tom Hanks and Audrey Tautou, and directed by Ron Howard. This film grossed 768 million American dollars worldwide, and a sizeable tourism market developed as a result of viewers' interest in the sites that featured in it, such as Saint-Sulpice in Paris, Temple Church in London and Rosslyn Chapel. This is termed 'mediatised tourism' because it is generated by media interest, whether print, film, television, or internet. Tourism research

---

67 Holden, John-Paul 2013 Rosslyn Chapel Unveiled After 16 Years of Work, *Edinburgh Evening News*, 5 September. At: http://www.edinburghnews.scotsman.com/news/rosslyn-chapel-unveiled-after-16-years-of-work-1-3077135.
68 Martine xiv.
69 Quigley, Elizabeth 2016 Visiting Rosslyn Chapel 10 Years After *The Da Vinci Code*, *BBC News Scotland*, 4 May. At: http://www.bbc.com/news/uk-scotland-edinburgh-east-fife-36170187.

Figure 11.5 Roslin Hotel. Photo by Donald Barrett.

suggests that the novel or film of *The Da Vinci Code* is the motivation for such tourists to visit places like Rosslyn Chapel, and that social media (Facebook, Twitter, Flickr, blogs) activity transforms consumers (tourists, visitors) into producers of their own narratives about the site, which in turn inspire others to travel. Maria Månsson contends that 'the power of scripting sites, which can be used as an inspiration by other tourists, is taken from the owners/producers and distributed further to include the tourists themselves. In some cases, as ... [with] the Rosslyn Chapel Trust, this consumer generated scripting is in direct opposition to the scripts of the site owners.'[70]

The attraction of Rosslyn Chapel, apart from Brown's bestselling fictional narrative, has always been esoteric, in the sense that Freemasonry, which was a dominant theme, was at the fringes of Christian culture. One of the most famous sculptural features of the Chapel is pair of pillars known as the Master Pillar (north) and the Apprentice Pillar (south). In *The Da Vinci Code* Sophie recognises

---

[70] Månsson, Maria 2011 Mediatized Tourism, *Annals of Tourism Research* 38.4, 1646.

them when she and Langdon first enter Rosslyn Chapel; she recovers a memory of having been there as a child with her grandfather. In the book her 'homecoming' to Roslin is a private, family matter, but as David Martin-Jones notes, 'in the film there is a much stronger sense of community, roots and belong evoked ... the movie suggests the entire village of Roslin is keen to meet the returned Neveu'.[71] In the book, Langdon informs Sophie of the prevalence of the pillars in Freemasonry: 'That's called *Boaz*—or the Mason's Pillar. The other is called *Jachin*—or the Apprentice Pillar ... In fact, virtually every Masonic temple in the world has two pillars like these.'[72]

Martine retells the legend of their creation, which he links to the Masonic tale of the murder of Hiram Abiff, architect of the Temple of Solomon. During the Chapel's construction, 'Rosslyn's master mason, having received instructions from his patron as to the design of an exquisite pillar, was hesitant to carry out the work until he had been to Rome for inspiration. While he was away, an apprentice, having seen the finished pillar in a dream, set about the work. When the master mason returned he was so jealous of his apprentice's achievement that he murdered the young man in a fit of rage.'[73] Yet the Masonic story attached to Rosslyn Chapel is itself fictional; modern Freemasonry was founded centuries after the Chapel was built, and 'Freemasonry has retroactively claimed the symbolism of Rosslyn'.[74] Sober architectural guides note that the Apprentice Pillar is not unique, but one among many European examples of 'twisted columns', though 'the realization of the idea at Roslin is uniquely luxuriant'.[75]

---

71 Martin-Jones 170.
72 Brown 569.
73 Martine 149.
74 Gunn, Joshua 2008 Death by Publicity: U.S. Freemasonry and the Public Drama of Secrecy, *Rhetoric and Public Affairs* 11.2, 245.
75 McWilliam 414.

Conclusion

For modern travellers influenced by media and with a preference for conspiracies and secrets rather than historically attested fact, it is easy to imagine Rosslyn Chapel, with its beautiful natural setting, ruined castle but a short walk away, and quiet, vaguely pretty village with two welcoming pubs, as being peculiarly opportunely sited, perhaps on land associated with druids or ley lines in the distant past. Since the rise of New Age beliefs in the 1980s and 1990s, earth energies and sites of power have been claimed for many notable tourist destinations, such as Glastonbury, Uluru and the Pyramids of Giza.[76] Interest in paranormal powers is often associated with conspiracism and secret histories; the groundwork for the success of *The Da Vinci Code* had been laid by Baigent, Leigh and Lincoln in *The Holy Blood and the Holy Grail* two decades earlier. The lawsuit that resulted when Baigent and Leigh sued Brown for plagiarism, which reached the High Court in Britain in 2006, in fact 'served to make the novel and film more popular'.[77] Baigent and Leigh lost; Brown identified *The Holy Blood and the Holy Grail* as merely one source among many that his wife, an art historian, consulted while researching for *The Da Vinci Code*.[78]

In the modern era the retreat of institutional Christianity as a dominant narrative, and the mainstreaming of a raft of alternative spiritual ideas that were never entirely extinguished by official religion, has resulted in the rise of private belief systems.[79] In the West, affluence fuels both individualism and consumerism in the crafting of experiences that are meaningful for individuals, and reading about and accepting conspiracies and secret histories, rather than being derided, is often viewed as experimenting with ideas and being open minded. Travel is a prime site of meaningful activity for affluent people, whose

---

[76] McDonald, Jeffrey L. 1995 Inventing Traditions for the New Age: A Case Study of the Earth Energy Tradition, *Anthropology of Consciousness* 6.4, 31–45.
[77] Tzanelli, Rodanthi 2010 The Da Vince Node: Networks of Neo-Pilgrimage in the European Cosmopolis, *International Journal of the Humanities* 8.3, 114.
[78] Button, James 2006 Deciphering Dan Brown, *The Sydney Morning Herald*, 4–5 March 32.
[79] Campbell 119–136.

understanding of the sites they visit is likely to be emotive and influenced by media (film, television, internet) rather than scholarly explanations. While historians, architects and cultural heritage experts seek to establish an accurate and factual narrative about structures such as Rosslyn Chapel, non-academics (including tourists) have more democratic ideas about which narratives will prevail.[80] The Rosslyn Chapel Trust, while grateful to *The Da Vinci Code* phenomenon that contributed so substantially to the site's popularity and prosperity, in fact authorises a very different narrative of family history, Christianity and medieval architecture. Yet the power of Brown's sprawling, esoteric thriller is now the dominant lens through which this fascinating medieval church is viewed and understood.

---

80   Holtorf, Cornelius 2011 The Changing Contribution of Cultural Heritage to Society, *Museum International* 63.1–2, 8–16.

About the Authors

Roxanne Bodsworth is a candidate for PhD by Creative Project at Victoria University (Melbourne). Her area of research is the representation of women in Irish mythology and she is writing a prosometric collection that is a feminist reconstruction of the tales told about Caer, Deirdre and Gráinne. Her first book was a verse novel *The Tangled Web* (1989) and her second, *Sunwyse—Celebrating the Wheel of the Year in Australia* (2003). Her poetry, short stories and articles have been published in a variety of books, magazines and journals. In her spare time, she is also a sheep farmer and celebrant.

Carole M. Cusack is Professor of Religious Studies at the University of Sydney. She trained as a medievalist and now researches primarily in contemporary religious trends and Western esotericism. Her books include: *Conversion Among the Germanic Peoples* (1998) (with Katharine Buljan), *Anime, Religion and Spirituality: Profane and Sacred Worlds in Contemporary Japan* (2015), *Invented Religions: Imagination, Fiction and Faith* (2010) and *The Sacred Tree: Ancient and Medieval Manifestations* (2011). She edited (with Alex Norman) *Handbook of New Religions and Cultural Production* (2012) and (with Pavol Kosnáč) *Fiction, Invention and Hyper-reality: From Popular Culture to Religion* (2017). She co-edits the journal *Fieldwork in Religion*.

Meredith Cutrer is a PhD candidate at University College Dublin, School of History, specialising in the late antique and early medieval periods, particularly in Ireland, Britain and Egypt. Her research interests include historical theology, exile, penance and historiography. She regularly participates in archaeological excavations, including digs in Tintagel, Glendalough, Vindolanda, Cap de Cavalleria and Kazakly-yatkan. She is part of a collaboration that is producing a translation and critical edition of the 'O'Donohue Lives'. Her PhD is generously funded by the Government of Ireland International Education Scholarship and the Irish Research Council Postgraduate Scholarship.

Stephen Joyce completed his PhD at Monash University in 2018. He specialises in the impact of Christian theology on the evolution of political authority in the early medieval West, particularly in relation to the British Isles. He is currently a Research Fellow on the Australian Research Council Discovery Project, 'Addressing Injustice in the Medieval Body Politic: From Complaint to Advice' (2019–2021), and acts as a Learning Skills Adviser at the Matheson Library. A monograph, *The Legacy of Gildas: Constructions of Authority in the Early Medieval West*, is forthcoming with Boydell & Brewer in 2020.

Bernard Mees is Deputy Associate Dean (Research) at the Tasmanian School of Business and Economics at the University of Tasmania. He is a historian of ideas and has written widely on early Celtic and Germanic epigraphy. His publications include *The Science of the Swastika* (2008), *Celtic Curses* (2009) and *The Rise of Business Ethics* (2020).

Constant J. Mews is Professor within the School of Philosophical, Historical and International Studies, Monash University where he is also Director of the Centre for Religious Studies. He has published widely on medieval thought, ethics and religious culture, with particular reference to the writings of Abelard, Heloise, Hildegard of Bingen and their contemporaries, including *Abelard and Heloise* (2005) and *The Lost Love Letters of Heloise and Abelard: Perceptions of Dialogue in Twelfth-Century France* (2nd edn 2008). He has edited and translated a range of medieval texts, and is currently completing a monograph,

About the Authors

A Scholastic Revolution: The Invention of Theology in Medieval Europe. His research interests range from the early Middle Ages to late medieval religious and intellectual culture, as well as the interface between various religious and ethical traditions.

Penelope Nash is an Honorary Associate with the University of Sydney. Her interests include medieval art, medieval Italy and Germany, women's power and biography. Her recent publications include '*Dominae imperiales*: Ottonian Women and Dynastic Stability', in *Dynastic Change: Legitimacy in Gender in Medieval and Early Modern Monarchy* (2020) and 'Maintaining Elite Households in Germany and Italy, 900–1115', in *Royal and Elite Households* (2018). Her 2017 monograph *Empress Adelheid and Countess Matilda: Medieval Female Rulership and the Foundations of European Society* compares two successful, elite medieval women for their relative ability to retain their wealth and power in the midst of the profound social changes of the eleventh century.

Cynthia Neville is Professor Emeritus in the Department of History at Dalhousie University and was recently appointed to the Graduate Studies program in the Department of History at the University of Guelph. She has written extensively on the legal history of the Anglo-Scottish borderlands in the period 1200–1500. She has also published a long list of award-winning books and articles about Gaelic lordship in later medieval Scotland and, more particularly, on the impact of Anglo-Norman and European ideas on the legal culture of twelfth- and thirteenth-century Scotland. She is a Fellow of the Royal Historical Society, a fellow of the Society of Antiquaries of Scotland, a Life Fellow of Clare Hall at the University of Cambridge and has held visiting fellowships in Scotland, England, the United States and Australia.

Tomás Ó Carragáin of the Archaeology Department, University College Cork, Ireland, researches the archaeology of early medieval Ireland and its European context (c. AD 400–1200). Among other subjects, he has published on the archaeology of Christianisation, archaeological approaches to ritual practice including pilgrimage, early medieval architecture and sculpture, the archaeology of territories and boundaries and the relationship between material culture and social memory. He is a member of the Royal Irish Academy and a Fellow of the Society of Antiquaries, London.

Lynette Olson is an Honorary Associate of the Department of History, University of Sydney. She is an early medieval historian whose interests, research and publication encompass the period as a whole (*The Early Middle Ages: The Birth of Europe,* 2007) with particular attention to the Celtic-speaking regions especially Cornwall and Brittany (*Early Monasteries in Cornwall,* 1989) and more specifically the early hagiography of Samson of Dol (editor of collected studies by various scholars and herself in *St Samson of Dol and the Earliest History of Brittany, Cornwall and Wales,* 2017).

Jonathan M. Wooding is the Sir Warwick Fairfax Professor of Celtic Studies at the University of Sydney. His research interests centre on pilgrimage, travel, monastic settlement and the cult of saints in the early Celtic world. His publications include *Communication and Commerce along the Western Sealanes* (1996) and *Living the Hours: Monastic Spirituality in Everyday Life* (with A. Grimley, 2010).

Index

Abba Moses 88
Abraham 83, 89
Áes Irruis Tuascirt 41
agriculture 38; *see also* farming
Alexander I, King 228
Alexander II, King 212, 214, 215, 226–227, 230, 236, 238–242, 245
Alexander III, King 211, 235, 242, 245
Alpine Celtic texts 16, 29
Ambrosianum 141–143
Amorites 81
Anglo-Saxons 36, 99, 173, 180, 211, 231; *see also* Garmon
Aon 58
Apollinaris, Sidonius 69, 177
Aquinas, Thomas 233, 235
Armes Prydein/The Prophecy of Britain 171, 173, 176–177, 179–187
Arthurian legend 252, 255, 256
Asa Itgen 58, 58
asceticism 79, 84, 87, 154, 157
Athelstan, King 184

Badon, Battle of 173

Barrind 89
Bernicians 173
Bible, the 78, 83, 85, 87, 90, 151, 160, 166, 167, 259
   Deuteronomy 82
   Exodus 83–86
   Ezekiel 136–137, 160, 164, 165
   Genesis 112, 261
   Hebrews 78, 83, 83, 87, 89, 91
   Isaiah 160, 164
   Jeremiah 134, 157, 159
   Leviticus 142
   New Testament 78, 82, 89
   Old Testament 78, 82, 128, 150, 176, 178, 262
Bitel, Lisa 190, 192
Bjarne, Bishop 209, 210
Boios inscription 32
Book of David 141
Book of Durrow *see* Insular motifs/objects: Book of Durrow
Book of Leinster 196
Book of Llandaff 68
Breatnach, Caoimhín 205

Breen, Aidan 126–140, 145, 156, 168
Bretons 178, 184, 184
Britain 153, 179, 180–182, 183
  Celtic 66
Britons 171–174, 177, 179, 181, 183, 186
Bromwich, Rachel 176, 179
Bronze Age 44
Broun, Dauvit 213
Brown, Dan 247, 255, 256, 262–270
  Da Vinci Code, The 248, 257–270
Burchard of Worms 220, 222

Cadwaladr 175, 182
Caesar, Julius 18
Caesarius of Arles 139
Cambrensis, Giraldus 64
Cambrian Archaeological Association 55
Campbell, Colin 256
Campbell, J. F. 197, 202
Camunic inscriptions 23
Carolingian derivatives 94, 101, 106–118, 122, 156
Carpenter, David 213
Carpet Pages 101
Carthach 145
Carthage 69
Carthaginians 128, 145
Cassian, John 78, 80–81, 84–85, 88, 132, 140–144
Celtiberian pronouns 27
Celtic Alps 16, 27
Celto-Etruscan text 16, 17, 23, 33
Charlemagne 98, 105, 106–111, 117
Charles the Bald 98, 119, 122
Charles-Edwards 36, 150
"chosen trauma" 181, 187
Christ *see* Jesus
Christian HIC IACET formula 48

Christianity 48, 154, 252–255, 259, 263, 269
Cistercians 60, 67
Claudianus, Claudius 69, 70
Clonmacnoise 38
codex 114, 119, 156
  Aureus 119
  Rabbula 114
Cologne Cathedral 117
contrition 217, 219, 242
Corcu Duibne 41, 43
Cormac mac Airt, King 194, 197
court culture 106, 112, 116, 119, 122, 175, 212, 223–230, 236, 240
Crivello, Fabrizio 119
crosses 40–42, 42–48, 51, 57, 61, 113–117, 123, 255; *see also* ring-cross
  Emlagh Cross 42, 44
  Gero Cross 116
  Latin Cross 42
Crusade, the 210, 251, 255
Crucifixion 113–117, 123, 253
Cymry 173, 184
Cynan 175, 182
Cyprian 125, 132, 138–140, 144, 156

David I, King 131, 167, 228, 235, 241
de Molay, Jacques 264
Dead Sea Scrolls 253
decretals 151, 152, 220, 225, 237–239
dedications 19–22, 25, 27, 31, 32, 66–67, 119
Deirdre 189, 192–196, 198, 199–207
Desert Fathers 78, 84, 84, 87, 89–91
Dingle Archaeological Survey 44
Dissolution, the 60–61
De xii abusivis saeculi see Twelve Abuses of the Age/*De xii abusivis saeculi*

Index

Ditoc 54, 58, 65–67, 75
Dobnorēdo 28
Dumville, David 172, 179, 182, 184–185
Duns Scotus, John 216

Easter 126, 139, 144
ecclesiastical estates 35–42, 47, 50, 144, 214
Echternach Gospels 102–105
Edwards, Nancy 57
Egypt 78–82, 84–86
Elijah 79, 87
England 211, 218, 221
  Cornwall 47, 63, 185
  Durham 222, 233
  Glastonbury 256
English
  Old 173, 176
epigraphy 15–17, 27, 30, 32
Eriugena, John Scotus 98–100, 119
esotericism 248, 255, 257–267
Etchingham, Colmán 36
Etruscan alphabet 16; *see also* North Etruscan texts
Eucherius of Lyon 78, 85

Faivre, Antoine 249, 257–265
farming 38, 50, 62, 63
Faustus of Riez 69
filigree 118
Finn 189, 195, 196–199, 205–206
Finnian of Molville 142–144
folklore 29, 191, 197
four-fold method of Scripture interpretation 80
France 100, 112, 252
  Arras 105
  Brittany 47, 177, 184–186, 187
  Laon 98

Normandy 70
Paris 234, 264
Reims 98, 111, 116
Franco-Saxon school 105, 112
Freemasonry 248, 251, 255, 267
Fulton, Helen 182

Gaehde, Joachim E. 112, 123
Gaelic 231, 240
Gaiseric, the Vandal 69
Galba, Servius 17
Gallo-Greek inscription 16, 26, 27
Gallo-Latin inscription 26, 27, 32
Garmon 179; *see also* Anglo-Saxons
Gaulish 25–28
  dedication 22, 25
  ieuru 22, 25
Gentiles 178, 185
Gerald of Wales 121
Germany 107, 117
  Aachen 106
  Kitzingen 113
Gildas 126, 131, 135–137, 141–147, 149–169, 171–183, 185, 187
  Collectio canonum Hibernensis 125, 139, 145, 150–169
  De excidio 126, 135, 143, 150, 158–169, 171–183, 187
  Fragmenta Gildae 150–164
Gobannos 29
God 78–79, 80–84, 86, 87–89, 119, 131, 133
Godescalc 106
gods and goddesses 15, 19, 29, 71, 259–263
Gooseberry Gardens 39
Gospel(s) 58, 101–121
  Lindau 116
  of St Luke 112
  of St Mark 105

of St Matthew 119
of St Médard 106
of St Willibrord 102
Trier 105
St Gall 114
Ebo 111, 119
Vienna Coronation 107
Gráinne 189-200, 202-207
Gratian 216, 233, 237
  Concordia discordantium canonum
  216, 225, 237, 239
Great St Bernard Pass 19-22
Gregory, Lady 192, 200, 203
Gregory the Great *see* Pope Gregory the Great
Grigg, Julianna 125, 143
Gruffydd, Lord Rhys ap 60

Hagia Sophia 122
hagiography 36, 39, 48, 64, 86, 186; *see also* Saints
Handley, Mark 58, 63, 68-75
Hanegraaff, Wouter J. 257
Hannibal's Wall 17
Hay, Father Richard Augustine 250-252
Herbert, Máire 193, 203
Historia Brittonum 172-174, 179, 180
Holy Blood and the Holy Grail, The 248-255, 269
Holy Grail 248, 252, 255, 262-265
Horace 68, 71
Howlett, David 73
Hrotsvitha of Gandersheim 95-96
Hull, Eleanor 191-192, 195, 201
Hull, Vernam 193

illumination, book 100-119
Insular motifs/objects 53, 72-73, 85, 94-97, 100-119, 122, 149, 153, 156

Book of Durrow 101-102, 107
gold buckle from Sutton Hoo 101
lions 102-107
swine 95
Ireland 35-40, 48, 64, 69, 102, 121, 125-129, 144, 150-153; *see also* Northern Ireland
Ballintermon, Co. Kerry 44, 48
Brackloon, Co. Mayo 44
Brigown, Co. Cork 38, 42
Camlin, Co. Tipperary 37
Dingle peninsula 41, 42
Fir Maige, Co. Cork 35
Inch Labhrainne, Co. Kerry 41
Inis Úasal 40, 42
Inishmurray 38, 41
Irish
  Middle 25, 193
  Old 193
Irish Literary Revival 189-192
Irish *peregrini see peregrini*
Iron Age fortifications 17, 28
Isidore of Seville 69-72, 129, 136, 146
Israel 82-85, 90, 128-131, 135-137, 162
Israelites 80-86, 90
Italian Celtic 17, 24, 107
Italy
  Alba Longa 95-96
  Rome 71, 95, 106, 139, 212, 223
iustitia (Lady Justice) 130, 139, 147
Ivo of Chartres 217, 222, 233, 242

Jack, Lloyd 63
Jankulak, Karen 95
Janson, Horst 116
Jenkins, David 72
Jeroboam 128, 131
Jesus 83, 87, 116, 252-255, 264
John the Baptist 79, 83, 265

Jonas 86, 91
Joseph of Arimathea 255
Julio-Claudian period 17, 32, 96
jury 226
justice 129, 134, 144, 147, 216, 218, 230, 238–246

Kinsella, Thomas 189, 206
Knights Templar 248, 251, 252, 264

Lady Gregory *see* Gregory, Lady
La Tène era 17, 28, 32
landholdings 35–38, 50; *see also* ecclesiastical estates
Latin 19–21, 24–27, 54, 68, 72–74, 113, 173, 177
law 139, 144, 213–246
  canon 139, 145, 151–152, 215–244
  positive 238
  royal 211–216, 229, 232, 235, 241, 246
  secular 214, 215, 218–221, 226–232, 236, 241
layfolk 136, 138, 143, 146
Lehmann, Edyta 199
Lepontic texts 16, 19, 23, 25
Lewes, Colonel John 55, 60–64, 76
libraries 232
Liddes inscription 16–19, 21, 24, 27, 31, 32
Life of Findchú 40
Lifshitz, Felice 113
Linderski, Jerzy 71
Lion of Mark 102
liturgy 139, 145, 153
Llanddewibrefi inscription 73
Llanllŷr House 53–67, 74
Llanllŷr inscription 54, 59
Louis the German, King 112
Louis the Pious, King 123
Lumberd 209, 242

MacCotter, Paul 36, 42
MacQueen, Hector 213–214
Magdalene, Mary 252–255, 259, 263–264
Majorian 69
Making Christian Landscapes project 36
Malcolm III, King 211, 241
Manching inscriptions 31
Martine, Roddy 251, 266, 268
Maur, Hraban 94, 123
Mayr-Harting, Henry 117
McCone, Kim 190
McKee, Helen 57
McKitterick, Rosamond 94, 118
McManus, Damian 195
McSweeney, Thomas 244
Mesopotamia 114
Meyrick, Samuel 61, 63
Mhac an tSaoi, Máire 198
Middle East 78
Milton, John 177
Modomnóc 54, 64, 67, 75
Monaincha 37
monotheism 259
mons Jovis (Mt Joux) 19
monuments 38–41, 44, 48, 53–58, 66
  and memory work 40, 76
morality 130, 132, 144, 147
Moses 79, 82, 86, 90
Murith, Laurent-Joseph 19
Musto, Jeanne-Marie 116, 119
Mütherich, Florence 112, 123

Naoise 189, 193–196, 200, 202, 204–205
Nash-Williams, V.E. 57
Ní Chuilleanáin, Eiléan 190, 198, 207
Ní Dhonnchadha, Máirín 197, 198, 204
Ní Shéaghdha, Nessa 196, 205, 206
noiarti 24, 26

North Etruscan texts 32; *see also* Etruscan alphabet
Northern Ireland *see also* Ireland
Armagh 38, 58, 140, 145

Ó Corráin, Donnchadh 36
Ó Duibhgeannáin, Dáibhídh 196, 205, 206
O'Grady, Standish 191, 196, 200, 205, 206
Octodurus, Battle of 17
ogham inscription 44, 50
ogham stone 48
Olson, Lynette 119
onomastic texts 16, 32
Orosius 178
Otto III 107, 117
Ottonian art and literature 94–100, 116–119, 122

Paphnutius, Abbas 84
Pauline Epistles from Kitzingen 113
plebs/plebes see layfolk
Padel, Oliver 63, 66, 178
paganism 39, 48, 177, 185, 256, 263
panegyric 69, 175
pastoral care 36
peregrini 77–79, 83, 87, 91
Photios, Patriarch 122
Poeninus, Iovus 15, 19–23, 25
poetry 69, 174, 176, 177, 192, 206
Poininos *see* Poeninus, Iovus
Pope Gregory IX 225, 237
Pope Gregory the Great 149, 151, 157, 164, 165
Pope Honorius 139, 242
Pope Innocent II 241, 264
Pope Innocent III 209, 224–230
Pope Paschal II 228

Prince of Deheubarth *see* Gruffydd, Lord Rhys ap
Priory of Sion 251, 252, 256, 260
Promised Land 80, 81–84, 85, 87, 89–91
Prophecy of Britain, The *see Armes Prydein*/The Prophecy of Britain

Queen Mary 250
Queen Victoria 251

Rabbula codex *see* codex: Rabbula
Ramsay, Peter 234
Recherches Archéologiques du Mur (dit) d'Hannibal (Ramha) 17
regio 181–182
Rennes-le-Château 252, 255, 258
Rhygyfarch 64
Rhŷs, John 53–57, 60, 64, 65, 76
Rhŷs, Maelgwn 62
ring-cross 55; *see also* crosses
Ritilos 19
Roberts, Brynley 184
Romanisation 16, 17, 27, 32
Rosslyn Chapel 247–252, 255, 265–269
Russell, Paul 75

Saints
  Anselm of Laon 217
  Augustine of Hippo 151, 157
  Bede the Venerable 83, 172–174, 180
  Bernard of Menthon 19
  Boniface 98, 113
  Brendan the Navigator 83, 89–91
  Brigid 121
  Columbanus 86, 88, 139, 142, 144, 149, 151, 154, 158, 186
  David 65–67, 184
  Honoratus 78

Jerome 121, 133, 134, 136, 138, 151, 161, 163
Luke 112
Mark 102–113, 127
Matthew 111, 118
Mochellóc 41, 50
Patrick, Bishop 125, 145–147, 149, 151–156, 168, 169
Paul the Apostle 78, 138–139, 161, 163
Peter the Apostle 58, 78, 161, 264
Samson of Dol 85, 186
Willibrord 98, 102, 112
Saint-Sulpice, Paris 259, 266
Salopek, Paul 181
Saul 128, 133
Scotland 47, 184, 209–246, 250–252, 265
  Aberdeen 232, 234
  Orkney 209
  Portmahomack 46
  Roslin 247, 250, 268
  Stirling 236
Scott, Matthew 234
Serapion, Abba 84
Sermon on the Mount 87
Sharpe, Richard 66, 150, 154
Sims-Williams, Patrick 57, 65, 173–175, 181–182
sin 87–88, 90, 131, 137, 161, 166, 204, 209, 216–222, 230
Sinclair, Henry 251
Sinclair, William 247, 250, 251, 255
Slovenia
  Ptuj 32
Solomon 128, 130, 133, 135, 166
standing stones 40, 42–46, 48
Stein, Peter 238
Stephens, James 201
stone circle 39

Strata Florida Cistercian monastery 60
suicide 193, 204
Swift, Catherine 48
Switzerland
  Argnou 19
  Berne 16, 27–33
  Martigny 18
Syria 114

Tallaght Martyrologies 64
Taylor, Alice 210–213, 230, 240, 245
Temple Church, London 266
templum 71–72
tesqua/tesquum 54, 68–75
tesquitus 58, 59, 65, 67–75
theology 78–80, 83, 214–222, 230–235, 239
Thomas, Rebecca 181, 182
topographical texts 36, 54, 59, 64, 69, 121
Topographica Hiberniae 64
Tudor-era house 55, 59–61
Twelve Abuses of the Age/*De xii abusivis saeculi* 125, 128–132, 134, 136–146, 147

Val Brembana 15, 22–26
Val Camisana 23
Val Leventina 16
Valcamonica 23
Vallis Poenina 18
Veneto 32
Verdun, Treaty of 117
vernacular poetry 175, 177, 180
Vikings 184, 185
Virgil 95
  Aeneid, The 96
Virgin Mary 259
visnet *see* jury
Volkan, Vamik 181, 187

Volto Santo 113
Vortigern 174, 180
votive 19–21

Wales 54, 64, 66, 74, 183
  Abergwili 57
  Llanllŷr 55–68, 75
  River Aeron 59, 62
  Talsarn 62–63
  Trefilan 62
  Tregaron 57
Watt, Donald 234
Weitzmann, Kurt 114
Welsh language 25, 28, 64, 177
Westwood, J. O. 55

William of Orange 250
William of Poitiers 70, 75
William I, King 224, 227, 230–240, 245
Williams, Hugh 178
Williams, Ifor 177
Winterbottom, Michael 154, 155, 174
Wright, Neil 174
Wrmonoc 177, 178
Wulfstan of York 171, 176, 218

Yeats, W.B. 191, 200, 203
Ynys Prydein 182; *see also* Britain

Zimmer, Heinrich 172

www.ingramcontent.com/pod-product-compliance
Lightning Source LLC
Chambersburg PA
CBHW071144160426
43196CB00011B/2003